TO THE PEOPLE,
FOOD IS HEAVEN

TO THE PEOPLE, FOOD IS HEAVEN

Stories of Food and Life in a Changing China

Audra Ang

Foreword by Ken Hom

Lyons Press
Guilford, Connecticut
An imprint of Globe Pequot Press

For those who shared their lives and their food
and especially for the people whose stories I didn't tell.

Copyright © 2012 by Audra Ang

Text design: Sheryl Kober
Layout: Melissa Evarts
Project editor: Ellen Urban

Map by Melissa Baker © Morris Book Publishing, LLC

Library of Congress Cataloging-in-Publication Data is available on file.

ISBN 978-0-7627-7392-3

Printed in the United States of America

10 9 8 7 6 5 4 3 2 1

CONTENTS

China

FOREWORD

There has been a proliferation of books on contemporary China, for it is one of the most riveting stories of our times: the renaissance of one of the world's oldest civilizations that has revitalized economically and socially and captured the imagination of the world. Its size and importance have an enormous impact on all our lives as witnessed by the number not only of books but columns in newspapers, magazine articles, and, of course, television programs. Often opinions divide between the negative—China will soon collapse—and the overly optimistic—China has found a new formula for eternal economic growth. The truth lies somewhere in between: not starkly black or white but in many shades of gray. I was thrilled to read Audra Ang's *To the People, Food Is Heaven*, a realistic work about a China I have experienced as well, and a book I would have been proud to have written.

Audra Ang certainly has the right qualifications as a former Beijing correspondent for the Associated Press, but like myself she is also an overseas Chinese. She thus brings another perspective to her unique experience of living and working in China—and what an adventure Audra takes us on! She has cleverly and brilliantly used one of China's greatest cultural heritages, its food, as the core theme of the book. After all, China's cuisine quite literally has changed world politics. As Henry Kissinger once said, "After a dinner of Peking Duck, I'll sign anything." Eating forms such an integral part of social and family life in China that the size of the Chinese population and what it consumes affect world food production and prices.

China was for the most part closed as it went through a century of political and social turmoil before transforming itself in the 1980s to re-emerge on the world scene as an economic dynamo, taking up one-third of the world's growth. This transformation has had a deep impact on China itself as its infrastructure, education, and society modernized. Foreigners began opening restaurants in China to take advantage of the boom, five-star hotels popped up to meet the demand of travelers from all over the world, and with them came a re-emergence of Chinese cuisine. As the ever-growing middle class demanded higher standards of cooking, enterprising restaurant owners and food companies rose to the challenge. Free markets inspired chefs and home cooks alike as they revisited old recipes and invented new ones. Chinese food has never been better than in China today, as Audra so rightfully points out.

However, this book is not only about food and cooking but how they form part of the fabric of Chinese life, even today, with China's incredible transformation. It is also a voyage of discovery: I did not know, for example, that millions of bed-and-breakfast inns were opening in the countryside as city dwellers flock to eat fresh food from the fields and to experience what it's like to live on a farm. The deep roots of this ancient cuisine inform every aspect of this change. I love, for example, Audra's touching description of her housecleaner, Cheng Ayi, and her cooking. I was genuinely moved by how Audra used food with the insight of how hard working and self sacrificing ordinary Chinese, like Cheng Ayi, can be.

At the same time, this is not an apologist book: It is unvarnished, with blemishes and all. In fact, I found it quite hard-hitting writing, worthy of any Pulitzer Prize winner. After reading the book, you feel the reality beneath the headlines—how China with its multitude of problems struggles to address them as it hurtles into the twenty-first century, well described in Audra's writing. I admire how the heartbreaking scenes are nevertheless lightened with evocative food and eating. There are passages where I laughed at the humor as she recounts cultural misunderstandings, such as those she encountered when she assumed that her young Chinese co-workers all drank tea. Like some of us, many are fans of cola!

But it is Audra's harrowing account of the Sichuan earthquake in 2008 that is one of the best on the subject. At times, I felt I was right beside her as she recounted her experiences, and yet food seemed to appear thankfully at the most dire moments. Survivors and relief workers told her that, despite the disaster, you still had to eat. You understand at the end of the book why cuisine is such an essential of Chinese life and culture.

This food strand appears again and again in Audra's book. Sometimes the description of the food was so vivid that I felt my mouth watering. At the same time, I found her writing wonderful and heart-warming. Her historical tidbits and the origin of some dishes offered invaluable insight even to someone like me, who has cooked and taught Chinese cuisine for so many years. Yet there were so many accounts of restaurants, dishes, and places that were so familiar that I felt we had almost been there together.

What makes reading this book so unique is the beautiful way in which Audra has woven people's lives with food. The strands not only complement each other wonderfully but seem to give strength and hope to the ever-changing dynamics of the world's fastest-moving country. It is a tantalizing portrait of contemporary China, a feast for the mind, heart, and stomach. I know you will find reading it as delicious and delectable as I have.

Ken Hom

Author's Note

The Chinese words in this book are written in *pinyin,* the system used to transliterate characters into the Roman alphabet. Most of the letters are roughly as in English, but there are a few exceptions, mainly:

Consonants	Pronounced	Example
c	*ts* as in *mats*	cai
q	*ch* as in *child*	keqi
x	*between* an *s* and *sh*	xinnian
z	*ds* as in *buds*	zongzi
zh	*dge* as in *budge*	Zhang

Vowels	Pronounced	Example
a	*ah*	Chang'an
e	*uh*	Cheng
i	*ee*	Li
o	*oo-awe* when consonant comes before	mapo (*mah-poo-awe*)
u	*oo* after most consonants	mu
u	after j, q, x, y, and sometimes l and n, pronounced like an umlaut is present, as in *few*	
ou	*oh*	hukou
ue	*y'were,* as in the contracted form of you were	Yueyang
ei	*ay* as in *lay*	Beijing
ao	*ow* as in *cow*	hao

This is a rigorous work of nonfiction. Documents, interviews, or photos support all material used in the book, but due to varying degrees of sensitivity about certain topics some people are only partially identified by name—or not at all. Chinese women generally do not take their husband's names, though for the sake of clarity I have identified some of them in relation to their husbands.

INTRODUCTION
Facing the Dragon

There's a saying in China—"To the people, food is heaven"—that perfectly captures the essence of the country's 1.3 billion citizens. It also strikes at the core of who I am as a Singaporean with Chinese ancestors. I live to eat; it's etched in my DNA.

While I'm a passable cook, what I love more is to nibble, savor, inhale, gnaw, devour, lick, sniff, share, and poke at food in its natural state or prepared by others. Sometimes, when faced with a particularly delectable dish, I hold a morsel of it in my mouth just for a few seconds to feel the flavors pool on my tongue. Then I chew, deliberately, to enjoy the swirl of tastes and textures. I eat when I'm happy but also when I'm sad.

In new countries, it's not museums or tours that excite me. It's supermarkets—slow, exploratory walks down aisles of produce and foodstuffs, some foreign, some surprisingly familiar, an anthropological dig with culinary discoveries. And outdoor markets filled with rainbow-hued pyramids of fruits and vegetables; buttery cakes and pastries; pungent herbs, spices, and cheeses; briny seafood on ice; and cuts of meat from animal parts I never knew were edible. And restaurants and street stands where the clang of pans, hiss of steam, roar of flames, and sizzle of oil sing to me a siren song. I love to talk about food, read about it, look at pictures of it, and I love people who love to do the same.

China is the place for all of that and more. There I hungered not just for food but also for discovering, forging, and holding on to connections. It wasn't always easy to find fulfillment—many efforts failed—but not once did I regret trying.

The view from my twentieth-floor apartment overlooking the Yabaolu area of Beijing, the Russian neighborhood. In the distance, on the right, you can see two lipstick-shaped office towers. The left one houses the current AP bureau.

I arrived in the middle of a punishing heat wave when temperatures edged past records daily. Like the deserts to the north, the air in Beijing was stifling and arid, the days bleached out by the sun. A coal-fired kiln encased the city. Nights offered no respite, and the sweltering darkness often grew thick with the aroma of grilled meats, sweat, and echoes of drunken chatter. One afternoon, it hit 105 degrees. I could feel my life force draining away on the seven-minute walk to work. Colleagues would have to peel my body—limp like an overcooked noodle—from the scorching asphalt. *How*, I thought to myself, *did I escape my equatorial hometown of Singapore and humid New York to end up here?*

This was how: In 2002, after twelve years in America—first as an undergraduate, then as a reporter and editor for the Associated Press—I ran out of ways to stay. My student visa had expired, along with a yearlong training allowance and a work permit renewed twice. The AP could have let me go, but luckily the higher-ups made me a China-based correspondent instead.

They sent me on a three-week test-run in July 2001. In June the following year, my permanent assignment in Beijing began, leaving me feeling apprehensive and ignorant. My family had roots in China, but I knew next to nothing about its history, culture, or people. No other city could replace my magnificent New York. *One year in Beijing,* I told myself, *then I would return to Manhattan.*

But I was wrong. My time in China began my most challenging adventure to date—as you'll see, life in America was a cakewalk compared to what I was about to experience—and a still-unfinished journey into my ancestral past. Professionally it pushed me to be tougher, more creative, and more resourceful. It piqued my curiosity and compassion. As so many people feel about New York, which I had already conquered, if I could make it in China, I could make it anywhere—and with some of the greatest food on the planet to fuel me.

I constantly straddled three cultures: American, Chinese, and Singaporean. In the early days, I awoke in a panic, thinking I was in my fourth-floor Brooklyn walk-up, late for work, imagining for a second having yet again to push past slow-moving herds of tourists congregating open-mouthed at Radio City Music Hall and the AP's more famous neighbor, 30 Rockefeller Center, home to NBC Studios and live broadcasts of *Today.* My stomach, always anxious to be filled, growled as my thoughts jumped immediately to an onion bagel, split, toasted, and slathered with lox cream cheese.

Then I realized I was lying under the covers of a double bed in a single room—that smelled vaguely of old cigarettes, blackout curtains drawn tight—at a hotel just off the Avenue of Eternal Peace, the main artery running through central Beijing. Outside lay a different sea of gray and grids, soybean milk and steamed buns, snarled traffic and frenetic pedestrians, where, after over a decade of standing out as an ethnic minority in America, I could dissolve into a crowd.

It was an odd cultural luxury that I didn't appreciate until after I left Singapore, where, as someone of Chinese descent, I formed part of the 75 percent majority. In Istanbul, groups of men called out *"Konnichiwa!"*—Japanese for "hello"—as I passed competing shawarma stands and clubs oozing their heavy thumping bass lines. Similar shouts have greeted me in a variety of Asian languages in my travels all over the world, from South Africa to Israel. Even in my über-progressive Park Slope neighborhood in Brooklyn, a group of kids once yelled from across the street "Connie Chung! Connie Chung!" I spun excitedly around, expecting to catch a glimpse of the broadcast journalist—only to realize, moments later, that they meant me.

After that, being "faceless" in China came as a relief, a gift of conformity that proved invaluable during the next seven years as I jumped into potentially sensitive stories. It made it easier to skirt the reach of authorities who zeroed in first on Western-looking reporters in their efforts to deter and detain. Suddenly my face had become the perfect undercover disguise.

However, despite my family roots in the country's south, I had been raised a world apart from most mainland Chinese, who thought that all Singaporeans had exorbitant wealth and that the island nation was spotless. It was strange being in a place where I looked like everyone but didn't have an immediate basis for connection. Everything was always at once oddly familiar and frustratingly foreign.

Customs, nuances, and the language were often lost on me. English—one of Singapore's four official languages—was my mother tongue. My Mandarin accent, initially a sibilant southern one, morphed into a strange hybrid when it encountered the guttural "er" sounds of Beijing's northern dialect. I was also an unmarried woman in her thirties living on her own and working a job that few understood—unusual even by the city's comparatively modern attitudes. Yet, in the best moments, it felt like the entire nation was extended family, kind relatives who, moments after meeting, invited you for tea and a chat.

I was only just beginning to understand what it felt like to be a tiny cog in a giant wheel. On the worst days, the pulsing crowds that left little personal space, the constant din, the difficulty of the simplest of tasks—because somehow, something always went wrong, whether an unnecessarily roundabout taxi ride or a botched repair job that only made the problem worse—made me boil with frustration and, at times, anger.

Communication itself, not just language, but the way that one human related to another, often resulted in a chaotic jumble of crossed wires, uncivil interactions, and plain stubbornness. Obstacles and red tape rose and stuck without need; *mashang*, which supposedly means "right away," usually signaled interminable delays. *Meibanfa*—"Nothing can be done"—reared its head time and again, when "yes" was equally and easily doable. No wonder people took desperate measures. It was a vicious cycle, and the build-up of daily *mafan*, troubles, took its toll.

There were days when, even with my comfortable expatriate existence and the strength of the AP backing me, I felt voiceless and overwhelmed. A permanent tension knot formed in my neck, and I developed a self-diagnosed syndrome that I called China Rage, which expressed itself in my equally frustrated friends. I saw red when police repeatedly stopped or manhandled reporters when we were trying to do our jobs. I fumed when Chinese guards at the gate to the compound where I worked blocked me daily from entering, demanding to see proof of identification, while my Western friends walked past undisturbed. Salting the injury, the guards said it was a security measure.

Once, I got into a shoving match with a woman who refused to stop jabbing my back while rushing willy-nilly with dozens of others to board a subway car.

"Stop pushing!" I yelled.

"You move faster then!" she screamed back, poking me hard in the ribs yet again.

I elbowed her, and she fought back. When the train picked up speed and she scuttled toward a rare empty seat, I narrowed my eyes and unleashed a steely glare in her direction. My traveling companion looked away and pretended not to know me. It's hard to fathom unless you've lived it.

But food and my lusty enjoyment of it wove themselves into daily life. It was the one surefire way to find common ground with people—along with some much needed sanity and comfort. Wherever I turned, someone was slurping noodles, tea, or soup. Guests often brought food as gifts when visiting friends, and their hosts usually welcomed them with something to warm their bellies. I once overheard a friendly argument about where to get the best barbecue duck necks turn aggressive. Luckily, the two parties agreed to disagree and arranged to meet for a taste test.

China has grand traditions of cooking and deliciously distinct regional cuisines influenced by history, geography, and climate, from the breathtaking heat of Hunan and Sichuan, to the delicate flavors of Guangdong and Zhejiang, to the underlying sweetness of Jiangsu and Shanghai. Coastal Shandong and Fujian specialize in seafood, while rugged Anhui features the bounty of its mountains and forests. Although lines have blurred in recent years because of greater mobility and wealth, you can still broadly divide the Chinese into wheat-eaters in the north and rice-eaters in the south. This translates to noodles, dumplings, and breads, topped or stuffed with meat and vegetables in places like Jilin and Shanxi, while provinces like Guangdong and Hunan cook separate dishes to accompany rice.

Ingredients also often contain hidden meanings. The Chinese character for fish, for example, sounds the same as the word for abundance, so a whole one, head, bones, and tail intact, ushers in wealth and marks a promising beginning and end of a year if eaten during New Year celebrations. Noodles—which represent longevity—are best left unbroken; and the longer the strand, the better, especially at birthdays. Preserved apricots are lucky because they sound like the words for happiness and prosperity.

Harmony between color, texture, and flavor reigns. Balance comes through aromatics like ginger, garlic, and spring onions, as well as seasonings like wine, soy sauce, vinegar, star anise, and sesame oil. Ideally, dishes appear in a certain sequence to complement other foods on the table as well as the setting in which they are presented.

These were near-impossible standards to meet on a daily basis if you weren't a chef, but I liked that they were there in the first place. In restaurants, names of dishes intentionally sound highbrow or exciting or pay tribute to nature or literature. Sometimes the names appeal to the ordinary citizen's sense of humor and celebrate everyday life. Some sound thoroughly unappetizing but turn out to be delectable—Ants Climbing a Tree: clear bean thread noodles and ground pork; Red Braised Lion's Head: a giant meatball in brown sauce; and Husband and Wife Lung Slices: sliced beef and tripe.

Literally translated, Saliva Chicken sounds terrifying . . . until you employ the better, more apt interpretation: Mouthwatering Chicken. A Sichuan specialty, the chopped, poached bird, bathed in peppercorn-spiked chili oil and served cold, quickly won me over with its numbing spice, kicked up with a sprinkling of sesame seeds and spring onions. My colleague Elizabeth Dalziel so loved the tasty oil that she gulped down a *bowlful* of it in Chengdu and suffered mightily—but with absolutely no regrets.

Eating in China is rarely an individual undertaking. People meet for dinner instead of drinks and share common dishes set in the middle of the table, plucking at bite-sized bits of food with chopsticks (often a communal pair) while catching up. I learned that if you want to serve another person food to show affection or respect, you flip the chopsticks around to offer the side that has not touched your mouth. I also came to understand that the careful preparation of a single dish, perhaps a comforting soup simmered and skimmed for hours, is a more common expression of love than a hug or a kiss.

What took longer to grasp was the delicate relationship in Chinese culture between eating, health, and inner balance, a tradition from ancient times that still has relevance today. Food generally has either hot (*yang*) or cold (*yin*) properties, and the equilibrium between the two importantly maintains a person's well-being. According to those beliefs, my irritability, impatience, and frequent headaches stemmed from too much "hot" energy within me, fueled by foods that I loved, such as ginger, lychees, meat, and anything deep-fried. I tried to "cool down" by eating more cucumbers, watermelon, and lotus root soup—but it rarely worked.

By the time I arrived in Beijing, the traditional Chinese greeting of "Have you eaten yet?" no longer seemed like a strange joke. Decades before, in the early 1980s, privately owned restaurants and food stands were just emerging. Before that, staples were rationed. State-run canteens dished out the slop of the day in chipped enamel bowls. The eating scene consisted almost entirely of a handful of noodle joints. Dining out after 6:00 p.m. meant going hungry. Most eateries were closing by then, their meager menus finished for the day.

Today, the city hums with eateries at every corner—between forty thousand and fifty thousand of them, open at all hours, offering cuisines from around the country. In my lifetime, people have gone from eating merely to fill their stomachs to dining as a self-contained experience. The traditional greeting now should be "What have you eaten today?"

The variety is bewildering and seemingly endless, from al dente hand-pulled noodles splashed with bracing black vinegar from Shanxi province in the north, to thumbnail-sized chicken pieces buried in a mountain of dried chilies from Sichuan in the southwest, to the rich braises of the east. Dumplings—fried, steamed, boiled—burst with savory fillings. In winter "hot pot" feasts, diners dip raw meats and vegetables into boiling broth flavored with anything from pork bones to curry powder to mushrooms.

Then there's the street food: fluffy buns, candied fruit, cumin-spiced lamb skewers, flatbreads slathered with salty bean paste, smoky roasted sweet potatoes, and the beloved *jianbing*—egg, lettuce, and crisp fried dough rolled in a flour crepe slathered with sweet and hot sauces: a Chinese breakfast burrito.

The international options are just as varied too, with many Michelin-starred and celebrity chefs making Beijing and its explosive wealth their destination.

Surrounded by this mouthwatering abundance, I began my new job, where assignments took me to virtually every province. I wrote about disasters, disease, and dissent and tried to put a face to the issues relevant to the country. It was as much about telling the story of the Chinese people as it was about telling the story of China.

I ate my way through a gamut of circumstances. During one bird flu outbreak, I couldn't resist an enormous platter of chicken with peppers in western China's Muslim region because it was a local specialty. Farmers, housekeepers, and dissidents treated me to bountiful home-cooked feasts. Police officers who detained me always made sure my teacup was full while interrogating me for hours. During the worst earthquake to shake the country in three decades, survivors pressed me to share what little provisions they had as aftershocks rocked the surrounding buildings.

It was only toward the end of my time in China that I realized how much those food encounters enriched my experience. They opened windows onto the lives of ordinary people and chances to enjoy the connection in a quintessentially Chinese way. They were key in some of my most human interactions and memories in the world's most populous nation, experiences that made endless hours of work worthwhile, that inspired and inspire me, that still leave a lump in my throat.

They also brought home the realities and the complexities of contemporary China, from the yawning rich-poor gap to percolating discontent over the lack of freedoms that many in the West take for granted. On many occasions, eating together offered an opportunity for people to tell their stories and air their grievances, a near impossibility in a country too vast for everyone to be heard and where criticism of the government or complaints about injustices often come at a price.

Connections forged during natural disasters, when resources were scant, and in rural areas, where enduring poverty means a hand-to-mouth existence for many, remain my dearest memories. The spirit, kindness, and generosity of the Chinese people shone, whether through a cracked bowl of rice or a bottle of water offered when there was literally nothing else left.

Those were the instances when I knew that food truly was heaven.

1

Welcome to Heaven

I threw up twice in my first forty-five minutes on Chinese soil.

It was July 2001, the start of my three-week trial at the AP's Beijing bureau. My US work permit was expiring, and my bosses were trying to figure out where to send me next.

You can blame the inauspicious introduction to my assignment on an inadequately chilled chicken salad sandwich served mid-flight, in darkness, somewhere over the great expanse between Chicago and Beijing. That thirteen-hour leg of my journey, which began at La Guardia Airport in New York, didn't bode well from the time that I boarded—to find myself stuck in a middle seat in the middle of a packed aircraft.

Luckily, I was sitting next to a very friendly Beijing-born woman living in Cleveland on her way to a tai chi conference at the martial arts school where action star Jet Li trained. She proffered a nectarine and told me all about her work as a scientist at NASA. The man on my other side alternated between wrestling obnoxiously for arm space and falling asleep on my shoulder. Any ill will toward him dissipated, however, when he offered me a single Pepperidge Farm Milano cookie. Food brings people together.

The rest of the journey consisted of completing the in-flight magazine crossword puzzle, about fifteen viewings of *Crouching Tiger, Hidden Dragon*, two of *Spy Kids*, and a lot of musing about what China would be like.

The feeling—*that* feeling—hit me minutes before we landed and sent me flying down the aisle to the bathroom. I gagged and retched yet again as the plane was taxiing, quiet enough in the cabin for everyone to hear the not-so-delicate noises my body was making into the airsick bag. The kung fu–NASA lady patted my back comfortingly as I heaved. I loved her. The final time came in an empty, fluorescent-lit bathroom before the imposing bank of immigration booths at Beijing International Airport. By the time my passport had been stamped, I had an empty stomach and a fresh start.

I was ready to enter the Middle Kingdom.

While New York and Singapore prepared me in many ways for the bustle-and-teem of a busy city, Beijing's seemingly endless sprawl still overwhelmed me for much of my first week. The municipality spanned about 6,500 square miles—about twenty-two times the size of all five of New York City's boroughs *combined* (or just a little bit less than Connecticut and Rhode Island put together)—and, at the time, was home to almost fourteen million people and eight million bicycles. By 2010, the population had boomed to almost twenty million, with migrants from other provinces contributing the bulk of the increase. Almost five million cars caused massive gridlock and air pollution that forced the government to cap new car registration in 2011.

The city had pockets of green, buildings that reached for the sky, and roads that often ran wide and straight, creating an illusion of space—but to me it was a near-impenetrable wall of traffic, noise, and people, many of whom curiously mixed friendliness and shyness. Most didn't speak English, and for the first time in my life I had to use my limited Mandarin skills on a daily basis. In Singapore, Mandarin for me was relegated to language classes in school and food stalls in the street . . . and that was about it.

In Beijing, I learned to begin all my conversations with "I am sorry that my Mandarin is not good" in order to preempt any misunderstandings on either side. People quickly and graciously reassured me that I was more fluent than I realized, a kindness I appreciated. Bestowed by my paternal grandfather, my Chinese name, Xiaoyin, means something poetic like "the sound of dawn," but I always joked that I was more like morning noise.

Fireworks arc and blaze over frozen Houhai Lake in central Beijing during Chinese New Year 2009. One of the most memorable fireworks shows I saw in the Chinese capital was in 2001, when they burst over Tiananmen Square after the International Olympic Committee announced Beijing as the host city for the 2008 Summer Games.

Reporting in a foreign language posed a huge challenge, and it didn't help that I often had the tact of the proverbial bull in a china shop. I asked direct questions and expected direct answers. But that is not the Chinese way. Because I had to speak in one tongue and write in another simultaneously, my notes became a messy stew of English phrases and bits of my own shorthand, generously sprinkled with Chinese script and *pinyin,* the system used to transliterate characters into the Roman alphabet. The latter two came in handy when I couldn't think fast enough or had to look something up later.

My questions lacked a certain nuance and subtlety, and my vocabulary hovered, at first, around the level of a ten-year-old's. Repeating every sentence back to the person who had spoken it to me, to make sure I hadn't misheard, probably made me sound even younger. As if Mandarin—the country's official language— didn't pose enough of an obstacle, China has hundreds of dialects spoken in villages, towns, cities, and provinces across the territory that we covered. I spoke exactly none of them and often had to rely on a local for help, usually someone younger who had learned Mandarin in school.

My colleagues were five men—three reporters and two photographers. Joe McDonald, the bureau chief, an American and a vegan, had a near-photographic memory. The news editor, John Leicester, a Brit, spoke English, French, and Mandarin with equal fluency. The other reporter, loquacious American Chris Bodeen, had an extensive knowledge and unquenchable thirst for Chinese politics. Chief photographer Greg Baker, a taciturn New Zealander, had lived in China for fourteen years and had his very own set of state security agents watching him. A fellow Singaporean, Ng Han Guan, whom everyone called Han, had a quiet stubbornness that made him one of the most dogged and successful shooters in town.

Then there was me.

Everyone welcomed me, incredibly intimidated though I was, and generously helped me settle into the job and my new life. Because I didn't know anyone else in the city, they also tried to make sure I was well nourished by taking me out to eat.

Han and Greg brought me to Xiaowangfu, a back-alley dive near my hotel, popular with both locals and foreigners. We feasted on dry-fried beans with preserved greens; rectangles of deep-fried silken tofu topped with a garlicky, spicy sauce; and giant pork ribs also deep-fried until crisp on the outside and tender on the inside, the meat flavored by a salt-and-pepper dip. We had hot tea and warm conversation, and for an evening I tasted what life in Beijing could be like.

Before moving to a modern office in 2007, the AP bureau lay in one of the embassy districts on the sixth floor of a hulking apartment building, among dozens built in guarded compounds in the 1950s, '60s, and '70s to house foreigners. Its balcony overlooked the frequently jammed Second Ring Road, a highway circling the heart of Beijing, and its walls were lined with bookcases full of yellowing books and publications and other old furniture left by previous correspondents. Our wooden desks were elephant-hide gray, and the equipment was old but serviceable. The two bathrooms had dingy showers that no one used, and, in the airy kitchen with a giant stove and a corner chair draped with a towel, our driver Shi Jie napped for most of the day. The homey feel was nothing like the corporate vibe of 50 Rock, the AP's former headquarters in New York.

At the mouth of a small but deadly intersection just a five-minute walk from the compound stood a couple of fluorescent-lit cheap-and-cheerful eateries with hearty food and no décor to speak of. One specialized in numbingly spicy Sichuan dishes like *laziji* and *shuizhurou*, respectively: bony bites of fried chicken lurking in a pile of dried chilies and thin-sliced pork in a bath of chili oil. Ted Anthony, who later took over from John as news editor, and I made frequent visits. A powerful thinker and writer and a staunch lover of all things porcine, he happily—and sweatily—consumed a small vat of *shuizhurou* at lunch, paired with an appetizer of cucumbers smashed with garlic and coarse salt, all washed down with something fizzy.

The place a couple of doors down served an equally delicious mix of northern and southern cuisines. The food was *jiachangcai*—homestyle cooking—simple, often oily fare, cooked quickly and eaten with rice. My favorites were fragrant and spicy shredded potatoes deep-fried to a brittle-crisp nest and seasoned with salt, sugar, and slivers of green onions and dried chili. Braised Two

Winters had bamboo shoots and *xianggu*, or what we know as shiitake mushrooms, in a savory brown sauce. They also served the prototypical peasant dish of eggs scrambled with tomatoes and a sprinkling of white sugar.

Also within walking distance was a Pizza Hut and a McDonald's, among the city's multitude of Western fast-food restaurants. KFC opened its first mainland franchise in Beijing in 1987; Pizza Hut came in 1990, and McDonald's in 1992. On some days, McDonald's deep-fried spicy chicken wings and a reconstituted egg drop soup with tiny shrimp—neither available on the American menu—proved strangely irresistible.

I slowly climbed the learning curve at work, swiftly switching gears from editor to reporter. In New York, the news I edited covered the fifty states. Now I had to think in the context of the world. We were responsible not only for mainland China, with offices in Beijing and Shanghai, but we also oversaw the bureaus in Hong Kong and Taiwan and wrote about North Korea and Mongolia.

Only by working there did I truly understand how far China's sphere of influence stretched and how fast it was widening. The country sits permanently on the U.N. Security Council, meaning that it has veto power as a player in every major decision the global body makes from sanctions to military actions—as seen recently with the bloody Arab Spring uprising in Syria. It also has a tremendous presence in Africa, so we monitored events unfolding in Sudan and Zimbabwe, where state-driven investments gave Beijing great political and economic clout. In Asia, we kept track of China's territorial disputes with India, Japan, the Philippines, and Vietnam, along with a tangle of alliances and subtle enmity. Not to mention the ever-morphing, see-sawing, passive-aggressive relationship with America.

In the midst of trying to figure it all out, then–secretary of state Colin Powell visited Beijing. I had never done a "pool" report stateside and didn't know how it worked until Joe, my bureau chief, explained that the press corps shared resources by taking turns sending reporters to cover an event where a limited number of media could attend. I was the eyes and ears for my colleagues who couldn't be there, then sent an e-mail telling them what transpired so they could include it in their reports. Just to be safe, I even included the color of Powell's suit and tie (navy double-breasted, dark red with stripes).

Even though roles are changing, being a wire journalist often means attending every press conference, staying until the last person leaves, and doing things that newspapers and other media outlets may not have the inclination or resources to do. We provide not only the fast and accurate foundation for stories but also the big picture and the smallest of details. It means working under tight deadlines, pressure-cooker situations, and often without credit. We alternated between day and night shifts, powered through weekends, and were on call around the clock, seven days a week. The first thing I did when I returned to the United States was to turn my phone to silent.

When reporting overseas, added obstacles like culture and language compound the frenzy. It also didn't help that our main office was in New York, twelve or thirteen hours behind us. The bosses came in fresh and demanding when we were at the tailend of a long day. It often meant writing a new story at 10:00 p.m., even though the shift started at 8:00 a.m., or staying up late to make calls to experts in the Western Hemisphere.

China was booming, but the Communist Party intended to maintain its stranglehold on political power. Chinese media is still largely state controlled, and foreign correspondents are viewed as complications to government efforts to monopolize the content and flow of information. At one point or another, every one of my colleagues told me stories about being detained, questioned, and threatened by authorities. We assumed that our office phones were being monitored, and mysterious cars with tinted windows—transport for state security agents—followed reporters on a regular basis. The extent of intimidation I experienced on that trip consisted of some shoving by paramilitary police in Tiananmen Square.

The first time I visited that historic venue I walked around for a few minutes before sitting at the base of a towering lamp-post. Around me, strollers, lollers, and picture-takers packed the massive square, bathed in fluorescent light that flooded the night sky. Dozens of kids on in-line skates zipped around, and kites thronged the air, which surprised me. I never associated them with China, but apparently, like so many things, the country receives credit for their invention almost three thousand years ago. One tiny girl was tugging at the strings of a butterfly-shaped kite twice her size—it was a miracle that it didn't carry her off.

That evening was my only visit for pleasure. Over the years, I walked through the square during annual meetings of the National People's Congress, the legislature, while trying to coax quotes from delegates, many of whom loathed talking to foreign media, especially American organizations. I skulked around during sensitive anniversaries, eyes peeled for protests and arrests, while trying not to be spotted by plainclothes policemen. I never returned with visiting friends or managed to watch the flag ceremonies at sunrise and sunset with thousands of other Chinese.

A couple of nights after my first visit there, I went back to Tiananmen to gather quotes and to be ready to describe the scene—what journalists call "color"—if Beijing won its Olympics bid. It was the city's second attempt to host the Games, an honor that would mark its full emergence onto the world stage. Worries over the country's human rights record had stymied the first bid.

There's no other way to put it: the air was electric. I stood in the heart of the crowd, barely able to breathe in the carnival atmosphere as thousands of people jammed against each other chatting, snacking, some even jumping up and down in excitement. It was probably the largest spontaneous gathering in the capital since the pro-democracy demonstrations in 1989. Remembering the bloody crackdown, I wondered for a second how events would unfold if Beijing lost its bid again.

As the time approached for the announcement from Moscow, where the International Olympic Committee was meeting, I called the bureau and held the phone line open to confirm what was being said. I gripped my pen, my hand shaky with anticipation, ready to start taking notes immediately.

The results, televised live, blared over a loudspeaker.

Silence.

Then a murmur rippled through the crowd followed by an eruption of cheers and screams when it became clear that Beijing had beaten Toronto, Paris, Istanbul, and Osaka for the honor. The square transformed into a sea of victory signs and fluttering miniature Chinese flags. Fireworks blossomed in the sky, showering the crowds with a confetti of paper and ashes. I couldn't wipe the smile off my face as I ran around trying to capture the ecstasy of the moment.

"This will be the best Olympics because the Chinese love sports more than anyone else in the world," shouted Lu Kexin, a nineteen-year-old waiter. Nearby, a group of students yelled "Beijing! Beijing!" and flashed victory signs with their fingers.

A similar scene was unfolding at an official outdoor ceremony in the city's west, where, about an hour before the IOC announcement, a handpicked crowd of thousands had gathered. After the decision, people burst into the national anthem as traditional lion dancers and ballerinas spearheaded festivities. President Jiang Zemin and other members of the cabinet and Communist Party politburo stepped into the spotlight as hordes of uninvited residents flooded into the venue.

"Comrades!" Jiang shouted to the crowd from the stage. "We express our deep thanks to all our friends around the world and to the IOC for helping to make Beijing successful in its Olympic bid."

On the Avenue of Eternal Peace, the city's ten-lane-wide east-west thoroughfare, the merrymaking lathered itself into one of the most spontaneous, unchoreographed, and happy gatherings of the masses in decades. It was an extraordinary sight, given the sensitivity of the area's history and the tight guard over the square. Citizens ecstatically cheered that China finally was receiving the popular recognition they felt it deserved. Jubilant residents danced on cars, drummed garbage cans, climbed street lamps, chanted victory slogans, and sang nationalistic songs. Two men—one shirtless—waved giant flags from the side-car of a motorcycle weaving its way down the road. Traffic stood still, the lights frozen red. Drivers turned off their engines while passengers leaned out of car and bus windows, high-fiving passersby.

Newspapers distributed late editions announcing the win with banner headlines in red, a color of good fortune reserved for only the most important news. The *People's Daily*, the party's main paper declared: BEIJING SUCCEEDS IN OLYMPIC BID.

Despite the extraordinary circumstances, the regime's security apparatus stepped in soon enough. Throughout the night, a phalanx of police stood guard around Tiananmen Square. By 2:00 a.m., they were herding crowds out of the area.

醬

Hot and rainy, the days steeped in a slow, yellow haze. I tried to explore and absorb as much as I could but felt like a sponge bloated beyond recognition with the constant stream of new experiences. While almost everything had a patina of "That's China!" charm, a couple of recurring themes gave me pause.

The first was a proclivity for public spitting that I realized was not just a local phenomenon but a national one. Everyone did it at all times of day in all kinds of weather in all locations. It happened in an elevator, at a restaurant, while swimming in the pool of a five-star hotel. The city government tried to curb the tendency before the Beijing Olympics by distributing "spit sacks" and threatening a $7 fine for each offending gob. Neither measure even registered among the population. Once, a health official whom I was interviewing about a respiratory disease hawked and nearly expelled phlegm onto the carpeted floor before catching himself.

The other head-scratcher was the ankle-high, flesh-colored nylons many women favored. They paired them with all kinds of footwear, from tennis shoes to sandals, and all kinds of outfits. Some said that only their mothers wore them, others that they kept the feet cool in summer. Most just shrugged.

When not working, I played tourist. Believe me, it was easier than explaining that I was a Singaporean working temporarily from Beijing for an American company whose name in Mandarin sounds like it has ties to the US government. Trying to see both old and new Beijing, I shopped at Hongqiao and Panjiayuan, the city's famous markets for pearls, antiques, and just about every imaginable knick-knack. I watched an acrobatic troupe jump through hoops, spin umbrellas with their feet, and toss heavy porcelain vats around with their necks. For hours, I wandered down walkways and around buildings of breathtaking beauty and ornateness at the Temple of Heaven and the Forbidden City.

One afternoon, I bought a ticket to watch Beijing Opera. While I didn't relish the thought of sitting through caterwauling, it was something I had to check off my to-do list. We sat at wooden tables and chairs, sipping tea and nibbling on pumpkin seeds. I liked the performance more than expected, especially the caked-on makeup, intricate costumes, and precisely coordinated movements. How could you not enjoy lines like: "May I commit suicide and my body hang from the rafters if I break my promise and let your secret leak out."

The highlight of my nightlife came on a Saturday, when a group of French expats took me clubbing. At the time, one of the hottest places among young Beijingers was a smoky club called Banana. (Its name in Mandarin sounded like bah-nah-nah too.) On the roof of an old shopping center, the club had a packed outdoor bar, complete with Chinese waitresses in blonde wigs and two guys selling grilled skewers of meat and vegetables. The dance floor was so jammed that all we could do was bounce in place to techno with an occasional Mandarin phrase thrown in: *thump-thump-thump-thump yi-er-san-si* (one, two, three, four).

At the end of my trip, I visited the Badaling section of the Great Wall. The area leading up to the wall formed a circus of tour buses, shops, and street vendors. It was Banana all over again—minus the techno. The crowds were mostly Chinese, which surprised me. Different tour groups—identified by baseball caps of various hues and guides holding up matching pennants—had gathered as well as clusters of friends and families on field trips. Together, they produced a cacophony of sounds: hawking and spitting, shouting into cellphones, hailing each other. They resembled an army of ants making their way along the imposing structure. I took a deep breath and joined them, squinting and sweating in the 100-degree heat.

It was terrifying. On the steep parts, at times, I was almost eye-level with the foot of the person in front of me. Everyone packed together so closely that, if one person misstepped or tripped, we all would have gone down. Guards posted at regular intervals screamed for people to move faster.

Suddenly, everything opened up, and we had room to move around. Women in heels (how did they make the climb?) and those flesh-colored nylon ankle-highs took turns posing for photos with smiles and umbrellas. Children ran about until their mothers chastised them. A small breeze blew as I gazed over the edge, taking in the astonishing vista. The monument was spectacularly, imposingly long, undulating as far as the eye could see through tree-laden mountains. The wall indeed was great, and I couldn't stop grinning.

醬

I ate well those three weeks.

One day my lunch consisted of shrimp and cabbage dumplings and pork and chive *guotie*, a pan-fried version, recommended by a taxi driver.

While researching a story about snakes, I visited a southern Chinese restaurant that served it braised. The waiter brought the reptile out to my table in a heavy cloth sack—still writhing. (I don't know what it looked like; my eyes were mostly shut.) He pulled it out, snipped off its head with a pair of scissors, and poured the blood into a bowl.

"Drinking it fresh brings you good health," he said.

I politely declined.

When the snake returned from the kitchen, chunks of it were sizzling in a thick brown sauce in a clay pot. It tasted like stringy, well-seasoned chicken, but even so I could only manage a little piece, bone still intact. The skin—shavings of black and silver—came last, slightly chilled and seasoned with sesame oil and chili. The chewy and crunchy texture felt like wood ear fungus, another popular addition to Chinese dishes.

Mr. Shi, the office driver, gleefully said that he could help with the story and invited me to sample his home-brewed snake liquor, a potent potion linked to virility, made by dropping a live specimen into distilled grain alcohol and letting it age for a few months. He stored the slightly cloudy liquor in a large glass jar, the snake curled in its depths. I took a sniff and pulled away quickly. It smelled like a gasoline-soaked attic. Mr. Shi, who also taught me how to make Coca-Cola chicken wings—empty a can of Coke into a pot, put in the meat, salt and some sliced ginger, cook until the liquid reduces into a syrup—poured a tiny amount into a glass and held it out as his elderly parents looked on. Like my father, I have no tolerance for alcohol, but I figured that, if I had to get sick, ingesting snake liquor was a good reason. Half a sip tasted so rancid that I thought it was going to burn a hole in my esophagus. Mr. Shi and his family seemed to find my watering eyes funny.

When friends took me to have *huoguo*, or hot pot (literally "fire pot"), we threw vegetables and paper-thin slices of raw meat and seafood into a cauldron of broth and watched the steam curl upward. I knew to keep the meat in the slotted spoon until it turned opaque and not to lose any of it in the soup, otherwise the pieces would shrivel up and overcook. The dumplings, on the other hand, didn't need careful watching; once they floated, they were done.

This was hot pot interface like I'd never had before. One side of the partitioned pot had regular chicken stock but the other had a burnt-red, lava-like, chili-based broth that bubbled like a witch's brew, a nod to the specialty of the southwestern municipality of Chongqing. Tears of agony tinged with delight flowed during dinner; everything tasted so good, especially with do-it-yourself dipping sauces put together with sesame paste, soy sauce, chili oil, cilantro, and garlic.

The flight home was uneventful—except the woman behind me threw up.

鬱

I returned for my long-term assignment almost a year later, in June 2002.

"If you do well there," my boss, Mike Silverman, told me days before I left New York, "the rest of your career is yours to write."

I took little comfort from his well-meaning words, echoed by pretty much everyone who knew where I was going. I was excited but mostly terrified—of how little I understood the country, of the unlimited potential to mess up, of disappointing the people who had faith in me, of not making friends, of being detained. As the list of worries and tasks grew longer, the hours I slept grew shorter.

Beijing was as crazy as—possibly crazier than—I remembered. Buildings were being torn down, and new ones took their place in the blink of an eye. Roads still teemed with chaos; everyone thought they had the right of way. I became a master of playing chicken with other pedestrians and bicycles and had learned to weave between fast-moving cars as if in a high-stakes game of Frogger.

Again the weather became unbearable; there were days so hot and dry that my rubber flip-flops softened on contact with the blazing pavement. The scorching air singed my nasal passages as though I had stuck my head in a 500-degree oven and inhaled. Keeping cool became an obsession. One happy way was to eat a semi-frozen, Jell-O–like concoction of questionable provenance called "Green Tongue" discovered in the ice cream section of a mom-and-pop store.

It was indeed tongue-shaped, wobbling and drooping suggestively on its stick when it warmed a little. "Shake your passion," proclaimed its brightly colored wrapper that described it as an "apple-flavored frozen stick." The fluorescent green color and the god-knows-what's-in-it texture put off most of my friends, but I could eat three in a row . . . and sometimes did.

For the first month and a half, home was a hotel room with a leaky tub, a small inconvenience balanced by the mini chocolate bar left on my pillow every night. I was still adjusting to my new home, new life, and new job. Instead of hopping on the F train, I hailed dilapidated Xiali-brand taxis. I shopped at wholesale markets instead of Key Foods and corner bodegas. This time, it was for real, not just a brief visit before returning to the comfort of New York.

Workers confiscated more than half of a box of books that I had shipped to myself from Singapore—mostly must-reads on China recommended by friends—when I picked it up at the post office. I was told to go to a counter set aside for inspections of incoming packages where a couple of postal clerks ripped open my box, dug in, and took a few to a back room without explanation. They waved away my questions with a simple "It's not allowed" and sent me on my way with a written receipt.

On another day I had to go to the headquarters of the Public Security Bureau—notorious for long lines and surly officers—to apply for my residence permit. When it was finally my turn, Officer Zhang Wei, the foreign press liaison, gave me a short lecture about the need to "learn the mother tongue," to "abide the rules of the country" and to avoid "unfortunate incidents with the police." Then he politely presented me with his card and told me to get in touch if I needed anything.

I couldn't wait to move into my new home in the heart of the Russian district, a few minutes' walk to work, and Ritan Park, a historic public space. The unit sat on the eighteenth floor (I later moved two floors up) of an ugly orange tile and green glass building with two towers and a lofty name: Beijing's Magnificent and Grand Garden, in Mandarin; in English, Palace Apartments. It rose far above the havoc of the city, 2,100 square feet spread out into three bedrooms, two bathrooms, new hardwood floors, and floor-to-ceiling windows in the living room. It was more rent than I had ever paid in my life, but it felt like a sanctuary to which I could retreat despite being within view of the Foreign Ministry, where our handlers worked and could literally keep an eye on us.

My colleagues Ted, Greg, and later Alexa Olesen all lived in the complex too. It was like having family close by.

A half dozen restaurants ringed the ground floor, including one that sold fresh hand-pulled noodles with meaty toppings like braised beef tendon and fried pork chop, a quick and inexpensive favorite with the lunchtime crowd. Another served hot pot and homestyle dishes, more of a dinner place, where families rubbed elbows around pots of bubbling stock cooking up meat and vegetables and munched on flaky buns topped with sesame seeds. In cold weather, the windows always steamed up.

Most intriguing were a pair of dueling outlets selling food from Wenzhou, a prosperous port city in eastern China notorious for its concentration of self-made millionaires. The cuisine is mostly seafood-based—thanks to its proximity to the East China Sea—mild and clean-flavored. In my building, both restaurants had all sorts of water creatures displayed, post-mortem, on ice, as well as walls lined with tanks of them swimming, wriggling, or lazing desultorily at the bottom. I picked the busier one for my first Wenzhou meal and reeled from the surly service and the din of hungry diners sucking on a variety of mollusks that I had never seen before while loudly toasting their pleasure with *baijiu*, a clear grain liquor with a vicious kick.

The other place, Little Jin's Seafood Restaurant, was quieter, had a friendlier staff, and, most importantly, had an equally impressive array of seafood. The best way to enjoy the selection, I learned, was to pick out the raw specimens as the cook—a short, smiling man in a white T-shirt, apron, and rolled up pants— looked on and to ask him to prepare them the way he thought was best. Manager Jin always took 20 percent off my bill.

My favorite dishes included a whole pomfret steamed to perfection in a shallow pool of its own fishy broth, flavored with a dash of soy sauce and a tangle of green onions; scallops, also steamed, agape in their fan-shaped shells, sat in their own juices, topped with glass noodles, minced garlic, and more green onions; curls of squid slices stir-fried with chives; and whole boiled shrimp with a dark soy dipping sauce.

Every meal there ended with a heaping plate of Fried Rice Vermicelli with Three Delicacies, an addictively tasty pile of noodles that had soaked up the flavors of its ingredients. The dish retained a delicious trace of what in Singapore is called *wok hei*, a hard-to-define smokiness infused into food cooked over roaring flame in a wok, the result of searing, caramelization, and other mysterious processes.

On summer nights, Manager Jin opened tables on the sidewalk and my friends and I ate until our bellies stretched as tight as drums, cars whizzing by and mosquitoes buzzing around our legs. Jonathan Ansfield, a keen and well-connected Reuters reporter at the time and one of my dearest friends, once downed a disconcertingly large order of fried silkworm pupae. A native of Milwaukee, Ansfield said it reminded him of his Mandarin study days in the '90s in China's northeast, where he regularly enjoyed roasted buns flecked with pepper flakes and cumin, and skewers of the insect sold by vendors beneath an overpass.

The Wenzhou batch, he said, was quite good and well seasoned, unlike some stale versions he had tried that tasted mealy.

Lindsay Beck, another close friend and Reuters reporter, decided to take the plunge. She put it in her mouth, whole, and scrunched up her face before sticking out her tongue.

"They're awfully . . . mushy," she managed after a few seconds.

Having avoided eating bugs on sticks—a popular street food throughout Asia—I succumbed to peer pressure from my dark-eyed, curly-haired friends. I gingerly crunched into one of the thumbnail-sized, brown-gray pellets, tasting a musty crispness that gave way to a layer that had the consistency of paste. I looked down at the cross-section of the pupa and saw its ashen insides, not sure which end I had eaten. Perhaps that was my mistake. I should've popped the whole thing into my mouth and not looked back . . . or down.

My apartment building lay in the middle of the Yabaolu district, a mecca for Russian merchants stocking up on Chinese-made goods at wholesale prices to be sold at home for huge profits. According to some accounts, the area was originally named Yaba Hutong, Mute Man's Alley, after a well-known resident but later changed to Yabaolu, Elegant Treasure Road. Its labyrinth of freight-forwarding services, warehouses, store-fronts, and malls advertised their wares in Cyrillic and sometimes Chinese. Their huge range offered everything from furs to shoes, toys to swimsuits, wigs to tea. Tall blonde women accompanied by men in leather jackets, no matter the weather, and Chinese pedicab drivers shouting in Russian to attract customers crowded the narrow, tree-lined streets.

When darkness fell, huge open-backed trucks parked on the side of the road as the grating *riiiiiiiip* of packing tape being wound around and around filled the air. Workers formed a chain and stacked the tape-wrapped bundles onto the truck bed, chatting loudly in their local Chinese dialect. As Yabaolu's reputation grew and more shops sprang up, the customer base expanded to include traders and shoppers from Central Asia, Eastern Europe, Africa, and the Middle East.

All those Russian merchants craved food from their homeland. Down an alley about six hundred feet from my apartment building sat a Russian restaurant with a signboard with Chinese characters that said BIG STUPID ELEPHANT. Inside lay a bar and restaurant designed to make a Russian appetite feel at home: vodka, hearty servings of sour cream–topped borscht, deep-fried and stewed meats with creamy or cheesy sauces, and mayonnaise-based salads of seafood, vegetables, and eggs accompanied by crusty brown bread. The décor was all dim lights, dark wood, and dingy carpets. On most nights, a floor show featured dances and songs that ranged from tacky to traditional to entertain the mix of couples, business associates, and the occasional hungry non-Russians like us.

Before I left Beijing, Chocolate, a glitzy new Russian nightclub, built a cult following, offering possibly the most surreal experience in town. In a suit and a Mohawk, a little person manned the deceptively nondescript front door—someone told me he was from the northeastern province of Jilin—and waved you through to the top of an escalator. Halfway through the descent into darkness, an enormous, subterranean space like a cross between *Alice in Wonderland* and a Baz Luhrmann movie opened up on the right. Chocolate had velvet curtains, oversized chairs, and paintings hung from the ceiling but facing the floor. One weekend floor show included pole dancers, a flirty African man in a bunny suit on a ten-foot unicycle, and a rotund blonde woman dressed as a nun who ripped off her habit to reveal skimpy lingerie before dragging a male customer to the floor to sit on him.

The borders of the Yabaolu neighborhood bled into other enclaves including traditional Chinese courtyard homes, a small Muslim community centered around a mosque, diplomatic compounds containing many foreign news agencies—the AP included—and an embassy district that included missions from America, Iraq, Japan, and North Korea. Because it was so hard to get any information from Pyongyang's secretive regime, we spent many hours camped outside the embassy in hopes of getting a statement from a representative or to be let in for a rare press conference when news was breaking, usually about the country's nuclear capabilities. Faced with photos of the "Great Leader" and the "Dear Leader"—Kim Il Sung and Kim Jong Il—the first consecutive father and son rulers of the North—and knowing what we did of the people's suffering, we grimly joked that the compound's barbed wire was there to keep people *in*.

My apartment faced north, above a *hutong*, the quintessentially Beijing warren of skinny, gray alleyways between courtyard houses packed with families living without indoor plumbing and with spotty electricity. In the fall, roofs sprouted a covering of drying *dabaicai*, "big white vegetable" (commonly known as Napa cabbage), the ubiquitous filler for soups, stir-fries, and dumplings. Shops squeezed together on a dusty path, selling everything from roasted sunflower seeds to plastic pails. It was always bustling and was the one place I enjoyed squeezing along with area residents, many of them tough bargainers not afraid to use their elbows or bodies to get the best product.

The *hutong* became my source for eggs and vegetables, often still encrusted with dirt from the fields. Despite the country's incredible economic progress, the urban and rural still overlapped in so many ways. On one of my first days in the middle of Beijing's notorious rush-hour traffic, a mule-drawn cart slowly made its way alongside bicycles and cars, steered by a farmer who didn't seem the least bit bothered by the bumper-to-bumper traffic. In second- and third-tier cities, the lines between city and country blurred even more.

Sadly, like many of its kind in Beijing, the *hutong* was razed to make way for a behemoth glass and tile building of indeterminate use. Over a couple of years, much of the old city disappeared, and the new took its place—sitting empty and unused.

As I got to know the area better, I frequented little shops that bestowed on me the title of *lao guke* or *lao pengyou*—longtime customer or old friend—because of how much and how often I bought from them. A friendly family from the poor central province of Anhui ran a fruit stand two minutes from my building. Like the nearby barbershops staffed with women in form-fitting ensembles who apparently did more than just cut hair, the stall remained open regardless of time or weather. Xiao Shi, a smiling young man with his nose always buried in a book when business slowed, helped me pick the sweetest clementines or the lychees without stems, lighter and a little cheaper because they were sold by weight. The family eventually accepted my 2:00 a.m., post–late shift fruit runs as part of my normal routine.

Just looking out my window taught me to watch for when farmers carrying their vegetables on bicycle carts set up at the playground by the high-rise apartment building across the street. With nothing more than some old hand-scales, a no-nonsense attitude, and a small wad of cash, they conducted a brisk business and often sold out by late morning.

❀

Some of my most treasured friends in Beijing came from the foreign press corps—dedicated, knowledgeable, tenacious, and often my direct competitors—and worked hours as long and odd as mine.

Those who lived there before I arrived made me feel at home from the start. Those who came later I got to know while showing them my favorite haunts and exploring new ones together. Reporters or not, all were gracious when I canceled on dinner plans at the last minute because I had to travel for an unexpected assignment or when the editing desk held up my story with questions and I showed up to parties hours too late. The last guests were donning their coats or everyone was already drunk, but they always welcomed me warmly and commiserated about pain-in-the-ass editors and bosses. When it really mattered, we shared our resources, checked one another's quotes, and worked together to push for access when there wasn't any. When it came down to it, it was always us reporters against them, the Chinese bureaucracy.

The expatriate lifestyle has certain central elements, no matter where in the world. In Beijing, however, something extra bound us even tighter. I'm not sure if it had to do with dealing with the daily frustrations and restrictions of an opaque government, the watchful eyes of neighborhood police, or whether it was just the thrill of living in one of the most exciting, controversial, and dynamic eras of one of the most exciting, controversial, and dynamic nations in the world.

We supported one another through homesickness, work stresses and pressures, broken hearts, and sheer physical exhaustion. We kept each other sane, sometimes with a hug or a quick phone call just to say hi. Other times it took the form of a hike or a weekend away, somewhere quiet to unwind. But the most memorable and comforting moments often came over food, whether gossiping over peanut butter and condensed milk toast at a Hong Kong diner or devouring sweet soy milk and fried dough sticks after hours of dancing.

For a handful of wonderful years, Ansfield and his wife, Amy Li, ran a bar in the historic Ritan Park, which offered one of the best slice-of-everyday-life experiences around.

Built in 1530, Ritan, or Altar of the Sun, houses one of Beijing's five historic altars (the others being Moon, Earth, Heaven, and Agriculture). Emperors from the Ming and Qing dynasties worshipped the god of the Sun and offered ritual sacrifices at the west-facing altar, a square platform built of white stones with nine steps leading to the flat top.

Present day Ritan still contains buildings and relics from the past, including the Slaughter Pavilion; the Dressing Hall, where the emperor changed his clothes or rested; as well as dozens of ancient trees, one said to be a 1,100-year-old cypress. But since it opened to the public in the late 1950s, the park, which contains about fifty acres of land, now includes a growing number of modern amenities, such as a climbing wall, children's amusement park, and fishing pond. It was a smallish park by Beijing standards, yet still a great respite from the crush of everyday life.

It was impossible to catalog fully the activities that people enjoyed there during the day. At any given moment, someone was fan-dancing or practicing different forms of tai chi, swinging a badminton racket, sword-fighting, singing, playing an instrument whose name I didn't know, napping, strolling, kicking around a feathered Hacky Sack, walking backward (to exercise different muscles), or, my all-time favorite, mass dancing. When the weather was warm enough, groups of mostly elderly men and women in baggy T-shirts and running shoes gathered in a large circle in the early evening and step-and-turned to traditional music blasting from an old boom box set in their midst. They laughed when someone misstepped and deftly worked around him or her. On other occasions there was ballroom dancing, figures twirling and dipping in the twilight.

After dark, the park grew quiet and eerie. Ansfield's bar, nestled in the confines of a small replica of Dowager Empress Ci Xi's Stone Boat at the Summer Palace, became popular with the expat crowd, especially us journalists. We gathered in all kinds of weather for drinks in the cozy space that overlooked a small, man-made lake. In winter, kids sledded on its surface, and in summer mosquitoes bred quickly in the murky waters.

With a cigarette in one hand and a beer in another, Ansfield, whose Mandarin skills far exceeded mine, usually engaged his customers in deep conversation. Aside from us, they were usually artists, musicians, diplomats, or families of tourists passing through the park. It was the place to celebrate a birthday or throw a party for one of the many people in our circle who was either leaving the city or coming back for more.

A couple of years in a row, we huddled in the warmth of heat lamps and rang in the new year with popcorn, dumplings, and sparkling wine toasts in paper cups.

33

"*Xinnian kuaile!* Happy New Year!" we shouted at the stroke of midnight, hugging and laughing in anticipation of the future.

Outside, it may have been cold and dark, but inside we had each other.

2

Farmer Tu's Last Chicken

Many in the country, however, had nothing.

Disaster and loss fostered my most memorable meal in China. Neither was immediately apparent that summer afternoon as Greg and I sat down to lunch at Farmer Tu's waterfront home, where milky green waves lapped gently at the edge of his property. Rice filled our bowls, the dishes simple and prepared with care: a freshly killed chicken lightly stewed in soy sauce; stir-fried garden greens; a small bowl of meltingly tender braised pork belly; and a fish, scaled in a flash and steamed whole.

The expanse of water outside the house shouldn't have been there, though. A river had overwhelmed nearby dikes and devoured a year's worth of crops. Tu's family lost everything. The chicken, sacrificed for strangers, was their last. It was a devastating scene, yet Tu and his wife worried more about making sure that we didn't go hungry after chronicling their catastrophe. When I learned what they had done for us, guilt ruined my appetite. But not partaking in my hosts' generosity might have offended them. So I dug in.

"We are just grateful you are telling our story, that someone cares about our plight," said Tu, a sun-browned man with sharp cheekbones, at the end of the meal. I asked what he was going to do to survive. He shrugged, lighting up a cigarette. "Borrow money from relatives. We can't do anything else until the water disappears."

❊

In 2002, early summer monsoons brought enormous amounts of rain to Hunan province, causing the Xinqiang River to crest its banks and flood the surrounding countryside, despite villagers' efforts to shore up area dikes. From his boat, Farmer Tu showed me the devastation as we zigzagged across his submerged paddy fields. AP/GREG BAKER

June usually signals the start of China's three-month monsoon season, when torrential rains pour onto steep riverbanks denuded by aggressive logging and trigger massive floods and mudslides that wash away crops, homes, and lives. Hundreds die each year, and the floods threaten the water supplies for countless more. The problem of overflow and destruction reaches an apex along the mighty Yangtze River, a north-south divide etched out by billions of liters of muddy water stretching from sparsely populated Qinghai province to cosmopolitan Shanghai.

In 2002, a couple of months after I arrived in China, something different was happening. The floods were hitting part of the country's arid belt, regions completely unaccustomed to dealing with so much water at once. It was an unusually strong manifestation of global warming. Winter had been balmy—the second warmest in half a century—and spring had seen particularly severe and frequent dust storms. Early summer monsoons had dumped immense amounts of rain on provinces with soil unaccustomed to a deluge of moisture. Almost a thousand people had died in nontraditional flood areas like the northwestern province of Shaanxi, the western desert regions of Gansu, and tropical Guangxi in the far south. Storms battered agriculture, transportation, power grids, and other infrastructure, causing billions of dollars in damage. Residents, many of them deeply poor, were blindsided.

Now, late in the summer, the government said the flood toll was shaping up to be as disastrous as 1998, when more than four thousand people died along the Yangtze. State media had been running increasingly breathless reports about rising waters and mass evacuations since June. In Hunan province, a densely populated farming region and one of the worst-hit with two hundred people dead, Chinese officials and experts were urging residents around Dongting, the country's second-largest freshwater lake, to brace for colossal flooding.

The Yangtze and four other rivers feed Dongting, about the size of Rhode Island and surrounded by hundreds of miles of dikes. Because Dongting rises with the rivers' flow, areas around the lake suffer chronic flooding. Land reclamation by settlers in the region had made the situation even more precarious as growing swaths of farmland meant less room for the lake to expand freely during summer rains.

Joe, Ted, Chris, and I gathered around the old television in our office to watch updates on Dongting from China Central Television. Reports on the twice-daily national newscasts said a million people were "affected." (I never got used to the frustrating vagueness of official Chinese figures; did "affected" mean their feet got wet or that property was damaged?) The broadcasts also aired footage of frenzied efforts by residents and workers to shore up the area's dikes and embankments with sandbags. It was dramatic stuff, and editors lost no time dispatching their correspondents into the field.

Joe volunteered me for the assignment because, the newest member of the staff, I hadn't yet traveled to another province. I didn't know what to expect on the trip but was impatient to see a new place and jump into action. My field experiences in Beijing to that point consisted entirely of one man running away from me when I approached him on the street to get a quote and a handful of press conferences, where I discovered that Chinese reporters received packets of money—usually a couple of hundred yuan—along with their press kits for "travel expenses." It was a standard practice in the country that you could construe as a way to supplement the income of the journalists who worked for cash-poor state-run publications . . . or as a bribe for favorable coverage, depending on how you wanted to look at it. Either way, I returned mine, glad for the experience of being mistaken for a local journalist.

Under official reporting rules then, foreign media could work outside Beijing only if given hard-won approval by the central and local governments. Few reporters adhered to the regulations, particularly when news was breaking. For their part, authorities usually assumed that we would show up, but sometimes it took a while before they made their move, depending on orders from above or how a situation was unfolding. It was a cat-and-mouse game, where they knew that we were in the area and we knew that they knew. It was just a matter of time before we found each other. For our part, it was essential to work fast. Disasters, even natural ones, were especially sensitive topics, and authorities kept an extra vigilance about excluding foreign reporters. On state media, however, the government sometimes exaggerated the danger and destruction in order to play up their efforts to rescue people or ameliorate their suffering. In that case, it was good public relations and a morale booster for the victims.

I filled a backpack with shorts, jeans, T-shirts, granola bars, notebooks, and my laptop, throwing in flood-friendly waterproof sandals and a Gore-Tex jacket at the last minute. Greg, the bureau's photo chief, was coming with me—and I was glad. He knew how the country worked. A prolific and thoughtful photographer, his sterling work ethic set the standard for every shooter in town.

We flew to Changsha, Hunan's capital, before catching a standing-room-only train that passed through the city of Yueyang, where rising waters were threatening to breach dikes and inundate surrounding farmland. We had heard that hundreds of residents had already been evacuated in deluged neighborhoods. More storms were coming.

So many people and a jumble of their belongings packed our train car that every breath I inhaled cost me an inch of personal space. Sunflower seeds and cigarette butts littered the area, perfumed as it was with the salty steam from beef-flavored instant noodles—a ubiquitous Chinese meal-on-the-run—and the occasional whiff of urine from the tiny bathrooms. The train stopped every few minutes to pick up even more travelers. My backpack, a buffer against pushy passengers, grew heavier by the minute, and my enthusiasm was flagging quickly.

❄

Yueyang has a special place in Chinese history as the birthplace of dragon-boat racing. According to legend, the Dragon Boat Festival takes place on the fifth day of the fifth month of the lunar calendar in memory of Qu Yuan, a wise and loyal minister who lived during the Warring States Period (475–221 BC). Originally one of the most trusted counselors of the king of the Chu state, Qu advocated making the Chu rich and powerful by joining forces with other states against the Qin encroaching from the northwest. But the king, swayed by jealous ministers' treachery, banished his adviser instead.

During his exile, Qu wandered the countryside writing mournful, patriotic poems about the fate of his beloved but corrupt and crumbling state. When he heard that the Chu had fallen to Qin invaders, he clasped a rock to his chest and drowned himself in the Miluo River. Villagers, who admired him as a righteous man, raced in their boats, trying to save him, but lost his body as the waters flowed into Dongting Lake. In one version of the legend, they splashed their paddles to scare away evil spirits and threw rice in the water to keep fish from eating Qu's body.

Today, rowers compete in long, colorful vessels with dragon heads along Dongting's shores every year as a reenactment of villagers' efforts to save Qu. Spectators feast on triangles of glutinous rice dumplings called *zongzi*. The rice is always sticky and usually wrapped in bamboo leaves. Fillings range from savory—fatty pork, black mushrooms, chestnuts, salted eggs—to sweet, including lotus seeds or mashed dates.

Much of Hunan, best known as the birthplace of Communist leader Mao Zedong, lies south of Dongting, hence the province's name, literally "South of the Lake." Mountainous and subtropical, Hunan is sometimes called Xiang, after a river that cuts through it. The region's bountiful plains, valleys, and bodies of water have given it the reputation of being "the land of fish and rice," like many of the areas downstream from the Yangtze.

Unlike the piquant cuisine of neighboring Sichuan, which pops with tongue-numbing peppercorns and the heat of dried chili peppers, Hunanese food features the more straightforward fire of fresh chilies, the saltiness of smoked meats, and the acidity of preserved vegetables. Hot and sour act as a key combination in the cuisine, the heat believed to cool the body by opening the pores in humid summer months and warm the body in colder ones. Dishes generally have thick sauces and rich colors, the result of lengthy braising, stewing, and double-boiling.

One of the most famous offerings is an obscenely unctuous pork belly dish so beloved by Mao that it was named for him. In his home village of Shaoshan, Mao Family Red-Braised Pork is said to be the product of a very particular and complicated recipe. Symmetrically sliced pork belly is steamed with star anise, rock sugar, and cinnamon before the meat is deep-fried then cooked in a pot with salted black beans. The golden result is fatty but not greasy, deliciously moist and tender.

Variations range from rendering the pork in hot oil, to using pressure cookers, to adding any combination of onions, ginger, garlic, Shaoxing wine, dark soy, fermented tofu, caramelized sugar, and chili peppers. The liquid often distills into a seductively dark lacquer that coats the meat. Many say that it was the "brain food" that helped the Great Helmsman defeat Chiang Kaishek, putting the Communists squarely in power.

❦

Greg and I arrived late at night in Yueyang, a picturesque metropolitan area of about five million people with mountains in the east, Dongting in the west, the Yangtze in the north, and other rivers in the south. Our hotel, a cavernous building, loomed softly in the darkness over the neighborhood's mom-and-pop shops. Its typical shiny, nondescript interior and bulky, dark-wood furniture tried to convey a sense of grandness familiar to midsize cities across the country. There were no signs of water or panic in the streets, but I was too tired to care.

At the breakfast buffet—standard fare of greasy stir-fried meats, vegetables, noodles, and buns, all heavily spiced—a posse of foreign journalists was silently sipping cups of instant coffee or concentrating on watery porridge and preserved vegetables, another morning staple. Greg made a round of introductions, and talk soon turned to the flood. A BBC cameraman said it wasn't as dire as the Chinese media were reporting. A handful of homes along the edges of the rising river and a few alleys were in bad shape, he said, but it wasn't the imminent calamity everyone had thought.

Many of the reporters with whom we had breakfast had the jaded, world-weary air of longtime correspondents. You could almost hear their eyeballs rolling back in mock exasperation. But surely the situation wasn't that calm. A government official had said that tens of thousands of people around Dongting had been displaced, and the state-run Xinhua News Agency was reporting that almost a million people were working around the clock to reinforce area dikes.

The sun blazed down narrow, dry streets lined only with a few skeletal trees offering little shade. Small eateries displaying slumbering fish and wriggling shrimp and eels in water-filled plastic basins were coming to life in anticipation of the lunch crowd. Barbers were giving sidewalk haircuts, and crowds gathered around chess and mahjong players. Customers belted out tunes on a karaoke machine set up in front of a supermarket to improve business.

Greg, camera gear slung on one shoulder, and I wandered down to the waterfront, where wooden fishing boats bobbed gently and residents milled around as on any other day. But something was wrong.

"Is that a roof?" I asked in amazement, seeing a triangle of tile poking from the murky brown-green water a few yards from shore. Other empty houses had water almost to the tops of their doors. Laundry hanging on lines dangled inches above debris-littered water. Toothbrushes and mugs sat abandoned on windowsills. Greg didn't answer, already recording the scene. Many of the residents watched him—the foreigner with a big camera and wavy salt-and pepper hair—as he shot frame after frame. Some shuffled out of the way, embarrassed or suspicious of the attention. Others simply stared into the lens.

"The people left their homes as soon as the waters started rising," a man called out from his boat, unasked.

We spent the next few days driving around and renting rickety fishing boats with motors belching smoke and noise as we cruised along the shore and waterways. The boats' operators, capitalizing on the situation, charged cutthroat rates. The occasional spray of water cooled my rapidly browning skin. The other reporters were right: Water levels had risen significantly, but there was no evidence of a deadly disaster. Even so, the damage in some neighborhoods was dramatic.

In those sections, the boatmen cut their engines, and we drifted silently through labyrinths of ghostlike canals where flooded homes and small businesses sat empty. In shuttered shops, water lapped at hastily stacked plastic chairs and tables. Unopened boxes of merchandise lay abandoned inside.

The people, however, were taking the upheaval in stride. A handful of residents, some in just their underwear, waded through hip- or chest-high water to recover belongings held high above their heads. Two shirtless men pushed a motorized tricycle precariously balanced on a plank of wood to the shore, passing a boy drifting, unperturbed, on a square of wood taped to two Styrofoam boxes. Minutes away, residents with water ankle-deep in their houses sloshed about, drying clothes and furniture in the sun. A young woman, her jeans soaked through, held tightly to a small white dog, both damp but no worse for wear.

In Chenglingji, the area's only major port, work had stopped, and buildings stood in five feet of dirty green water. In some parts, we floated eye-level with the tops of roofs and trees. Residents living on the ground floor in a row of two-story apartments had moved their lives upstairs.

"Of course it's trouble," said Wang Guoqing, a dockworker. "But what can we do? *Meibanfa*." Nothing can be done.

Daily life continued in the afternoon heat, a tinny soundtrack provided by transistor radios and small-screen televisions. Men smoked and read newspapers as they napped on cots set up in makeshift bedrooms. Others threw baited hooks off their balconies and called excitedly to their friends when they caught something, usually small fish that flashed silver in the sun as they writhed desperately. Chickens and geese circled nervously in converted pens, formerly storage rooms, as children played nearby with dolls.

"The floods come fast, but they also go down fast," Wang said optimistically.

More storms were predicted, so we wanted to see how people were preparing for the rain. We stopped on Junshan Island in the middle of Dongting, a former Taoist retreat turned tourist attraction famed for its bamboo groves, golden tortoises, and pricey tea. Thousands of sandbags at the shore, five to six deep, lined the edge of a park, workers in straw hats stacking them against the rising waters.

The tip of the roof of the park's ticket booth peeked out above the waterline. Lavish temples and elaborately decorated pagodas stood empty. Water had flooded the neatly trimmed grass and pebbled paths, and giant blue pumps were sloshing floodwater back into the lake.

Near sunset on another day, residents shouted *"Nihao!"*—"Hello!" from their balconies and second-floor windows. They assumed I was Greg's translator, a misconception on which he played often because he knew it annoyed me. Curious, they asked a flurry of questions about his background, a couple of which I answered before saying, "You should ask him. He speaks Mandarin!"

Greg chuckled but kept silent. They waved as we floated off.

One afternoon, while driving along a pockmarked side road near Yueyang, we spotted workers in green army fatigues on a long levee piled high with white sandbags. A red-and-yellow banner, the colors of the Chinese flag, fluttered nearby, reading CITIZEN SOLDIERS EMERGENCY RESCUE TEAM. It was just after lunch, and the sun was blazing. Another group of men, shirtless, was cooling off in a striped tent, half-dozing in the heat. When I popped my head in, they looked at me suspiciously and demanded to see the journalist identity card that Beijing issues to foreign reporters, an unusually savvy move. Even after they saw my credentials, they were wary. Yang Yang spoke grudgingly, saying that he and four residents had been living in the tent for more than a week and were performing "danger checks" for leaks every six hours. At night, they slept on the dike, smoking and talking between shifts.

"These are our homes," he said, pointing to a cluster of squat brick houses below the embankment. "We have to protect them. Wouldn't everyone do the same?"

One of his friends made a call on his cellphone. I found Greg, who had wandered off, and warned him that the workers might be calling the cops. I had no idea if that was the case, but a couple of other foreign reporters had already been detained while filming in the area. We got back into the car, erring on the side of caution.

Later that afternoon, miles away at another dike off a highway, a blue-and-white public security car pulled up at a nearby snack stand just minutes after we arrived. Had we been followed, or was it just coincidence? We made a beeline for the car, and our driver sped us away so fast that we nearly skidded off the road.

❈

A violent, thundering storm shook the hotel windows, and lightning streaked the skies on the second to last morning of the trip. The sun hadn't risen yet, and only a few people were on the streets. Some ran by, hunched over, heads uncovered. Holding my jacket's hood in place, I walked down to the edge of the lake, slipping a couple of times on the wet sidewalks. With the recent break in the rain, water levels had been dropping in our week there, but, despite the ebb, the lake level still stood at a depth of nearly 114 feet, well above the danger mark of about 108 feet.

The big, warm raindrops felt good after days of relentless sun. After about three hours, the storm abated into a steady drizzle. Greg and I headed into the rural areas surrounding the city. We stopped occasionally, trying to assess the situation, but no one seemed overly concerned.

❈

Mid-afternoon we randomly turned onto a driveway, drawn to a cluster of two-story, cement-and-tile houses sitting by the water. The homes seemed enviably close to the shores of the Xinqiang River, which feeds into Dongting. Trees, grass, and garden vegetables sprang from the dusty ground. Downy yellow ducklings wandered the yard before waddling in a panic toward the water when we approached.

Four men, a teenage girl with braids, and three young children soon emerged, curious about the strangers in their yard. One of the men called out a greeting. Greg took photos as I said hello and asked if the summer rains had affected them.

Farmer Tu, a slight man wearing a thin, striped shirt, sleeves rolled up, and gray trousers folded to his knees, pointed toward the water. "Our crops for the year, everything we've worked for, are gone," he said with a heavy Hunan accent.

"Crops? Were they far away?" I peered into the distance but couldn't see any paddy fields.

"Right there," he pointed again. "Under the water."

His idyllic waterfront property turned out to be a disaster zone. Too small and too fragile, embankments here had failed to hold back the floods. The rain-bloated river had swallowed their livelihood for the year. The quiet destruction was the most jarring image I had seen so far.

Tu offered to take us out on his boat to show us the area. He donned a white hardhat, grabbed a bamboo pole almost as tall as he was, and paddled with steady strokes, zigzagging across his submerged paddy fields. At first, he spoke only when I asked him questions, but he soon warmed up to the tale of the villagers' ultimately futile efforts to shore up the surrounding dikes the week before.

"We worked so hard to add sandbags every day in hopes of keeping the water back. Young and old, we all helped, except for the littlest of children. We worked night and day. . . . Every minute, every second we fought," he said, mimicking frantic stacking. "We brought our food there, we ate there, and we slept there. The water levels just kept getting higher."

In the end, the villagers could do nothing but watch as water overwhelmed the levees and engulfed crops with floods that rose to thirteen feet in some areas.

"The water just kept coming," he said. "We tried our hardest, but it wasn't enough."

Some two thousand people were evacuated from the area as homes were submerged, leaving only the tips of power poles visible. Most residents left with little more than bare essentials, seeking refuge in schools and with relatives.

Tu's home remained intact, but the loss of his crops left him $3,500 in debt—a monumental figure considering that rural residents in China made an average of $290 that year.

"My heart aches. I have five mouths to feed and no way to do it. I don't even have the money to move my family to higher ground. . . . Even if the floods recede, there's no way to earn a living. We'll have to beg. We'll become beggars."

He fell silent.

Waves splashed against the side of the boat. We cruised past more rooftops peeking out from the opaque green water. The village's flood prevention office had water up to its windows. A boy on a boat made of wooden planks tied to a pair of rubber tires paddled past.

I didn't know what to say, so I kept asking questions and listening to his answers. I didn't realize until later that many Chinese, especially in poor rural areas, enjoyed the chance to vent about their struggles to eke out a life for themselves. It was a novelty not only to speak openly, but to have someone listen to them in a country where citizens are not consulted formally about the way it is run and can be punished for being too vocal.

At the end of the afternoon, Tu issued a casual invitation. Please, he said, join us for something to eat. I agreed, keen to continue the conversation with him and his friends. Tu shouted out to his wife, who waved from a window. We docked and entered the couple's home, already fragrant with savory smells escaping from pots and pans. Hot oil occasionally popped above the rhythmic thump of a cleaver in the kitchen, which once overlooked the fields.

One of Tu's neighbors showed us around the sparsely furnished house, which had plain concrete walls and floors. Tu's father stood on an upstairs balcony looking out onto an overcast sky and a stretch of floodwaters surrounded by mountains. He nodded and smiled but said little.

Less than an hour later, my stomach growling savagely, we sat down to plates of chicken, pork, and fish. The Tus piled rice into our bowls, offered tea and rice wine, and, along with a dozen other neighbors, watched us intently. No one else was holding chopsticks. The food was just for us. The significance of the meal escaped me because I was so green. The abundance of meat and variety of dishes signaled a luxury usually afforded only on very special occasions, like Lunar New Year, the country's biggest holiday. Even then, this spread was rare for a rural family.

Despite their misfortune, the Tu family had pulled out all the stops and shared their limited provisions without a thought. They sat down at the table only after I insisted that we wouldn't touch a mouthful unless they ate with us. I couldn't find words to express our gratitude sufficiently.

They hadn't killed their last chicken in vain. Its meatier pieces, pale brown from a soy sauce bath, tasted dark and gamey. Tu and his wife crunched into bone and tendon while Greg and I gingerly pulled at the skin with our teeth. From small ceramic bowls we drank a soup made from the bird's bony bits. Its eggs, scrambled quickly in hot oil, had turned a gorgeous shade of sunshine yellow. We picked tiny bones from the fish, netted from a small pond nearby and steamed to flaky perfection, its flesh infused with the subtle, heady taste of cooking wine. The pork, dense and salty, made a perfect foil to our rice. Mao would've been proud.

As is customary, Tu and his wife put choice pieces of food— a chicken drumstick, a delicate fish cheek—in our bowls. We ate gratefully and heartily, but it was the gentle, down-to-earth company that made the meal. We chatted about our vastly different lives. Cigarette in hand, Tu spoke of long days in the field and how hard it was to make ends meet. "We wake up at 5:00 a.m. and stop work around 7:00 p.m., rain or shine," he said. "We work that way every year to survive."

I told them of my heritage and how I was still trying to understand my place in China's chaos. They delighted to see that I wrote with my left hand, a rarity in the country. In ancient times, the character for "left" had bad connotations. *Zuodao*—"left path"—for example implies illegality or immorality. Decades ago, being left-handed was frowned upon because it was nonconformist. Now, many Chinese considered me smart because I was different.

Before long, the inevitable arose: "Are you married?" they asked. I shook my head. "Do you have children?" they asked Greg, who also replied in the negative. They looked at us pityingly. They had lost their annual income and were heavily in debt, but they felt that it was we who had tragic lives.

❈

The sun was beginning to set, and it was time for Greg and me to return to the hotel. I desperately felt the need to help the family in some way, even if just to pay for the meal. I pulled some money from my wallet, but Tu pushed the notes away roughly. It was an embarrassingly clumsy gesture on my part after the generosity they had shown. Tu finally accepted two packs of cigarettes I bought in Changsha thinking they might be a way to bond with farmers.

He walked us to our car; the good-byes were brief, awkward. There were no handshakes, no hugs, no kisses. What do you say to a family who has lost so much yet remained so open? I didn't want to leave yet. I felt like there was more that I could do—and should.

As we drove off, I turned to wave, but Tu was already gone.

Big Red Fish Tale

I always joke that I reported mostly on the three D's in China: disasters, disease, and dissent. I didn't do happy—but I wanted to. Then, like a gift from the heavens, a headline appeared one day in the *China Daily*: EXPLORATION FOR "LAKE MONSTERS" TO LAUNCH IN NW CHINA.

I couldn't believe my eyes. Lake monsters? *Fun!*

"For hundreds of years there have been rumors that mysterious creatures that devour livestock live in the lake. Horses, cattle, and sheep are said to go missing near the lake every year," the article said. Excitement pinged in my chest.

I was looking forward to revisiting Xinjiang, the massive resource-rich region with borders touching Mongolia, Russia, Tajikistan, Kyrgyzstan, Kazakhstan, India, Pakistan, and Afghanistan. I had been there once before in 2003 to cover an earthquake and loved the dusty, arid area around the Taklamakan desert, but Kanas Lake lay in a heavily forested nature reserve in the northern tip, a whole new ballgame.

All lake monster roads led to Professor Yuan Guoying, director of the Xinjiang Scientific Research Institute of Environmental Protection and a passionate scientist known for his ecological expertise. Well versed on the region around the lake, he himself had seen the creatures on more than one occasion. Yuan, the unofficial clearinghouse for the phenomenon, had written numerous articles on the topic. Even better, he was leading a group to the area in a matter of weeks, part class reunion with his university buddies, part package tour to commemorate the twentieth anniversary of his first sighting of the *huguai*—the term in Mandarin for lake monsters. Best of all, he had given the green light for us to join him.

At the Big Red Fish restaurant, owners displayed a massive specimen of the hucho taimen, *a giant member of the salmon and trout family that locals call* dahongyu—big red fish. *Caught in a nearby river, reportedly in 1999 and purchased for around $600, this five-foot-six-inch trophy fish weighed 103 pounds—and more than paid for itself with the tourist traffic it drew.*

Yuan and other scientists said the *huguai* were likely *hucho taimen*, a giant, flat-headed specimen from the salmon and trout family known for its intimidating size and aggressive predatory skills. Locals simply called them *dahongyu*—big red fish. Their bodies were either bright silver-white or a shadowy gray, with rust-hued tails and razor-sharp teeth that they used to devour other fish. Known to hunt in packs and even prey on mice, bats, and birds, they have earned the nicknames "river wolves" and "terror trout." That sounded close enough to monsters to me.

"Villagers are afraid of going to the lake," Yuan said. "I said it was rubbish at first. The next day, I saw them. I had to eat my words."

But there was still a niggling doubt. What he had seen and what other people had reported didn't quite jibe with descriptions of the muscular *taimen*, which spawn mostly in the fast-moving rivers of Russia and Mongolia, highly prized by sport fishermen. No one knows how big the colossal fish can grow, but the largest on record, caught in Russia, clocked in at almost seven feet long and a hair over 230 pounds. The biggest caught in Kanas, by comparison, had been a paltry four feet, nine inches long.

Witnesses at the lake, however, have told of enormous shadows as big as trees and boats, some up to thirty-five feet long, cutting through the water. One account describes a silhouette as long as seventy feet leaping out of the depths when an earthquake struck the area in 2003.

Even China Central Television jumped in the fray, showing a grainy video filmed by a tourist in 2007. "From this clip you can clearly see a group of unknown bodies swimming in the water," the commentator said about the fifteen shapes, which looked like small boats speeding through the water, creating a huge wake. "They look like a naval force. It's a magnificent scene.

"The last time the Kanas monsters were spotted, it was on an evening in 2005. A tourist who was taking photos suddenly noticed that huge, fast-moving waves were appearing on the calm surface of the lake in front of them. There was even some rhythm to the appearance. Not long after, a pair of black, deep-water creatures more than thirty-three feet long appeared on the surface of the water."

So were the lake monsters really the *taimen*? Or a mutation? Or an undiscovered species?

※

Our trip began one morning in August 2005 at the main gate of the Xinjiang Science and Technology Cadre Training Center in

Urumqi, a sprawling city of glass-and-tile buildings. Three teachers, a nurse, a local reporter, a college student, a lab technician, and her mother were waiting to board a tour bus parked along a curb. A handful of Yuan's university buddies and their wives were also coming along. A scholarly bespectacled bunch with a quiet humor, they paired clothes in muted colors with sensible shoes. It was going to be roughly a 550-mile, fifteen-hour bus ride, and already the early morning sun was blazing.

A compact man with an unlined face and penetrating voice, Yuan was graying at the temples but looked younger than his sixty-six years. He waved to Greg and me and introduced us to the other travelers, who smiled and nodded. We received bottles of mineral water and the choice of bright orange or white T-shirts that said KANAS LAKE MONSTER in curling blue Chinese script. I picked a white one, put it on, and posed for the first group photo.

Wild beauty surrounded the rough road to Kanas. Fields of sunflowers and herds of grazing horses, fat, woolly sheep, and camels lazing in the grass brightened endless stretches of desert scrub and rugged mountain peaks. It felt like a different country.

Yuan played a documentary for us to watch, CCTV's *Chasing the Kanas Lake Monster*, featuring Yuan and two other experts. The program opened with a montage of photos, including a glimpse of the fog-wreathed lake, eyewitness videos of sightings, and a shot of Yuan in a yellow rain jacket standing atop a mountain taking photos while looking over the water.

"Some say that this lake monster can command the wind and rain and lift towering waves as if it was a huge, fierce fish. Some say it's an ancient life form that used to live in the lake and is still not extinct," the narrator said as a graphic of plesiosauri flashed across the screen.

"In 1980, I stayed two months on the nature reserve and heard from the local Tuwa people that there are creatures in the lake that can swallow cows and eat horses," Yuan said in the video. "They regarded them as gods and worshipped them. At that time, there were also stories of people who said they had caught a very big fish. Reportedly thirty-seven horses could not drag it away. Its head was so big that if you used its skull as a pot to make rice, it could feed an entire village of people. When we heard this story, I laughed and said 'It's just a story.'"

Five years later, Yuan returned to do ecological research on the Altay Mountains, following the range from east to west and finally, into a valley to the shores of Kanas Lake. When he arrived, he heard that a research team from Xinjiang University had discovered fish whose heads were about five feet wide and twice as long. "I heard this and it was beyond me. I said 'No way. There's no way there's a fish that big. I don't believe it.'"

The next day, Yuan and his team wanted to try their own luck at spotting the fishy colossus, so they made their way to the Fish Viewing Pavilion on the lake's west side, hundreds of feet above the water. From that position, they saw "groups and groups of reddish-brown dots on the surface.

"We felt it was so strange at the time. What are these things? I thought maybe it was a type of aquatic algae, patches of rust-colored algae bloom. As I was thinking about this, they took the binoculars and . . . said 'Big fish! Big fish!' As they were shouting, I suddenly thought of what we heard yesterday, and I hurriedly snatched the binoculars to take a look. The groups of reddish dots were really several fish heads."

The screen filled with a video of something red frothing in the water backed by dramatic music. "Their mouths were really big," Yuan said, pointing to his own mouth. "Around where they were breathing, there were circles of ripples. Their eyes were huge. They were definitely groups of fish heads."

The host of the program asked Yuan how big he thought the fish were. Yuan said he conferred with one of the Xinjiang University professors who thought the largest one was possibly fifty feet or longer.

In 2004, late in the morning when the sun was high and hot, Yuan had his second sighting. This time, it happened when his group was on the way down the mountain. "We saw in a bay what looked like very long rolls of black plastic at the mouth of the lake. Not only that, one was in the shape of an archer's bow. We didn't think at all it would be fish because it looked too much like plastic sheeting that was very wide and very, very long. At 10:00 a.m., the light from the opposite side was slanting down and glinting off the surface.

"I thought to myself 'What sort of stupid person would scatter plastic onto the lake?' As I was thinking this, there were five people with Henan accents standing beside me—four men and one woman. I remember clearly. They were exclaiming 'It's moving! There are seven of them!'"

The group's observation startled Yuan, who realized that he was seeing a dorsal fin of some sort but wasn't sure about how the fish were configured. "I looked again and was wondering if it really was seven fish. But I couldn't see clearly. I couldn't see if it was a trick. I said 'Let's take a picture first, and then we'll see.' . . . I took this shot. Four fins. The shimmer had gone below the surface, and only the fins were apparent on the water." The photo he held up showed an aqua curve of water with four blurry white dots clustered close to shore. It was impossible to tell what they were, but Yuan was so earnest, so convinced, that I wanted to see what he saw.

"Their bodies weren't actually moving. They were quietly resting in the water and when the wake broke against the shore, that's when they started going under and sank. They didn't cause any waves. It really was too bad. In my heart I wanted to stay longer to take a photo if it surfaced again. But there were so many people around, and they couldn't wait for just one person. In the end, I had no choice and went back down."

Toward the end of the program, Yuan defined the simple truth of what the pursuit of the lake monsters meant to him. "In 1985 I saw them, and then in 2004 I saw them again. Every time I go there now, I have to go up the mountain to watch the surface of the lake in hopes that I will see them again. My destiny is with the *taimen*."

漢

The story of the *huguai* encapsulates both ancient myth and modern moneymaking. The lair lies in a 200,000-year-old lake in the wilds of China's undeveloped western frontier, the legend of the mysterious and powerful monsters kept alive by oral traditions of the indigenous Tuwa tribe that lived along the shores. Yet tourists—mostly wealthy travelers from cities—come in droves, packed in shiny buses and toting an array of electric gadgets in hopes of a sighting. With them, they bring noise, litter, and money.

These packaged outings showcase how far thirty-plus years of economic reforms have taken China. People have moved forward enough to afford the luxury of looking back. Many Chinese have more time and cash now to explore a rich legacy of deeply rooted superstitions and myths once condemned as offenses to Communist dogma.

During the Cultural Revolution, the campaign to destroy the "Four Olds"—old ideas, old customs, old habits, and old culture—resulted in the mass destruction of books, artwork, temples, family heirlooms, statues of Buddha, and other religious and cultural relics. Superstition, myths, and the occult were considered harmful because they encouraged folk beliefs in nature and gods instead of the Party. Telling those stories became taboo because leaders believed that they could harm social stability and national unity.

But since reform in the late 1970s, superstition and sorcery have staged a strong comeback, particularly in rural areas. Officials frame the revival of folk beliefs in economic terms, as a way to build local identity and culture to lure tourists and improve people's livelihoods. The making and chasing of myths has become big business, with visits to areas known for paranormal sightings a common element in tour packages costing hundreds, sometimes thousands, of dollars.

Even conservative state media, including CCTV and the party mouthpiece *People's Daily* newspaper, are giving credence to the paranormal, devoting numerous dispatches to those topics. They had a colorful cache of phenomena from which to choose.

✿

In central China's Hubei province, hundreds have claimed to have seen a half-human, half-ape form more than six and a half feet tall, his body covered with matted gray, red, or black hair. The creature, known as *yeren* or "Wild Man," is said to have made its home in the remote and mountainous Shennongjia Nature Reserve. While there was little evidence beyond claimed sightings, scientific expeditions in the '70s and '80s found hair, a footprint, and a sleeping area that may point to the *yeren*'s existence.

Late in 2010, Xinhua News Agency published a story about how an association of scientists and explorers was planning to recruit people from around the world to join an expedition to find *yeren* once and for all. Applicants had to be between twenty-five and forty years old, in good physical health, and with a basic knowledge of biology and how to use a camera. The project had no timetable because organizers first had to raise $1.5 million in funding.

UFO sightings have also been treated with great seriousness. Just weeks after my Xinjiang trip, China played host to the World UFO Conference in Dalian. The *China Daily* described a "cult-like crowd" gathering at the opening of the event, which featured footage of sightings and first-person accounts of alien abductions. Gu Xingwen, a taxi driver, said he had been plagued by a sudden headache after dropping some passengers off late one night. "I pulled over. Then, out of nowhere, a beam of strong light shone on me, and I passed out," the newspaper quoted him as saying. "When I reopened my eyes, I found myself on another street."

In 2010, a series of unidentified flying objects spotted across the country made the news. While some were explained away as rockets, planes, or lighted kites, question marks remained over others. The most high-profile incident shut down an airport in the city of Hangzhou in July. Xinhua quoted an employee of Xiaoshan Airport as saying that a "twinkling object was first spotted over the city's sky . . . however, the object did not show up on the airport's radar."

Chinese reports mention Scotland's Loch Ness monster, Nessie, when discussing unidentified creatures spotted in various lakes around China, including in Qinghai, Tibet, and Hubei, near Wild Man territory.

One of the more documented mysteries surrounds the monster—or monsters—in Tianchi, a crater lake in Jilin province, which borders North Korea. Soldiers have reported seeing a creature with a black head, horns, and a scaly back—a description reminiscent of ancient depictions of dragons—breaking the surface of the water. A television reporter said he shot a twenty-minute video of "six seal-like, finned creatures swimming and frolicking in the lake for an hour and a half, before they ducked out of sight."

"They could swim as fast as yachts, and at times they would disappear under the water. It was impressive to see them all swimming at exactly the same pace, as if someone was giving orders," the reporter, Zhuo Yongsheng, said in a *People's Daily* story. "Their fins—or maybe wings—were longer than their bodies."

One scientist said the creatures were likely mutated offspring of trout stocked by North Korea decades ago. Kim Li Tae, a senior researcher for the North's National Academy of Science, said he was one of the researchers who released nine trout into the lake—close to where leader Kim Jong Il reportedly was born—in 1960.

漢

When I met Professor Yuan, he had been to Kanas Lake ten times—not just to try to find another piece of the monster puzzle, but also to keep an eye on the area's ecological balance. A respected environmental scientist, he had led expeditions with British and German counterparts to study the habitats of the critically endangered wild camel in Xinjiang's Lop Nur Desert, where he helped to establish a sixty-thousand-square-mile nature reserve for the animals. He has provided expert opinion on issues ranging from expanding deserts and river systems to the feasibility of natural gas and water pipeline projects.

But he is best known for his sightings of the *huguai*. Over the years, Yuan has written books and numerous essays on the topic and spoken at conferences and on television shows. No article about the lake monsters lacked his retelling of what he saw. People have sent him piles of photos and letters describing what they had seen, including one witness who spotted a fin almost three and a half feet high speeding through the water.

Yuan felt that having a specimen in hand would be key not only to gaining better insight to the area's ecology and environment, but also to protect the creatures. "But where would I even begin to look in this huge lake?" he asked.

For lunch, we stopped at a small restaurant for platters of hand-pulled noodles topped with a tomato-based sauce thick with bits of lamb, onions, bell peppers, and eggs, as well as *shouzhua fan*, rice studded with lamb, carrots, and raisins. Both are staples in Xinjiang, whose inhabitants are predominantly Uighur Muslims, a Turkic-speaking ethnic group.

The food is mostly meat-based—no pork of course—and heavily seasoned with chilies and cumin. In Beijing, Xinjiang cuisine largely meant either skewers of *yangrou chuan'er*—perfectly spiced pieces of lamb between bits of crisp fat eaten late at night, hot off the stick, at a hole in the wall—or a feast at a handful of good restaurants. The meal often included a simple salad of cucumbers and tomatoes, piles of *chuan'er* and rounds of a sesame seed–flecked flatbread called *nang*, perfect vehicles for sopping up the oily, fiery red gravy of *dapanji* or "big plate chicken," in which cut up pieces of whole bird were cooked with garlic, chilies, and chunks of potato.

Yuan's group polished off the food as they chatted about monster sightings and their expectations for the trip.

"If I see it, I see it. If I don't, I don't," said Zeng Jianghai, a retired professor of social studies and researcher of soil and environmental protection, between bites. "Of course as people who study science, we want to understand how this came to be. We want to understand the mystical quality of it. This does not follow the natural order of things. It's a coldwater lake. How a fish got so big is of interest to everyone."

For others, it was a matter of turning childhood stories into reality. "A long time ago, my mother told me about the *huguai*," said Liu Ting, a nineteen-year-old student with a wide face and wide eyes. "I was always curious. I watched television programs on the topic. I know it's pretty rare that they will make an appearance. . . . I don't know what they are. I only know they are something very big."

Wang Lan, a twenty-five-year-old nurse in a red baseball cap, brandished a pair of binoculars excitedly. "I really wanted to come here with this group. I've heard the story since I was a child. All along I thought it was a dinosaur. Then last year I heard it was a big red fish. I wanted to try to see for myself."

Scientists who have sighted the creatures of Kanas are skeptical that they are anything other than the big red fish. Jiang Zuofa, a professor at Heilongjiang Aquatic Research Institute said without a doubt that "the so-called lake monsters are actually a kind of fish called the *hucho taimen*."

"I went to the lake for scientific research twice between 1988 to 1990. I saw about thirty to fifty of them together in the lake from the top of the mountain. They were about more than three feet in length and the largest of them were between ten to thirteen feet," he said over the telephone. "We believe it is possible for them to eat chicken, goose, and sheep—but it is impossible for them to eat cattle. The rumor of the monster eating cattle is an exaggeration."

Chen Yifeng, a professor at the Institute of Hydrobiology at the Chinese Academy of Sciences, didn't believe that the *huguai*—or Nessie or any other mysterious lake monster—was an undiscovered species. Anything that large would dominate the food chain and would need to consume large quantities of fish, shrimp, and other food. That, Chen said, would make it impossible for it to escape detection for long periods of time, especially in areas explored by many experts.

Our group's search for the extraordinary meant stops at tourist sites with unusual and bleak landscapes. In Karamay, which means "black oil" in Uighur, we stopped at Black Oil Hill, formed when thick crude overflow mixed with grit and dust and slowly solidified, growing higher over the centuries. A nearby chain of natural ponds of crude oil had inky, glossy surfaces that mirrored the sky.

We also visited the "Ghost Town of the World," a prehistoric lake turned desert turned dramatic geographical wonder filled with plateaus and ridges made up of brown, gray, and reddish strata eroded by the elements into fantastical shapes. The area, showcased in *Crouching Tiger, Hidden Dragon*, took its name from the shrieking winds and sand storms that blew through the rocks, drawing comparisons to taloned demons, wailing ghosts, and howling wolves.

That afternoon, the wind kicked up, warm and dry, but not strong enough to rouse the supernatural. Rays of late-day sun piercing through low, dark clouds eerily backlit the alien landscape.

While talking to Yuan about his quest to find the *huguai*, I began to understand what it's like to chase a white whale. China was as elusive and ineffable. I was constantly trying to interpret and analyze what I wrote about, but all I seemed to have were contradictory pieces of a puzzle and occasional glimpses of the bigger picture. The country was so large, so varied, changing so fast that it was impossible to peg. Maybe, like Yuan, I just had to keep meeting people and telling their stories—and hope for the best.

蕃

Roughly fifteen miles long by one mile wide, and more than 4,300 feet above sea level, the stunning milky green crescent-shaped Kanas could take on shades of old jade, storm-gray, or almost-black, depending on the angle, season, and light. It sits in Xinjiang's northernmost tip, where China, Mongolia, Russia, and Kazakhstan converge in snowcapped mountains thick with forests. The area is known for spectacular sunrises, especially after heavy rains, when sunlight and water droplets reflect and refract in a combination that produces surreal, multicolored rings called Buddha's Halo.

The lake has a maximum depth of 603 feet. Yuan and other scientists know of eight species of fish in the lake, including the carnivorous and nearly extinct Chinese paddlefish, which looks like a swordfish and sometimes is called the elephant fish because of its snout. Fishermen have reported catching paddlefish up to twenty-six feet long, though scientists have recorded specimens only about half that size.

"Only the *taimen* are capable of growing into giants," said Yuan.

Throughout the summer, up to four thousand tourists flock there daily. All day long, boats of different sizes chug and buzz along the lake, packed with *huguai* spotters. A jam of people gazing at the poetic beauty of the surroundings—and hoping for a glimpse of something out of the ordinary—burdened a wood and metal pier stretching like a finger into the water.

"It's a beautiful tale that attracts visitors," said He Yuejin, a teacher from Hunan.

His friend, Li Puqing, was more skeptical. "I think it's impossible for a fish to grow so big in there. There's no way it can live that long."

Surprisingly there was scant monster publicity at the site. A souvenir shop had just one book about the lake that mentioned the *huguai*. The park's spokeswoman, Zhao Yuxia, gave a cautious response. "We believe there are unidentified creatures in the lake, but we can't say for sure what they are. We've never seen them with our own eyes."

Even so, because it was a nature reserve, there were measures in place to protect the area's wildlife—whatever they may be. Fishing and swimming were banned, and boats had to obey a strict speed limit. There was also a cap on the number of visitors allowed daily.

On that gorgeous day, we strolled on a narrow wooden walkway that hugged the shoreline, shaded by trees. The mountain air was crisp even in the heart of summer. I kept looking out at the water, which changed color every few minutes.

"It's so green and milky, and it looks so nutritious. It must be good for fish!" squealed Wang Lan, the nurse, as a wave broke near us.

The group walked briskly, exclaiming over plants and flowers, and taking photos of each other with mountains and water in the background. At a grassy knoll close to the water, we stopped to take another requisite group shot. Then we hiked past cows to the top of a nearby peak. On one side, a breathtaking vista of the Kanas River wound through a sea of trees and verdant land, like an emerald snake. On the other, a wide expanse of lake glistened. People pulled out cameras and cellphones to snap photos as Yuan began reliving his sightings from a nearby cliff.

I asked if there had been reports of people disappearing or boats being overturned linked to the creatures. Yuan laughed and said he'd heard of no such thing, adding cheekily: "We used to swim in the lake, but after 1985, after I saw the monsters, I never swam there again. I would've been a delicious morsel without my clothes!"

The sun was slowly sinking behind a mountain as we walked back down, but we didn't leave, hoping that the quiet darkness would tempt the *huguai* to make an appearance. The moon was barely a sliver in the sky, and a faint glow from the day's remaining light made surreal silhouettes out of the trees at the top of the mountains.

A few of us huddled on the edge of a floating wooden dock, speaking in low voices as our eyes scanned the water. Yuan stood off to the side, standing by a railing, slightly pensive.

Liu Ting, the student, trained a weak flashlight beam on a spot in the water close to the dock. She exclaimed as she saw tiny, silver fish dart at hunks of bread they had dropped into the lake. "Look! There are so many of them!" she shrieked. Then petulantly: "But where are the lake monsters?"

Forty minutes passed. A breeze kicked up, and everyone drew their jackets closer.

"We can wait all night," said Yuan, unfazed. "Let's see if this is our fate."

※

In the end, no creatures—*huguai* or otherwise—broke the surface.

On the last day of our visit, we braved the crowds. We lined up early in the morning, squeezing in with tour groups and families standing under the sun. We moved at a snail's pace on the long trek up seemingly endless steps to the Fish Viewing Pavilion.

Anticipation was building within our group. After all, this was our last chance to see anything. For about thirty seconds I allowed myself to get carried away and imagine what I would write if I saw them. Then reality set in. I looked down at my little pocket-sized camera and sighed, knowing that it wouldn't be powerful enough to capture a sighting even if there was one.

"Look! It's the lake monster!" joked one man. Hundreds were milling around, crowding, and elbowing each other. Even though we were out in the open, I felt claustrophobic. It was like this at every major attraction. At the top, visitors jostled for an unobstructed view of the snowcapped mountains, the lake, and the forever blue of the sky, yelling for friends to snap pictures.

Breathless, Yuan stood on a nearby bluff overlooking a curvy portion of the shore, hands shielding his eyes from the sun as he gazed down onto the water. A pair of binoculars hung from his neck, and his video camera hung from his right shoulder. The lake was a sheet of silver. Tiny boats bobbed in the distance, and everything looked normal. "It's hard, it's hard," he muttered as he started the camera. "They can be anywhere."

He moved between a couple of vantage points. "Our luck isn't good today. We aren't seeing anything," he said softly, almost to himself. Then as consolation: "But they don't come out much. It's hard to get a sighting."

After an hour or so, downcast, he gave up. "All right. We're done here."

As he began his descent, he took one last look at the lake.

Nothing.

舉

On our way back to Urumqi, we stopped at a well-known restaurant called Big Red Fish, the popularity of which hinged on a 103-pound specimen on display, a trophy the owner reportedly bought in 1999 from a local fisherman for the princely sum of 4,000 yuan (around $600). The five-foot-six-inch-long big red fish reportedly was 128 years old, caught in a river near Kanas Lake. Word spread, and the place soon became a tourist destination; the fish ended up paying for itself.

We sat at a table in front of the glass tank displaying the preserved fish. It looked leathery and desiccated with a mile-long, dead-eye stare. Its mouth lay open, as if taking a breath. Even through the glass, it was obvious that its teeth were terrifyingly sharp. It was at once ferocious and sad.

Soon steaming plates of food were placed on the lazy susan in the center of the table, a mix of Han and Uighur cuisine. There was lamb in several guises, greens, tofu with fish slices, piles of steamed buns, and a huge bowl of rice. The centerpiece was a whole fish, steamed. But it was disappointingly small, nothing like the gigantic specimens we had been discussing during the trip—or even like the one in the glass tank, which now mocked us.

Professor Zeng was fatalistic as always. "There are no regrets. There is a time and place to see things. You can't fix a timetable."

Yuan poured a shot of *baijiu* for everyone. He thought for a moment and simply said: "To the Kanas Lake big red fish."

❀

The next day, Greg and I began a search for poultry farms in the area. Bird flu was raging through Asia, and Xinjiang had reported a few cases of sick ducks and geese. Our bureau chief wanted a story on how farmers were dealing with the crisis.

The fun was over.

3

Dissent Is a Dish Best Served Cold

Seven men and one woman gathered around a wooden table laden with food, heads bowed, hands clasped.

"Our people have suffered so much," prayed Wang Meiru, who was hosting the Easter lunch. "So many of them are in prison. So many of them are in pain. Please, God, be with them." With a resounding "Amen!" a meal with some of China's most enduring dissidents began.

It was April 2004, and tracking SARS—the mysterious respiratory disease that originated in Guangdong and traversed the planet—had taken up most of my time the year before. Deep into the swing of things, I had been busy with a slew of stories, from an eye-opening trip to Tibet to the fall of a cherubic, chain-smoking orchid tycoon detained just days after North Korea named him head of a planned free-trade enclave on the Chinese border.

But I was increasingly focusing on stories about ordinary citizens harassed and imprisoned because they were speaking out against the government, pushing Party limits through petitions or by advocating change in the system. It was my first real brush with defiance and its eye-opening consequences. Suddenly my job became much darker.

No one is born an activist. Many in China fall into the role—and persist at it—when they realize that they can, and want to, make a difference, like lawyers who risk accepting cases considered politically sensitive by the government. There were also the longtime political dissidents, mild-mannered, often intellectuals who suffered from chronic and acute illnesses, manifestations

On Easter Sunday, 2004, I shared an incredible meal with eight dissidents. Collectively, the group had endured hundreds of detentions and decades of prison time. An unmarked car and a small van not far from the house kept us under surveillance the entire time.

of the physical toll of dissent. Holding onto hope, they spouted gallows humor as they shouldered their weariness and pains like war veterans.

Personal tragedies propelled many more into action, like residents who had lost their homes to development, or parents who found no recourse when infant formula adulterated with melamine sickened their babies. Inconsolable grief and the need for answers drove them. They cried and marched in protest, their efforts raw and physical.

At the core of all these people lay an unshakable conviction and sometimes a questionable stubbornness that kept them going. At times it resembled a form of madness. Was it worth it? Could answers be found or change be wrought from within the authoritarian regime? Almost everyone I interviewed said "yes" to the first question as a case for the second. Some vowed to die trying. Perhaps that's what the Chinese government feared most: a perfect storm of cause, fervor, and frustration.

The leadership's grip on dissent swung between tight and tighter, unrest routinely extinguished by well-equipped and well-funded security forces. In March 2012, China's declared expenditure on public security jumped 11.5 percent to $111 billion, eclipsing the country's official military budget for the third year in a row.

Although a law safeguarded citizens' rights to assemble and demonstrate—promulgated just months after the brutal crushing of the 1989 pro-democracy demonstrations around Tiananmen Square—authorities never issued the permits for which people had to apply if they wanted to stage a rally. On the contrary, those who filled out applications regularly found themselves the targets of police or security agents despite constitutional promises of "freedom of speech, of the press, of assembly, of association, of procession and of demonstration."

The bottom line for all the stories I wrote was the same: People hungered to be heard and acknowledged. The Party brooks no challenges to its authority, and anyone who threatens, appears to question, or simply doesn't toe the Party's line is disciplined.

Laws exist, but there is no rule of law, despite what leaders and officials insist. The stories of surveillance, detentions, beatings, and torture are too frequent, too relentlessly similar. I tried my best to be objective, to tell both sides of the story, to consider if nuanced contradictions or layered exceptions played a role in events. But authorities routinely refused to acknowledge abuses and rejected international pressure as extraneous interference with internal matters.

Unlike the West, which believes that human rights hinge on individual freedoms, China defines the concept in terms of improving living conditions for its 1.3 billion people, ignoring civil and political rights by maintaining control over speech, religion, political activity, and independent social groups. A country's human rights policies, Beijing believes, should take into account its own level of economic development and social systems.

I had interviewed Ren Wanding on human rights a couple of times on the telephone before meeting him on Easter weekend in 2004. Then sixty, he had spent years in prison and labor camps as punishment for his fight for a democratic government and the release of political prisoners. Personable and patient with my stuttering Mandarin, he had invited me for a meal with some of his friends. He didn't say much on the phone beyond giving me directions on where to meet him.

On Easter Sunday, photo colleague Han Guan and I took a taxi to the designated point. In a pastel-colored striped shirt and black trousers, Ren greeted us warmly as he got into the car and gave further directions. I tried to ask questions, but Ren told me to be patient.

When we reached Wang Meiru's house, a breeze was blowing through the courtyard of her home, tucked in a maze of fruit trees and farmland ninety minutes northwest of central Beijing. Roosters wandered by caged rabbits, and birds were singing merrily as some of the country's most diehard dissidents met to offer mutual support and voice their discontent.

Smiling, Ren and Wang led me to a sun-filled living room, its walls covered with hand-painted poems and scenery painted on scrolls.

"Lunch will be ready soon," Wang said, her hands wet from washing vegetables.

I settled onto the couch with Ren and Ye Guozhu, a man who had been battling authorities since he was forced from his home to make way for development for the Beijing Olympics.

Ren handed me his emerald green business card, which highlighted his life history and achievements chronologically. The list began in 1979, when he drafted a human rights manifesto and went to prison for four years. It included his 1994 Robert F. Kennedy Human Rights Award. The list ended in 2002, when he proposed building a "culture of democracy."

We sipped tea—and waited.

醬

When lunch was ready, the ten of us sat around the long wooden table set with platters of whole green chilies blistered in hot oil, soy sauce–stewed pork belly and hard-boiled eggs, fried salted peanuts, sliced cured pork, shredded pickled vegetables, cherry tomatoes and cucumbers with mayonnaise, and sautéed beans. At each end of the table lay a washbasin-sized metal bowl brimming with a soup made of a whole fish, scaled and chopped, and slightly bitter leafy greens. Cold beer and bottled water also washed down mashed tofu flecked with spring onions, stir-fried pork with celery, and crisp vegetable fritters.

Wang, sixty-two years old, plump, and carefully made-up, was the only woman among the activists. The rest could have been anywhere between forty and sixty, an academic-looking bunch in dress shirts and glasses. Yet collectively, they had logged hundreds of detentions and years of prison time over the past two decades. The police, who had them under tight watch, had beaten or put them under house arrest for speaking out or writing essays critical of the Party.

"We have all suffered at some point. Our rights have been trampled," said Yang Jing, accused of spying and imprisoned for eight years for helping print the *April Fifth Forum*, a well-known reformist magazine during the landmark Democracy Wall movement. The journal, edited with two other activists and mimeographed in their apartments, had mild political and social commentary, but it candidly treated sensitive subjects, such as freedom of expression.

71

For a few heady months in 1978–79, Party leaders encouraged the public to criticize Mao Zedong's unsuccessful policies during the Cultural Revolution, which had ended in 1976, and a leftist political faction—including Mao's wife—that gained prominence during that time. At first only a few pro-democracy posters covered the drab brick structure in central Beijing designated for the purpose, but soon, encouraged by reformist statements by ascendant Party leader Deng Xiaoping, students and workers filled that wall with proclamations and poetry, establishing similar walls in other cities.

The "Beijing Spring" ended when Deng consolidated his hold over leftists in the Party and cracked down on the poster activity. Police arrested the movement's leaders, including many of Yang's friends. He published numerous appeals on their behalf, pressing for their release. In 1981, police arrested him too.

Unlike the others at lunch that day, Yang wore metal-framed sunglasses, a gray T-shirt and jeans, and a black baseball cap squeezed backward on his head. He looked more like a retired rocker than a former steelworker who, for slipping a note to a fellow prisoner, had spent ten months in solitary confinement in a six-foot-square permanently lit cell. While in solitary, he kept track of time by reading the *People's Daily*, which prison guards gave him every day to study. Toward the end of his sentence, he worked in a factory making plastic sandals and willed himself not to think too much about his impending freedom.

Released in 1989, Yang came home to an eight-year-old son born after his arrest who believed that his father had been on a research project in the South Pole. His muscles wasted, Yang not only had to readjust to daily life but also to the death of his father and the animosity of a brother who couldn't forgive him for being imprisoned. He spent much of his time in the family's small Beijing home. Another brother gave him tickets to a movie about spies and how to escape from jail.

Even fifteen years later, when I met him, Yang still spoke of the fates of his fellow *April Fifth Forum* editors, Liu Qing and Xu Wenli, the latter a former electrician arrested two days after Yang and sentenced to fifteen years. "This cause goes beyond personal benefits. It's for the good of the people," Yang said. "Our hearts are calm. What we do is something of value."

And if struggle ends with death, "It's a necessary sacrifice," Ren, the man who had invited me to lunch, said with quiet conviction. A former accountant at an equipment installation company, Ren appeared pensive and intense for most of the meal. But the few times he smiled, his face lit up with an innocence that tugged at my heart.

In 1978, he had been one of the most dedicated participants in the Democracy Wall movement, authoring a bold nineteen-point human rights manifesto calling for the abolition of corruption and secret police among other actions. He also formed an unofficial group called the China Human Rights League.

Police arrested him in 1979 as he was posting yet another notice on the wall. He spent the next four years in a cell less than ten feet by ten feet, where he wrote essays about political liberalization on rolls of toilet paper.

Released in 1983, Ren resurfaced at the end of 1988 with renewed vigor during the run-up to the tenth anniversary of the Democracy Wall movement. He approached foreign journalists like a peddler, pulling from his denim book bag page after page written in cramped handwriting.

"The Democracy Wall dared to expose the problem of life-long tenure in office, the fact that 'ownership by the people' is state ownership, the existence of unemployment and surplus labor, and many other economic truths" about China, he wrote in a November 1988 essay in the English-language *South China Morning Post*, based in Hong Kong. He urged foreign countries to invest in China only if the Communist government made progress on human rights.

Ren also penned an open letter to the U.N. Human Rights Commission and followed it soon after with four new pieces of work denouncing the Communist Party as a narrow-minded bully, appealing to the world to show concern for human rights in China.

"If one just thinks about things and doesn't have the freedom to speak out, then there's no freedom," he wrote.

Ren continued his calls for political change and the release of his friends as the demonstrations blossomed around Tiananmen Square in the spring of 1989. "People are praying for the awakening of a legal system," he told a group of about two thousand listeners in the square one day in April. "This is a historical necessity."

It was no surprise when police took him less than a week after the bloody June 3–4 crackdown that crushed the protests. Authorities charged him with counterrevolutionary sabotage, commonly used against political dissidents and implied opposition to the Communist system.

Although he played no leadership role, Ren received a seven-year sentence for his speeches, the most severe punishment handed down to the group accused of leading the rallies. State media said it was because Ren "showed no repentance." The stubborn stance echoed one of his earlier pieces, where he had written: "What I do is just. I remain blameless."

Two years before Ren's release, under increasing pressure from Washington to show progress on human rights, Beijing played for reporters videotapes of four prominent dissidents linked to the Tiananmen protests celebrating with their families in prison to show that they were in good health and being treated humanely. Two others were shown enjoying servings of roast meat, seafood, or cake with friends and family. Ren appeared sharing a simple meal of fried fish and vegetables with his wife and daughter—but he was grim-faced.

While he was serving his sentence, Ren's wife and teenage daughter suffered government harassment themselves, including periodic detentions. Authorities sealed the door to their

Beijing apartment, forcing them into a life of drifting from one temporary residence to another.

Ren emerged on June 9, 1996, thin and weak, with a host of health issues that his time in prison had aggravated: cataracts, retina damage, and back problems. Despite being free, Ren found himself under constant surveillance. Officials warned him against leaving his home when foreign dignitaries—including President George W. Bush in 2002—came to town, monitoring his phones and e-mail. But he remained outspoken and active in creative ways, like acting as the bridge between foreign journalists, including me, and other Chinese dissidents. In 2000, President Bill Clinton had mentioned him in a speech about the importance of China's impending entry into the World Trade Organization and how it had the potential to move the country in a new direction for economic and, perhaps, personal freedoms.

"Ren Wanding is one of the fathers of the Chinese human rights movement. In the late 1970s, he was thrown into prison for founding the China Human Rights League. In the 1980s, he helped lead the demonstration in Tiananmen Square. In the 1990s, he was thrown in prison yet again," Clinton said. "Yet, he says of this deal, 'Before, the sky was black. Now it is light. This can be a new beginning.'"

If I didn't know what Ren and the other activists had survived, their proclamations about dying for freedom would have sounded a lot like bravado. Yet their actions, their years of dogged determination to be heard no matter the cost, belied an underlying backbone of steel—or a misplaced faith in the possibility of change.

※

"If I don't die, who will?" Ye Guozhu said from across the table.

In 2003, Ye and three generations of his family, like thousands in the Chinese capital, were evicted from their homes as the government began clearing land for the 2008 Beijing Olympics.

Handsome, intense, yet worn-looking, Ye had been beaten and detained scores of times by police for protesting the loss of his house and restaurant and for the insufficient compensation his family received, leaving some of them homeless.

Later that year, his younger brother, despairing of their plight, attempted suicide by jumping into a narrow canal flowing past the Imperial Palace on the northern edge of Tiananmen Square. He was sentenced to two years in prison for disturbing social order.

"This government is a savage, brutal one. It is like a hoodlum. It has absolutely no sense of human rights," said Ye as he sipped a glass of water. "We have to shout out for the sake of the people who have suffered because there are so many of them."

Jobless and homeless, Ye lived off friends who let him stay with them for short periods of time. With bags under his eyes, he spoke in passionate bursts, gesturing wildly, his voice breaking as he listed wrongs against ordinary citizens: Tiananmen Square, Olympics evictions, police abuses, and more. At one point, he wept while discussing one of the homeless families he knew. "They have no hope. They have no money, no jobs, no way to survive."

He took care to separate the regime from the country, though. "We are Chinese. We love China," he said simply.

Despite the tranquil surroundings and abundance of food, the mood was somber. Between puffs of cigarettes, talk between friends continued along a jarring track—arrests, torture, and deaths of fellow dissidents. With the fifteen-year anniversary of Tiananmen just weeks away, the activists believed that it was only a matter of time before authorities stepped up their surveillance.

"You won't be able to see us in a month," Yang said matter-of-factly.

Ren and the others pointed out an unmarked car and a small van a few feet from the house. "We are being watched," they said.

Government control in China takes many forms, including shadowing by plainclothes security agents and phone taps that lead to disconnected calls if the conversation ventures into forbidden territory. What the government considers taboo arbitrarily changes with each situation. During sensitive periods, like political anniversaries or legislative sessions, authorities take vocal rights advocates from their homes and hold them at secret locations until the occasions pass and the activists no longer pose a threat.

"To venture out near the Tiananmen anniversary would be asking for a beating," said Wang, whose words flowed like a stream as her hands played with a silk handkerchief and adjusted her spectacles.

A devoted Christian, Wang belonged to Beijing's underground house church movement, where millions worship privately in homes to avoid detection, as Catholics did in sixteenth-century England. China requires all religious groups to register and accept Communist Party oversight, allowing worship only in government-sanctioned churches, both Protestant and Catholic. Many unofficial congregations still openly hold services with an evangelistic, charismatic flavor. Their unity and fervor—a potentially explosive mix—don't sit well with the leadership.

This is why Wang cried while praying before our meal. Over the years, many of her Christian brethren, taken away by authorities, faced a variety of charges. Wang's daughter, a lawyer, died after being thrown from a building in 2001 in an incident that authorities have yet to explain. A godson went to prison at the height of the 1989 Tiananmen protests for carrying a six-foot-tall crucifix. She had appealed so many times to officials for resolution and justice in both cases that they blacklisted her. Police kept her under close watch and regularly harassed her, which prevented her from leading a normal life.

During lunch, though, she anxiously labored to make her guests feel at home. With the help of a couple of homeless children whom she had adopted, she cooked part of the meal outdoors in two giant woks fired by coal. Her moves economical and balletic, she pivoted between counter and stove while stirring hot broth in a pan.

When a neighbor dropped by unannounced, the conversation hushed to ensure that he had nothing to report to the neighborhood watch committee, an Orwellian vestige of grassroots policing from the Mao era. He hovered at the gate, peering occasionally at our group as Wang made small talk. We were doing nothing wrong, but I stealthily moved my notebook out of sight. Han, who had been snapping dozens of photos, quietly set his camera on a nearby chair and picked up his chopsticks.

After the man left, Xiang Nanfu, another of the democracy activists, spoke thoughtfully as he chewed on a chili. "This is indeed a rare occasion. Only here do we have the freedom to say what we want. Outside, there are ears everywhere."

❈

Within weeks, as the Tiananmen anniversary drew close, most of them couldn't leave their homes. Ren was allowed out only to buy groceries. In August, Ye applied for permission to organize a "10,000 People March" to protest the evictions. Police quickly arrested him, and he received a four-year prison sentence for "provoking and making trouble."

Human rights organizations said that Ye finally was freed in October 2008 after being forced to sign an agreement accepting compensation for his eviction. Since then, he has dropped quietly off the radar.

In the years after that Easter lunch, I asked Ren if there were plans to get everyone together again, but each time he said it was impossible. His health had taken a turn for the worse, and the others were either in prison or under surveillance.

"Things are harder now, and I'm being watched at my home," he told me. "That lunch from 2004, it's not going to happen again."

❈

Controls notably tightened after 2002, when Hu Jintao took over from Jiang Zemin as general secretary of the Communist Party and China's president. It's unclear if there was a direct connection—anything to do with the government is predictably opaque—but not only were established political activists being monitored vigilantly, but authorities began casting a broader net to include lawyers, artists, journalists, and academics as well.

It blossomed into a full-fledged and often terrifyingly covert battle to eradicate any trace of dissonance within the "harmonious society" that Hu and his inner circle of power had adopted as their legacy. Authorities targeted villagers who had made the pilgrimage from the countryside to the capital in a last effort for recourse after being ignored or mistreated by local officials, a centuries-old practice dating from days when people could petition the emperor.

Sometimes it seemed like my colleagues and I were looking over a cliff onto a sea of people with an ocean of grievances. No one seemed to want to listen, yet the petitioners didn't give up. Those unsuccessful in getting Beijing to address their concerns tried the foreign media almost every day, either calling or faxing us in hopes that perhaps we could help resolve their issues and make their problems disappear. After traveling hundreds of miles, many camped out in squalid conditions in a makeshift village across the highway from the State Council's petition office in southern Beijing. They stayed for weeks, sometimes months, cooking on hot plates and sharing an outhouse with hundreds of others.

The most determined would find our office and show up at our door, dusty and looking lost, almost always clutching a stack of photos and documents as proof of some kind of wrongdoing by a local official or authority figure that was not within our scope of coverage. Many were old and would sometimes go down on their knees, weeping, to beg for an audience.

As years went by, the petitioners grew savvier about calling us shortly before a protest to maximize the time that reporters, photographers, and television crews needed to get to a venue and to minimize the chances of authorities breaking things up. On those occasions when cynicism took over, it felt like a symbiotic relationship: They got the exposure they wanted, and we got quotes or footage that fulfilled our news needs.

Police and state security often showed up anyway. The agents usually didn't try to hide who they were. They wore dark street clothes and no expressions. While uniformed police dealt with crowd control, security agents impassively surveyed the situation, often photographing or videotaping demonstrators and bystanders. Sometimes they held a satchel under one arm that contained a video camera to monitor events. They didn't answer questions, but they also didn't seem to care if we took photos of them.

Ultimately, the petitioners were detained or beaten and sent back to their towns. A growing number of them are thrown into "black jails," unofficial venues—rooms in shabby hotels or abandoned factories—where they are held and often abused before provincial officials or thugs-for-hire round them up and force them home.

Beijing has long defended its hostility to political opposition and tight rein over anything that might foment dissent—the Internet, churches and spiritual groups such as Falun Gong—as essential to protecting China's breakneck economic growth and the peace and safety of its people. For a while, it seemed like those targeted by the government had some hope, thanks to a small group of lawyers willing to risk taking on politically sensitive cases. But even that faded as authorities began to clamp down on the legal sector.

"The people who hurt them, the people who are high up, they really don't want us to exist. But we believe that conscience triumphs over the black and evil forces," said Xu Zhiyong, founder of the Open Constitution Initiative, better known by its Chinese name, Gongmeng, a prominent public interest legal center. "We are upholding social justice. We're helping the weakest people."

I met Xu and some of Gongmeng's lawyers on the day that Beijing's Civil Affairs Bureau shut down their research center. Officials confiscated computers and other equipment, saying that the facility, which did legal research on public welfare and offered legal aid, hadn't registered itself properly. The closure sounded the death knell for the organization, which closed its doors shortly thereafter when authorities issued a huge fine for "taxes owed."

At the same time, fifty-three lawyers known for tackling politically sensitive human rights issues lost their licenses, effectively banned from working. The Beijing Municipal Bureau of Justice said the lawyers didn't pass an assessment by their firms or failed to register with the bureau.

Our meeting took place in a restaurant serving the food of Xinjiang, the restive western region where authorities—facing sporadic bursts of violence from a separatist movement and ethnic tensions between Chinese and Uighur Muslims—have kept a tight watch. By the time I arrived, the lawyers had finished eating. All that was left when I sat down were bowls of untouched rice, a half-empty bottle of Sprite, and a couple of plates with reddish grease stains, evidence of the cuisine's spicy overtones.

All casually dressed in short-sleeved shirts and T-shirts in the summer heat, the lawyers showed a surprising calm and focus as they exchanged information and tried to figure out next steps, smoking cigarette after cigarette. Every few minutes they fielded calls from friends and colleagues.

"This goes against the law in a powerful way," said Li Xiongbing, a Gongmeng lawyer who defended Falun Gong members. "I'm most concerned that the authorities are going against the principal of law and are cracking down on people in the legal profession. Where is our country going now?"

"We have lost the trust of the government and Party," grimly added Jiang Tianyong, portly with a thick head of spiky hair. "That's why we have this situation today. But we feel like we have completely followed the law. I feel like China's laws have cheated us."

For many years, Jiang taught middle school, but in 2005 he started practicing law. He listed the people he had defended: Tibetans, Falun Gong members, and parents who lost children in the Sichuan earthquake. "The relevant government departments have specially warned me not to take the cases." He could still do legal consulting or work for an NGO if the situation didn't improve.

I asked if other attorneys could help take over his caseload.

"Theoretically my clients can fire me and hire other lawyers. But the reality is, whom can they hire? Who else can take their cases? . . . The number of people in our profession who would is already so small, but under these circumstances, who would dare do it?"

When I told him that he and the other lawyers were brave, he demurred. "There are people who are far braver than I am, especially my clients. I feel they are the ones with true courage."

I asked him what I ask many activists: Why do you do what you do, especially since it puts you and your family at risk?

"It's not that I look for these cases especially, but more perhaps that they find me. And when they do, I don't avoid them, and I don't turn them down."

Why not turn them down? I pressed.

"People refuse these cases for their own reasons. The reason I don't refuse them is that these people have the right to hire a lawyer, and according to the law I have the right to accept what they entrust me with. And some of the people who find me, they have been refused by other people. . . . I feel honestly that when they find me they are in a desperate or angry state of mind, they have a lot of grievances.

"They know they have a right to a lawyer, but so few lawyers will provide legal service to them. I think so many of these desperate people still hold on to the last glimmer of hope, so if I refuse them, too, I'm not sure what choices they will make after they leave me. They may be disappointed by their country's legal system or may choose to take extreme measures we see in the media like bombing the courts that we've seen or killing people. . . . I hope that by providing my legal service to these people, they will feel that China's law is useful, that it can be used."

❖

China's booming number of Internet users surpassed America's in 2008 to become the world's biggest. In January 2012, the number of Chinese Internet users surged past a half billion and growing.

One blogger who lives in rural China poetically captured the profound impact that access has made on his compatriots: "If there were no Internet, they would probably be like me 10 years ago, trapped by high mountains and deep valleys, and could only look up to the sky from a well. They would be isolated by artificial and natural barriers, lonely and helpless . . . their wailing heard by no one and their struggles seen by no one. The Internet came from heaven and served like a time tunnel, changing everything."

While most Chinese still go online to download music, use search engines, read news, and buy things, a burgeoning, ever-changing community of netizens is using the web to find like-minded people and air opinions, a growing number of which question or criticize official policies.

Online forums have helped mobilize people and disseminate information from diverse and numerous sources, becoming a new arena for expression in its purest form, a way to be heard as never before on social, political, and personal issues. This unprecedented access to a voice has become a nightmare for a government determined, at all costs, to prevent large-scale distribution of information that can unite people and communities against it.

In many ways, the chaos of the Chinese corner of the Internet mirrors the unwieldy nature of life on the mainland: It's crowded; its inhabitants have something to say and want to be heard; the situation is potentially explosive—and the government is trying its best to keep everything under its thumb.

The Party relies on a multifaceted strategy to control content and monitor online activities at every level of service. Government agencies and private companies employ hundreds of thousands of people to support the mammoth effort, which authorities allege is aimed at stopping the spread of pornography, gambling, and other harmful practices. Of course sensitive political and social topics fall very much under the stringent rules.

Automated technical filtering forms the foundation of those censorship efforts. Domain names, Internet addresses, and web pages containing taboo keywords, phrases, or topics have been identified and barred. Hundreds of banned words include "dictatorship," "democracy," "freedom," "truth," and "riot police." Censored issues span criticism of top leaders, independent evaluations of China's human rights records, violations of minority rights in the autonomous regions of Tibet and Xinjiang, the Falun Gong, the Tiananmen protests, and various dissident initiatives that challenge the regime.

During extremely sensitive incidents, the government has gone so far as to shut down entire communications systems, including Internet access and mobile phone service to prevent the spread of unofficial accounts of events and more unrest. While traveling in Tibetan areas during antigovernment demonstrations in 2008, we couldn't send or receive text messages, but the problem cleared as soon as we left. The service provider told us that systems in that area were "under maintenance."

Ever-changing lists of directives come from political bodies that oversee Internet content, most prominently, the Central Propaganda Department and the State Council Information Office. They ensure that media and cultural content don't contain any material inconsistent with the Communist Party's political dogmas. Below lie a stable of offices and ministries that regulate news websites and control the amount of coverage—if any—of negative stories like environmental and natural disasters, tainted food scandals, and deaths in police custody. Specific instructions go out, often many times a day, on how to highlight or suppress opinions and information.

Chinese journalists and bloggers often sarcastically refer to the instructions as well as other censorship orders as directives from the Ministry of Truth, after one of the four ministries in George Orwell's *1984*. People employed both by websites and the government manually read and censor content as well.

To beef up public support for the government's position, authorities have employed commentators to shape and sway public opinion by posting pro-government remarks and leading online discussions along Party lines. Sometimes, these commentators—called "50-cent Party" members after how much they are rumored to earn for each post—report users who have posted offending statements.

Dozens of people have been imprisoned for Internet-related "crimes" such as posting photos and articles highlighting corruption and sensitive topics like school collapses in the 2008 Sichuan quake. In December 2011, Chen Wei and Chen Xi, veteran dissidents (not related), received sentences of nine and ten years in prison respectively for inciting subversion because they posted online essays criticizing the government.

The intrusive system of censorship has generated resentment among Internet users, who have come up with creative new forms of online resistance, mobilization, and expression that continually morph to stay one step ahead of the state. Users post images of text rather than text itself or jumble Chinese characters so they read vertically rather than horizontally. One of the most ingeniously cheeky ways they're circumventing the censors is by using puns and homonyms in place of banned words. As a result, a whole new system of double-speak has emerged in jokes, songs, poetry, and stories that dig at the Party and its policies.

The first and most well-known example is that of the "grass mud horse," a mythical, alpaca-like animal whose name in Chinese, *caonima*, sounds almost like "fuck your mother." The creature first appeared in cartoons and videos in which it battles and eventually defeats the "river crab," a homonym for "harmony," a catchword used by the leadership while blocking content in order to "build a harmonious society." Internet users now refer to censorship as "being harmonized."

The idea of the grass-mud horse trouncing the river crab caught on so fast that within weeks, the *caonima* had become the de facto mascot of Chinese netizens fighting for freedom of expression.

It took government censors a while to catch on because the phrase was so common, but many experts believe it was a key reason why YouTube was blocked in the mainland in March 2009. Censors also removed postings related to *caonima* and forbade forum managers from promoting any threads on the topic.

釁

Hu Jia, one of the country's brashest activists, had regular run-ins with authorities—but he was always helpful, businesslike, and very willing to talk to foreign reporters. Sometimes, our calls were disconnected, a sign that we had crossed the censors' line of acceptable conversation.

Born in 1973 in Beijing to parents who were among intellectuals persecuted during an anti-rightist campaign in the 1950s, Hu played the role of protector even as a child. If his friends were beaten by their parents, he chastised the parents. If he saw beggars on the street, he gave them all his money.

In 1996, Hu graduated from the Beijing School of Economics, where he had become interested in environmental issues after reading about an elderly Japanese man who came to China to plant trees on the barren plains of Inner Mongolia. Moved to do the same, Hu later founded an AIDS awareness group after meeting Wan Yanhai, an activist pressuring the government to deal more openly with the disease. In December 2002, he was detained for four days while trying to deliver toys and winter clothes to AIDS orphans in Henan province.

"It was the first time in my life my freedom was restricted, the first time I had been searched, been threatened," Hu said.

From that point, he headed down a path typical for many dissidents. When the government gave little ground on causes dear to him, he began to see China's problems as rooted in authorities' lack of respect for human rights. He fought back, focusing on the broader issues of freedom in his country.

In the beginning, it appeared an unlikely role for the bespectacled, slightly built vegetarian. A Buddhist who admired the Dalai Lama—a figure much reviled by Beijing—Hu sometimes shaved his head, giving him a monk-like appearance. But he was also tenacious and soon exercised an outsized influence from his airy, fourth-floor apartment, even while under house arrest.

Using the telephone and the Internet, he tirelessly detailed the arrests, harassment, and detentions of other activists to a network of dissidents, reporters, and diplomats in China. Hu acted as one of the first points of contact when Chen Guangcheng, a blind activist who executed an extraordinary escape from suffocating and abusive house arrest in eastern China, fled to the US Embassy in Beijing with the help of sympathizers. In a photo both touching and full of hope, longtime friends Hu and Chen, who incurred the wrath of local authorities for exposing forced abortions and sterilizations in villages as a result of the country's one-child policy, clasp hands and smile broadly.

In January 2006, Hu married Zeng Jinyan, whom he had met while she was also doing AIDS volunteer work. A month later, security agents seized him, pulled a hood over his head, and drove to an unknown location. He was held for forty-one days and questioned about a nationwide hunger strike that he helped organize to protest violence against dissidents.

I met him at a Starbucks in Beijing's central business district three days after he was released. Dressed in dark olive pants, a blue flannel shirt, and a khaki-colored fleece-lined jacket, he arrived a few minutes late, citing the usual detail of plainclothes agents. He nodded toward a pudgy man in a brown shirt, circling the vicinity like a listless shadow as we talked. The man carried a satchel under his arm, which he pointed in our direction as he rested against a nearby railing, obviously recording details of the meeting. Another man peered out from behind a wall near an elevator bank but quickly withdrew when he saw me staring back.

"Ignore them," Hu said—but it was hard because they were menacing and yet so clownish. I got our drinks, a bottle of orange juice for Hu and a tea for me.

He spoke animatedly, vividly recounting his experiences, at one point twisting his arms to show how roughly his abductors handled him.

"I can't keep quiet about this," he said. "I must take these actions to file a lawsuit and let them know that the Chinese people will still let their voices be heard."

Hu had been under surveillance to prevent him from having contact with Gao Zhisheng, an outspoken lawyer who had launched a symbolic, rolling hunger strike campaign in early February that had gathered several thousand participants. At least half a dozen people who participated or had ties to Gao were subsequently detained.

One February morning, four ferocious-looking men—not the usual ones who followed him—had abducted him from the street in an unmarked car. They snatched his glasses, put a hood over his head, and pulled his arms behind his back. The harder he struggled, the tighter they held him. "I kept breathing. I tried not to vomit. I could not see anything but could feel them accelerating."

They brought him to a hotel room where they let him rest after taking his cellphones and tape recorder. When he awoke, a group of eight policemen was watching him. He asked what they were doing, and they said that they were following orders.

"I'm a free citizen. I want to go home. You can't keep me," he said, but they ignored him.

Later that afternoon, Hu broke a vase over his own head, hoping that the men would take him to a hospital—but they only cleaned up the glass shards. An officer told him that he couldn't leave because they were under orders to hold him but wouldn't give him any other information. Plainclothes officers repeatedly interrogated him, asking him for details about the fast, how it was organized, about his connections with Gao. They flanked him and made threatening motions while questioning him—but he refused to give them answers.

He refused food and drink the first five days of his detainment but was told that if he didn't eat he would be force fed. For the next thirty days, he ate watery gruel and lost over twenty pounds. He sucked in his cheeks, putting his fingers in the hollows to illustrate his point.

"I didn't think they would hold me for this long," he said, sipping his juice. "I thought they would let me go and not drag this on for so long. In this life, I never thought I would feel this kind of hunger, this dizziness. I was always thinking about food. I couldn't sleep, I couldn't see, I couldn't walk. I didn't want my wife and family to see me this way. On the thirtieth day, I started eating a little. I tried to get better."

They moved him to another location, a hotel room with rats, where they allowed him to take walks. Once, he went on one for almost fifteen miles in the rain. "I wanted them to understand my will."

At the end of March, Hu was hooded again and dropped off about two miles from his home. His captors gave no reason for their actions. They took his diary to erase any trace of his captivity.

"There's no use in fighting," one of them warned. "You've suffered so much for so long. We understand that your friends and family are so worried. If you don't want this to happen again, stay away from sensitive activities. We will do this again if you do."

Hu looked at me defiantly. "I will keep doing this because it emphasizes China's lack of human rights."

❋

Hu had been under house arrest for 223 days when, on a December afternoon in 2007, he was taken from his home. Zeng, giving their infant daughter a bath, heard nothing when nearly two dozen plainclothes police swarmed their apartment, confiscating laptops, cellphones, bank cards, and books before quietly whisking her husband away.

It could have been because he participated via webcam in a European Parliament hearing, in which he said it was "ironic that one of the people in charge of organizing the Olympic Games is the head of the Bureau of Public Security, which is responsible for so many human rights violations."

While in prison, Hu was awarded the 2008 Sakharov Prize, Europe's highest human rights honor. Many considered him a frontrunner for the Nobel Peace Prize that same year. *Time* magazine had named Zeng one of the world's top 100 influential people the year before. Her blog and tweets provided precious snippets of information while she was under tight surveillance by state security agents. In June 2011, Hu was released from a three-and-a-half-year prison sentence for sedition.

"A sleepless night, Hu Jia reached home at 2 a.m.," Zeng tweeted. "Safe, very happy."

Efforts to quash unrest aggressively increased when the success of the Arab Spring in the Middle East and Northern Africa inspired attempts at a Jasmine Revolution in China. The government, already on edge about swelling domestic discontent over corruption and the vast economic divide, responded with one of the most sweeping campaigns of repression since 1989.

The call to action came from anonymous appeals issued on the Internet, urging people to stage peaceful demonstrations—just strolling and smiling, one posting said—on Sundays in Beijing, Shanghai, and a dozen other major cities. Participants were urged to shout: "We want food, we want work, we want housing, we want fairness," common complaints in China.

My colleague Gillian Wong, a resourceful and tireless reporter, tracked down one group of organizers. The network of twenty highly educated and young Chinese in and outside the country said they were fed up with the inequalities and injustices seeping from the Communist Party's autocratic rule and wanted a shift toward democracy.

In the end, more onlookers than protesters filled the streets. Security forces massed, and text messages and Internet appeals for protests were censored. Even jasmine flowers—their sweet scent and pure white petals deeply entwined with China's history and culture—became contraband.

Dozens of Chinese bloggers, Christians, writers, activists, and lawyers disappeared, were detained, or were arrested as a precautionary measure. Many more were questioned or harassed. Authorities even rounded up people without long histories of activism. No one was above scrutiny or punishment.

Ai Weiwei quickly became the most high-profile target of the crackdown. A globally renowned conceptual artist, he had helped design the distinctive Bird's Nest Stadium for the Beijing Olympics before souring on the games. Well known for his intolerance and criticisms of the Communist Party, he gave them the finger both figuratively and literally in his work.

In 2008, Ai recruited volunteers on Twitter to compile the names of thousands of students who died in the Sichuan quake. He created an affecting installation piece out of nine thousand children's backpacks that covered the facade of a Munich museum, forming the Chinese characters for "She lived happily for seven years in this world."

For years, Ai, the son of one of China's most famous modern poets, seemed largely immune to the public security apparatus. Then, in April 2011, he was prevented from boarding a flight to Hong Kong and was whisked away to an unknown destination. His detention sparked an international outcry.

Ai spent almost three months in police detention before being released, visibly thinner and temporarily subdued. Officials slapped him with a $2.4 million bill for fines and taxes that he allegedly owed.

Authorities also put intense pressure on foreign journalists covering the Jasmine Revolution, the worst in at least a decade. Officers phoned dozens of correspondents telling them to "obey regulations," and plainclothes security agents also assaulted several television reporters. They kicked one in the face and cracked his ribs and repeatedly slammed another's leg in a van door. The Foreign Ministry summoned many for questioning and threatened some with the revocation of work visas. Chinese news assistants were contacted and asked to report on journalists' behavior. The e-mail accounts of half a dozen reporters were hacked, and one lost Internet access altogether.

Even with the power of the Internet, which imprisoned Nobel Peace Prize winner Liu Xiaobo called "God's present to China," the tides of change were being held at bay, albeit shakily.

Since 2009, Liu has been serving an eleven-year sentence for "inciting subversion of state power." A poet and literary critic, Liu was one of the chief architects of *Charter 08*, a manifesto calling for a peaceful end to single-party rule, a new constitution, and an independent judiciary. It was modeled after *Charter 77*, drafted by rights advocates in then-Czechoslovakia, which led to the 1989 Velvet Revolution that swept away that nation's Communist regime.

When Liu was awarded the Nobel Peace Prize in 2010, an empty chair represented his presence at the ceremony in Oslo. From prison, he wept and told his wife, Liu Xia, that he dedicated it to the people who died in the Tiananmen protests of 1989. During those demonstrations, Liu had staged a hunger strike, then negotiated the peaceful retreat of thousands of students before the full wrath of the crackdown, preventing bloodshed on a much larger scale.

Police watch Liu Xia, also a poet, and have prohibited her from seeing anyone but a handful of family members—the leadership's way of preventing her from becoming a rallying point for activists. She is effectively under house arrest without phone or Internet access. She saw Liu two days after the announcement from Norway, then went for months with no communication.

⁂

In 2006, Gao Zhisheng, the pugnacious Christian lawyer who started the rolling hunger strike which Hu Jia joined, blamed security forces for an attempt on his life.

A military vehicle and another car, both with license plates covered, followed him as he drove home one night. One of the cars overtook him and braked suddenly, forcing him to stop. When he got out, the second car sped from behind to hit him. He jumped for his life into a roadside flowerbed.

When I asked him if he knew who was behind the incident, he said: "In the abstract, it's the Chinese Communist Party, but in reality I have no idea."

The vehicles raced off but returned and followed him as he drove home. A newspaper covering the license plate of one car blew off, and he recognized the number as belonging to a vehicle that had followed him in the past.

"I've been threatened before," he said, his voice strident with emotion, "but this time they wanted to kill me."

In 2010, he was released after being held secretly by authorities for fourteen months. My bureau chief, Charles Hutzler, interviewed Gao at an empty teahouse in Beijing under the watch of plainclothes police.

Once named one of the country's ten best lawyers by the Ministry of Justice, Gao seemed broken. Normally talkative, forceful, and spirited, he looked weary and subdued, dressed all in black. He told of being moved from hostels to farmhouses, apartments, and prisons in Beijing, his native province of Shaanxi and Xinjiang, where he lived for many years. Several times three officers hooded him, stripped him naked, and beat him with holstered handguns. When they tired, they rested after tying his arms and legs with plastic bags and throwing him to the floor.

He was kept in a room with lights always on, made to sit motionless for up to sixteen hours, and told his children were having nervous breakdowns. Twice a day, he ate rotten cabbage. They bound him with belts once and covered his face with a wet towel for an hour to make him feel like he was suffocating slowly. With brutality excessive even for China's often abusive police, Gao's captors committed other atrocities that he wouldn't describe, saying that it was worse than when security forces held burning cigarettes to his eyes to cause temporary blindness and electrocuted his genitals.

Two weeks after talking to Charles, Gao disappeared again. For almost two years, no one heard from him or what had happened to him. Many, including his wife and family, feared he was dead.

Then in December 2011, the Xinhua News Agency announced that Gao was being sent to prison for three years for violating his probation after receiving a three-year suspended sentence in 2006 for subversion. Xinhua didn't give any details on Gao's alleged violation—puzzling since he was surely under constant supervision since his release. Legal experts said that timing played a part in the decision. Gao's five-year probation was set to expire in a week. Formalizing his detention was one way to keep him locked up and have a ready answer for queries from foreign governments.

Gao had asked Beijing police at one point why they didn't just put him in prison. "They said 'You going to prison, that's a dream. You're not good enough for that. Whenever we want you to disappear, you will disappear.'"

4

The Great Migration

My former housekeeper Cheng Ayi—Auntie Cheng—makes the best fried chicken in all of Beijing. Her recipe begins with wing drumettes and a simple marinade of cooking wine, salt, sugar, black pepper, and ginger slices that infuses the meat with a subtle, savory fragrance and the tiniest kick. Like most Chinese cooks, measurements are irrelevant to her. It's all about instinct and experience. The chicken sits in a bowl for about an hour as the flavors set in. Then it's time to fry.

"Getting the oil at the right temperature is the most important step," she said. "I put a tiny piece of meat in it, and if it bubbles and floats I know it's ready."

She painstakingly transferred each wing from the bowl to a plate of plain flour for a light dusting before dropping each individually into the wok of canola oil. The stove fan roared, and the oil sputtered and bubbled. She used long wooden chopsticks to turn the pieces to ensure even browning, instinctively knowing when they were done. Within minutes they emerged a deep red-brown, and she drained them on paper towels.

When eaten still warm, the slightly crunchy greaseless exterior gave way to briny-sweet, ginger-kissed meat. Plucked cold from the fridge the next day, it was like having an instant picnic in my twentieth-floor apartment. They were the perfect snack.

Cheng Ayi also made killer braised pork ribs with a thick brown sauce studded with bits of dried chili and star anise; garlicky stir-fried greens; and shrimp with leek, red bell peppers, and a perfectly balanced sweet-and-sour glaze. But she seemed genuinely surprised each time I told her how much I loved her food.

Dinner with Cheng Ayi, my housekeeper, and her friends in Beidian, a migrant enclave on the outskirts of Beijing. The meal had strong, simple flavors, from the smokiness of cured pork to a hint of licorice in the chicken. The egg custard was warm, soft, and comforting.

Cooking was just something she did every night for her family and twice a week for me. She made enough to last a few days and put everything in plastic containers in the fridge. Having a home-cooked meal within easy reach, regardless of my work schedule, offered a supreme comfort.

I was willing to try whatever she liked to cook as long as it had lots of protein and no onions. She whipped up scrambled eggs with thinly sliced shiitake mushrooms and stir-fried ground pork with garlic bolts that looked and tasted like thin, shaved green asparagus stalks. When I asked her to make a typical favorite from her home province of Anhui in central China, she presented a dish taught to her by her mother.

She shaped ground pork into meatballs and browned them in oil before quickly frying them with a handful of salt-preserved greens, minced ginger and garlic, and a tiny bit of soy sauce and water. When all the liquid was absorbed, which took about ten minutes, the dish was ready. The tart saltiness of the vegetables cut the rich meatiness of the pork, and both textures crunched pleasantly.

Occasionally her cooking was far too greasy, and although I asked her to cut back she couldn't break the habit. For her, it was a reminder that she was living in better times. "Before, we had no money, so we had no oil, and the food wasn't good. When there's a lot of oil, the food is delicious."

When I brought ingredients home from a trip, Cheng Ayi gamely incorporated them into the rotation of dishes, many of which she learned to cook from other households she cleaned. I enjoyed *mapo doufu*, Sichuan's quintessential tongue-tingling tofu concoction, after I picked up packets of *Pixian douban*, a spicy fermented bean paste, from the airport in Chengdu. The *douban* sauce acted as a fiery, salty, earthy foil to the bland tofu. Occasionally, she added mushrooms or ground pork to give the dish more body. Dried scallops and abalone from Xiamen ended up sweetening and adding delicious depth to chicken soup simmered for at least two hours. Ayi's other soup, made from pork rib and lotus root, kept me warm on many winter nights.

During a trip to Singapore, I thought of her fried chicken and was inspired to try something new: seasoned flour. Ayi considered the sachets I excitedly showed her and took it to the next level. She used the same chicken marinade on pork ribs but added chili powder for extra kick before frying up a batch with the seasoned flour. Another classic was born.

藩

Cheng Ayi and I met in 2003 when she was working for my friends John Ruwitch, a well-regarded Reuters reporter, and his wife, Anh, who is extremely particular about cleanliness. Their apartment was always impressively spotless. At the time, I was looking for a new cleaning lady because my last one didn't cook and did a lackluster job when she showed up at all. It had taken a while to warm to the idea of hiring domestic help, but it was a necessity, given my irregular work schedule.

I went to Anh's for dinner, and Cheng Ayi was in the kitchen, chopping and frying. She had worked for a French family who gave her the cookbook from which she got the idea for her fried chicken; an Italian family who told her about pasta and tomato sauce; and Anh, who is Vietnamese-American. From her, Cheng Ayi learned to make *goi cuon*, the fresh rice-paper rolls filled with vermicelli, pork, shrimp, spring onion, and lettuce.

Cheng Ayi has a round face, beautifully smooth, sun-browned skin, and slightly rosy cheeks. She had pulled back her hair, jet-black and straight, into a bun. When she smiled, her eyes crinkled, and when she laughed it was a full and happy sound.

I babbled to her in my best Mandarin, hoping that I was making sense. I realized only after a while that she spoke mostly her Anhui dialect. We were both self-deprecating about our language abilities, which put me at ease. Although she was only nine years my senior, I called her "ayi," pronounced ah-yee, the term used for housekeepers in China, which also means "auntie."

Our lives and jobs differed enormously, but we both knew what it was to be far from home. At the time, Cheng Ayi had been in Beijing cleaning homes for thirteen years, making a living to help support a husband (who came to the city a few years later) and two children still in a village outside Hefei, Anhui's capital. Leaving them was hard, but it meant an uninterrupted education and a brighter future for them. While she longed to see them, it was a necessary sacrifice that many in her position made, and Ayi was a practical woman. "It's very hard to make a living back home. Money is tight so we have to go to other places for temporary work to earn enough to pay for our children's education," she said.

Cheng Ayi once asked her daughter: "Do you miss me when I'm gone?"

"No," the pretty pre-teen replied. "I miss Dad, but I don't miss you. You've never been around."

She came to my apartment on Wednesdays, when I was at work, and on Sundays, when I was usually collapsed on the couch or in bed. She moved quickly and efficiently as she dusted, wiped, swept, washed, and rinsed. Everything was tidy and spotless after she left. She even rolled up plastic bags from supermarket purchases into neat little balls.

Cheng Ayi brought her daughter a couple of times to help when the girl was on break from school. I wasn't home the first time, and it was only weeks later that I found a note that she secretly wrote to me, lost among stacks of bills and random pieces of paper on my dining table: *"Hong xiaojie, nihao!"*—"Miss Ang, hello!"—was all it said in small, childish, precise lettering. Another time, mother and daughter stood side-by-side at my bathroom sink, hand-washing some clothes I had left out. "Don't wash the bright colors with the light colors," Ayi said patiently above the splash of water. "Wring it dry. A little harder—but don't wrinkle it."

In between cleaning and laundry, Cheng Ayi cooked. Although I never asked her to, she kept meticulous records and receipts for the ingredients she bought. I usually gave her money every couple of weeks, and she kept track of how much she spent, down to each penny. The fourth of eight children, she was semi-literate, her scrawl revealing that she had had only a few years of education.

Except for a greeting or a question, she rarely spoke when she worked. Once in a while, her cellphone rang, and she had a booming conversation—such stentorian levels of talking are the norm in China—with whomever was on the other end of the line. Despite a generally jolly demeanor, Cheng Ayi was no pushover. She always held herself with pride and never let anyone treat her like a peasant in a society that's still very class-conscious. She held her own against security guards trying to stop her from entering my building and argued with uncooperative taxi drivers. Annoyed with family members, she unleashed a torrent of angry words, none of which I understood.

It was a thing of beauty to behold her haggling at wet markets over a few cents, harassing vendors in a loud, scolding voice. Everything was too expensive, and the produce was never good enough. It's a bargaining ploy that many Chinese use and I tried to imitate—with varying success. She once made a stallholder pull out vegetables from a box behind the counter because the ones on display were wet—a trick used to make them look fresher and weigh more.

She worked hard seven days a week, cleaning up to three homes a day around the city, many of them rented by my friends, other reporters to whom I had introduced her. At one point, her schedule was so full that she couldn't take on new clients. Every day she squeezed onto buses so packed that she had to stand for the entire two-hour journey between homes.

Various bags often weighed her down. She had her purse, plastic bags of groceries if she had to cook for someone, and at least one overstuffed bag made of cloth or the ubiquitous woven nylon in a red-white-and-blue plaid. Sometimes they contained hand-me-downs that we gave her—clothes, shoes, appliances—and I always did a double-take when she showed up in one of my old sweaters or T-shirts.

My friends and I paid her extremely well by Chinese standards—totalling about $1,000 a month, more than most farmers or factory workers earned in a year—but she frugally saved the bulk of her earnings for her family and for repairs on her home in Anhui. She always took the bus and ate only a plain steamed bun or two for lunch even though I asked her to share the food she cooked for me. Some of that probably stemmed from the Chinese habit of being *keqi*, a concept of politeness and standing on ceremony that sometimes gets taken to extremes, when people said no, even when they want to say yes.

Cheng Ayi once guiltily told Anita Chang, my AP colleague and food-loving soulmate whose home Cheng Ayi also cleaned, that she sometimes snacked on McDonald's ketchup packets that Anita had accumulated from late-night deliveries. I used to save empty bottles for her because she sold them for cash. It turned out, though, that the ones I gave her were worthless because no one wanted dark colored glass. She got the most money from clear plastic.

Eventually, her thriftiness paid off. She made enough to plug the leaks in her house in Anhui and build a second story. She also bought another home in the county seat for her children to live in when they get married.

Cheng Ayi also cooked for some of her other clients, whipping up homestyle dishes they all loved. For Anita, she made scrambled eggs either with tomatoes or yellow garlic chives, stir-fried chopped lotus root, braised pork belly with tofu skin cut into strips and tied in knots, and a simple but delicious appetizer of chopped cucumbers mixed with mashed garlic and sesame oil. For Tini Tran, another officemate with whom I always ate well, she made the same anise-scented pork or chicken that she made for me, and winter melon and spare rib soup. The fried chicken was a big hit. "Tasty and sweet . . . yet spicy," my unabashedly carnivorous friend Marsha Cooke, the Asia bureau chief for CBS News, wrote in one ecstatic email. "Not greasy nor loaded down with batter. Her chicken IS the definition of FINGER LICKIN' GOOD."

Scott McDonald, my news editor, paid for Cheng Ayi to attend cooking classes where she learned to make eggplant parmesan with homemade tomato sauce, pizza, banana bread, and apple pie.

"You want a woman from Anhui to learn how to make you apple pie?" I asked, incredulous.

"I eat Chinese food all the time, so I wanted something different at home," Scott said. "The eggplant is her signature dish, and she rocks with it. The right amount of tomato, so it doesn't dominate the dish. I'm happy when I come home on a Monday and that smell is in the kitchen. She does lighter stuff like a tossed salad on Thursday."

For someone who once listed a bar as his favorite restaurant, Scott sounded almost like a foodie when discussing Cheng Ayi's culinary skills. That's how much we appreciated her cooking.

I had to eat my words after she made the apple pie for me one day. It was tasty, with a semi-flaky crust and a filling not cloyingly sweet. I asked what she thought of the eggplant parmesan of which Scott was such a big fan.

"I tried a little of it, and I liked it very much," she said after a small hesitation. Then she smiled sheepishly. "But I have no idea what I'm cooking, really. These ingredients are really unfamiliar. I have to go to a special store to get the cheese."

❀

Cheng Ayi's home province of Anhui, an impoverished region carved up by mountain ranges and the great Yangtze and Huai Rivers, features lots of wild game and herbs in its food, considered one of the eight traditional cuisines of China, although it is less ubiquitous than Cantonese or Sichuan food.

I had been to Anhui only once, to interview doctors about an outbreak of hand, foot, and mouth disease that had sickened thousands of children. But less than twenty-four hours after my arrival, I was diverted to Sichuan, where a massive earthquake had struck, and I never had a chance to explore Anhui's local fare.

Fans say its flavors perfectly blend surrounding provinces: the oily sweetness of Zhejiang and Jiangsu, and the lightness and subtlety of Shandong. Strictly monitored cooking temperatures retain the flavor, nutrients, and color of the fresh ingredients.

Commonly used ingredients—game, mushrooms, bamboo shoots, and dates—come from surrounding mountains like Huangshan, famous for its distinctive, cloud-wreathed granite peaks and views of stunning sunsets. Many dishes are braised or stewed in a dark brown soy-based sauce for succulence, though occasionally they can be heavy with oil, believed to lubricate the skin and bowels. Ham, crystallized sugar, and a variety of dried foods like sea cucumber add texture and depth.

A dish synonymous with Anhui cuisine is Li Hongzhang's Hodgepodge, a soupy, anything-goes stew named after a Qing dynasty statesman and Anhui native who, as the story goes, asked his kitchen to throw whatever they could find into a pot of chicken soup to make an impromptu creation when more guests than anticipated showed up for a banquet he was hosting. It's common to find bits of squid, dried bean curd, chicken, fish, ham, and vegetables in the mix. Another favorite is the silky Bagong Mountain tofu, made with spring water and famed for its fine texture and pure white color.

The area around Huangshan, in the province's south, is considered the root of Anhui cuisine. A local delicacy often presented as a gift is called Drunken Crabs, made by packing brush-cleaned crustaceans into a jar with wine and seasonings, including soy sauce, salt, garlic, ginger, and sugar, and sealing it for a week to allow the crab to pickle and the flavors to absorb. The best time to do this is in fall, when the crabs are fat and fresh.

Another crowd-pleaser is a chicken dish named after Fuliji, a northern Anhui town where an eighty-year-old recipe is said to be the foundation for the distinctive flavor of the bird. Traditionally a healthy, strong chicken is made to drink clean water before being slaughtered. After, it's hung up to dry, glazed with malt sugar syrup, and deep-fried whole in sesame oil until tawny. Next, a pot of water is heated with a sealed gauze pouch filled with spices like star anise, cumin, black cardamom, ginger pieces, Sichuan peppercorns, and dried orange peel. When it comes to a boil, sugar, salt, and the fried chicken are added. The liquid is returned to a boil, skimmed, and then cooked gently for five minutes before being covered on reduced heat. In all, the bird is cooked for four to six hours until the meat is fall-off-the-bone tender. The stewing liquid should be saved and used again.

Cheng Ayi hails from a village on the outskirts of Hefei, the provincial capital, known for dishes like Cao Cao Chicken, named after a devious and brilliant warlord and flavored with cinnamon, ginger, and medicinal herbs. Legend has it that Cao's chef stewed the chicken with the nourishing herbs when he saw that his master was worn out from battle. Within days of savoring the specialty, the warrior regained his health.

Most of these restaurant-style dishes were unfamiliar to Cheng Ayi, however. Her table is more rustic, her family enjoying staples like stir-fried chilies, tofu in soup, stir-fried kidney beans with sliced pork, and braised eggplant.

"I eat anything," she laughed when I asked what her favorite dish was. "While we were growing up, we were poor. It was pitiful how little we had to eat. There was hardly any rice. It was mostly sweet potatoes, a little corn, foods made with flour. There was very little meat. Sometimes we raised chickens and we ate the eggs. Nowadays, we eat a lot more meat on a regular basis—although the price of pork is so high that we've had to cut back."

The only break she ever took was during Lunar New Year, the country's biggest holiday, when she visited her hometown in central China for three weeks. Despite *hongbao* (packets of money) we gave her as a bonus, Ayi insisted on a grueling train journey that took two days during a time when millions of others were doing the same in the world's largest annual movement of humans. Because of this, Chinese media often call migrant workers *houniao*—migratory birds. If lucky, Cheng Ayi would get a ticket for a seat; more often than not, it was standing room only for much of the way. But as always, Ayi was prepared.

"I buy a small stool and squeeze in with the crowds," she said. "It's too hard to stand for two days. I don't sleep. It's too hard to sleep while sitting on a stool."

Eventually, the whole family reunited for a celebratory New Year meal that included the meatball and salted vegetable dish she made for me.

"I'm always so excited to get home," she said. "I feel happy and comfortable. When I'm in Beijing, I think about going back to see my mother, I think about going back to see my children."

The rest of the year, Cheng Ayi lived in a tiny room in Beidian, a small village on the outskirts of Beijing's city center. Her husband and son, who moved to the capital when the latter finished school a couple of years after she started working for me, shared the space. Her daughter remained in school in Anhui, looked after by her grandmother.

I spent three days in Beidian, snapping pictures for a photo project on urban living, wandering around with Cheng Ayi and her friends from Anhui who had also made their way to the capital in search of high-paying jobs and a more prosperous life. They cooked wonderful meals and welcomed me like a long-lost sister. It was a tough, sometimes hand-to-mouth existence for them, but most thought it far better than the farm life that they would otherwise be living.

Those women form part of the more than 220 million people moving in droves, mainly between the underdeveloped heartland and the affluent urban hubs along the eastern coast, as well as Beijing and Tianjin in the northeast. The jobs they find are usually in construction, manufacturing, or the service industry. In theory, this flow of people is mutually beneficial. The cities are desperate for labor, of which there is a surplus in the countryside, especially in recent years as a result of modern farm practices and obsolete state-run factories leaving many unemployed.

An agrarian society for millennia, China for the first time has more people in cities than the countryside. Some estimates predict the number of urban residents will rise from more than 665 million in 2010 to one billion in 2030.

The dramatic increase in the size of the "floating population" of migrant workers on the move over the last twenty-five years has resulted in social consequences increasingly harder for the government to ignore. Although I always picture groups of farmers gliding around on clouds like fairies in traditional Chinese tales, the term "floating population" categorizes people who live away from their place of residence as defined by *hukou*, the government's strict and complex residency permit policy modeled after *propiska*, the Soviet internal passport system.

Used by the Communist Party beginning in 1958 to regulate and restrict the mobility of citizens between cities and the countryside, the rigid system has become the foundation of a near impenetrable barrier between the haves and the have-nots, which critics have lambasted as China's version of apartheid.

The *hukou* system takes shape in a brown booklet with gold lettering that details a person's birthplace, current residence, marriage status, moves, and education. In the past, it has dictated the two most important factors that determine status: location, which specifies the city, town, or village to which a citizen belongs, and the urban or rural classification.

An urban *hukou* means a long list of opportunities and state-sponsored benefits, from employment to retirement pensions, subsidized housing to free education and medical insurance. The holder of a rural *hukou* receives access to farmland but very little else. Children feudally inherit their parents' status.

The specific rural-urban classifications have decreased in significance in recent years, but the *hukou* location remains key, spurring Chinese from the country to migrate to cities. Because these migrants are still technically residents of their rural hometowns, they often face higher medical fees, pay more for daily expenses like tickets to city parks, and cannot receive most socioeconomic assistance such as subsidized housing and public health insurance. If parents can't afford to pay private school fees, their children often lack access to free education in local communities. Governments regularly shut down schools specially established for children of migrant workers, saying the facilities are substandard and that the children should attend public schools. But those schools are usually too full to take more students. Officials justify these antimigrant measures by saying that the influx of people is stretching city resources to the maximum.

The discrimination has taught an especially bitter lesson to low-skilled job-seekers from the countryside who already face a litany of woes for working and living outside their designated hometowns in hopes of building a better future. They move constantly, trying to find continued employment, adapting to unfamiliar foods and climates, struggling to manage an uncertain life always in transition.

Older migrant job-seekers often stand out with their weathered skin and clothes. They are often treated like second-class citizens and blamed for increases in petty theft, drug addiction, overcrowding, and pollution. While many have relatively decent living conditions, home for others can be a squatter camp, crude and crammed shacks on construction sites, shared beds, chairs at Internet cafes, or the streets. They don't see their families for months or years, underscoring a lonely existence in a place where they cannot replicate a sense of community. Cellphones become lifelines.

Workers toil for paltry salaries—their national average hovers around $250 a month—often under appalling conditions. Not only do they take jobs in factories, restaurants, and on construction sites, but they accept positions too dangerous or too menial for others to contemplate: sifting through dumps for recyclables, coal mining, collecting garbage, peddling coal.

Employers chronically exploit them, flouting labor laws by docking or delaying pay, refusing to provide copies of contracts, enforcing grueling hours with few days off, charging for substandard living conditions without heat or proper bathing facilities and minuscule or inedible portions of food, and failing to pay for medical or accident insurance. Workplaces filled with exhausted and undernourished workers—who have very little redress because they have no proof of contract or residency status and can't afford the time or money to resolve problems—often have high rates of injuries and deaths.

Cheng Ayi's husband, Mr. Liang, moved around Beijing from site to site, taking temp jobs wherever he found an opportunity. Once, when he worked at a plant nursery, Ayi brought me a potted orchid with succulent, deep green leaves, a gift from him. His latest job was at a construction site, where he put in grueling hours for bosses who were withholding his pay.

"They owe us money. We've been asking them, and they keep putting us off, saying that they will pay him in good time," Ayi said, showing a flash of anger and resignation. *Meibanfa*. Nothing can be done, and she didn't want to talk about it anymore. Still, Ayi and her husband, who both still have their Anhui *hukou*, were more fortunate than most. They lived together in Beijing, and she made a good wage from her job.

Ongoing abuses by factory owners and municipal officials have given rise to widespread grievances and anger, which are chipping away at social stability. Unhappy workers amass to protest, and demonstrations have turned violent, shattering the popular stereotype that migrant workers are simple country folk subservient to authority and will endure hardship without complaint. Leaving home and working in new environments, on the contrary, have opened their minds to protest tactics and labor rights.

Increasingly, workers under thirty, who make up about half of China's working population, have attitudes and expectations very different from their parents', much less willing to tolerate harsh terms and conditions. Never hungry or cold, they grew up with greater prosperity in families limited by the one-child policy and won't do the sweatshop jobs their parents endured that turned the country into the world's factory floor. They are more used to getting their way and won't hunker down on assembly lines for little money. They also have no intention of returning to their villages, presenting a challenge to a government intent on limiting their access to housing and education in already overburdened cities.

It's looking more and more likely that the tide may turn in favor of the migrant workers as the demand for labor grows and demographic shifts lead to shortages and more leverage for workers. But like everything else in China, by just how much is anyone's guess. The 2010 census showed that children under fourteen years of age, the country's future workers, comprise only 16.6 percent of the population, meaning that the labor shortage will deepen in coming years. Further pressing the situation, migrant workers increasingly are finding jobs closer to home as poorer interior provinces gain prosperity and farm-friendly policies make it possible to stay in rural areas.

The government's massive stimulus package has also created more jobs across the country and overshadowed the allure of coastal factories. Some twenty-four provinces and municipalities raised their minimum wage by an average of a whopping 22 percent in 2011 to attract more workers.

Calls for the reform and abolishment of the *hukou* system have been growing, although those advocating change acknowledge that it must come slowly to prevent disruption and chaos. In an editorial unusually critical of a government policy, the online version of the *People's Daily* denounced the concept of *hukou* as politically outdated and said that it "runs counter to the principle of justice."

When I pressed Cheng Ayi about the difficulties of being a migrant, she had some trouble answering because pondering such matters meant the luxury of time and energy she didn't have. "It's OK. It's not hard," she finally said. "I think it's harder to live in Anhui because there we can't earn any money." She added with a laugh: "I'm actually very lucky."

緊

The first time I visited Cheng Ayi's Beijing home was a winter Sunday when we made our way to Beidian together. It took her two hours to get home by bus from the city center, but it took us just twenty minutes to get there by car. The village resembled a warren of alleyways—a completely different world from the sedate, tree-lined embassy district in which I worked and lived. Some streets were so narrow that a couple could barely walk hand in hand, while in others a small truck could barely squeeze by. Homes and shops jammed up against one another.

It was one of many enclaves that had sprung up in the capital's rural northeast in recent years as migrants inundated the city. In

Beidian—an archaic term for the northern area outside the suburbs of the capital—the population of permanent residents had grown from eight hundred in 2003 to about one thousand people in 2008, but the number of temporary dwellers was much higher and harder to track. At the same time, urban sprawl was gobbling surrounding communities, and many people had lost their fields and homes to development. Their struggle to make a living never ceased.

By day, the dusty but paved streets of Beidian buzzed with a chaotic mix of people, bicycles, and roadside vendors. The energy was infectious, and I couldn't stop snapping pictures as I tried to take it all in. Cheng Ayi briskly led the way to her home, one in a series of rented rooms—averaging about thirteen by thirteen feet—in partitioned single-story brick and concrete buildings with corrugated tin roofs. The cheapest went for just under $30 a month.

Big metal gates sealed off the compounds, and the courtyards filled with all kinds of odds and ends: mops, empty paint cans, sacks of fertilizer, drying clothes, vegetables. Cheng Ayi's room had big windows covered with old newspapers as an added layer of insulation. A pile of bricks topped with a wooden board next to her door served as a makeshift table on which sat a row of shoes and slippers, an assortment of pans, and a flowerpot in which a single yellow bloom was thriving.

A double bed for her and her husband commandeered one end of the room, while a smaller one, her son's, took up the left side along with an old computer. I had met him once before, a couple of years earlier, when he sat in my living room for about a week keeping watch over workmen renovating my bathroom while I was at work. With a thick head of hair, a pug nose, and a sweet, close-lipped smile, he was about twenty, soft-spoken and with his mother's eyes. He never touched the snacks and beverages I left him, but watched a little television or read a book that he brought with him. At the end of the job, I tried to pay him for his time, but he adamantly refused. "This is something we can do for you. I cannot take your money," he said firmly, his arm blocking my efforts to hand him some cash.

They had placed a television on a dresser and a coal stove against the opposite wall, along with a table that held a green hot water flask, a rice cooker, and various condiments. There were no closets or cabinets, so plastic bags filled with belongings were stuffed under the beds, and clothes protected in coat bags hung from wires nailed to the wall.

"This is my home," Cheng Ayi said with a trace of embarrassment. "It's a mess, and it's small." I told her I was glad to be able to visit and thanked her for arranging the trip. Unlike a lot of Chinese I met, she never seemed fazed by my profession or worried about answering my questions. She said it was fine if I wanted to take pictures of life in the village and offered to introduce me to her friends if I wanted to talk to them.

I asked her where the bathroom was, and she said the public one that everyone shared was probably too dirty for me. I assured her that it was fine, but she refused to give me directions.

"Just go in here," she said, handing me a small bucket lined with a plastic bag before turning her back. "We do it, too. Go ahead."

I had relieved myself under far more challenging conditions while reporting—in the ruins of earthquakes, in an outhouse over maggots wriggling on a pile of waste, over a drain with women squatting in front of and behind me doing the same thing at the same time, and twice in the sty of a grunting hog separated from me only by a thin piece of plywood—so this was no big deal.

We visited one of her friends a couple of compounds away. Zhang Ayi, who had a round face and wide smile, welcomed me into her home with a cheerful greeting. Her long hair hung down the back of her short black down jacket, and she wore black jeans tucked into black boots with silver buckles. Zhang Ayi's room, bigger and newer, had an airy interior and tile instead of a concrete floor. A consummate host, she immediately poured glasses of fruit juice that reminded me of Hawaiian Punch and served plastic bags full of snacks: peanuts in their shells, roasted watermelon and sunflower seeds, and individually wrapped mandarin oranges. She, too, cleaned for a living but had scored a job at one of the embassies.

Both women said they had some shopping to do, and I eagerly jumped at the chance to explore food options in the area. We walked briskly through alleyways until we came to a small indoor market next to a bathhouse advertising free saunas. No more than half a dozen stands displayed amazingly fresh and plentiful fare at prices a fraction of what we paid at city supermarkets. An eye-popping assortment of vegetables in all colors filled boxes and plastic baskets: green bell peppers, two kinds of eggplants, zucchini, and silk and bitter gourds. There were at least six kinds of mushrooms and a host of leafy greens whose names I didn't know. Carrots, cauliflower, chilies, chives, cucumbers, leeks, lotus root, onions, pumpkins, taro, tomatoes, turnips, and *wosun* ("asparagus lettuce") rounded out the selection.

One stall sold tofu products, not just firm white blocks but also dried and pressed into sheets, cut into strips, deep-fried into airy cubes, and smoked to a tobacco-brown hue. Adjacent stood the pork vendor, a fittingly porcine woman with at least a dozen cuts of meat for sale—from belly to ribs to trotters—as well as livers and kidneys piled high on metal plates. The only implements she had were a weighing scale, a grinder, and a well-honed blade.

Zhang Ayi loaded up on pork and greens, and we began our walk home. As we rounded the corner, she headed straight for a bicycle cart that I hadn't noticed before. It was a surreal dream come true—a plastic display case filled with metal trays of impossibly perfect-looking roast ducks balanced on the back. Each bird was a uniform red-brown and shiny in a way that indicated that the skin was completely rendered of all fat and exceptionally crackly. I stared transfixed until the kind-faced vendor, who wore a clean white butcher's apron, asked Zhang Ayi for her order. After she placed it, the man picked up one of the roasted ducks by the tip of a drumstick and brought it around to the back of the cart, where he had set up a workstation that included a round, wooden chopping block and a table with an electric scale, a variety of bottled sauces, and a plastic canister of lethal-looking chili paste.

With a cleaver he first hacked off the duck's head, then began work on splitting the body down the middle before separating the thigh and drumstick and chopping it up for us. It was the juiciest, most tender part. Next he placed the meat in a bowl lined with a small plastic bag and splashed the pieces with a dark soy-based brew and sesame oil before topping it with a healthy dollop of the chili.

We strolled without talking, passing a little girl in a pink jacket standing outside a bike repair shop. She stared at us then shyly looked away. A small van, weighed down with huge, jade-green heads of Chinese cabbage, honked for us to get out of the way. It was cold, but the sky was a rare clear blue, and the light was golden.

Back at Zhang Ayi's, she set the bags of food on a small table outside her room next to a tiny one-ring gas burner and began preparing dinner, usually eaten early in China. Cheng Ayi helped her wash *xiao baicai*—baby bok choy—at a communal sink made of cement. Neighbors also making evening meals soon joined them. The smell of burning coal filled the air, and oil sizzled as cut-up vegetables fell into flame-blackened woks. Windows steamed as rice-cookers bubbled away.

Zhang Ayi sliced white tofu into slabs before cutting the smoked version into matchstick-sized pieces. She poured a couple of glugs of cooking oil into her wok and wilted the *baicai* over high heat, adding only a touch of salt. The smoked tofu and rings of green chilies went into the pan next, with more oil. The raw heat of the chili as it hit the hot fat smelled amazing. Cheng Ayi returned to her room, where she had been cooking a milky tofu soup and had reheated some braised pork ribs. Around 5:00 p.m. we sat down to eat.

Like the other meals I'd eaten in Chinese homes, this was a special occasion feast, and I was a guest of honor. The two aunties heaped rice in my bowl and insisted that I eat the meat first.

"Mmmmmm!" I said after I took my first bite as they looked on expectantly. They laughed. "Mmmmm. Mmmmmmmm. *Haochi!*" Delicious! I said, enthusiastically popping the rest of the piece in my mouth. The skin still had some bite, and the salty-spicy sauce perfectly accompanied the gamey duck, which had absorbed the flavors. I put a piece in each of their bowls and urged them to enjoy the poultry with me.

The sun had long set by the time we finished. Only light streaming from the windows of the rooms within illuminated the courtyard. A stillness was settling over the village as we said our goodbyes.

※

I bought my first digital camera in 2003, a tiny point-and-shoot that I carried everywhere, from the streets of Beijing to neighborhoods in Kabul and Islamabad. I hoped it would sharpen my ability to notice things in ways both big and small, as if looking through landscape and microscopic lenses. I learned to look at the same thing from different angles, always surprised at the new perspective I gained. Invaluable for work, the photos helped me reconstruct situations and add layers of detail, but the camera also became one more thing to juggle while taking notes and wielding my tape recorder.

For me, getting a good shot was a lot more about luck, timing, and instinct than getting a usable quote for the story. It froze a mood, an expression, or a detail for eternity, and the moment had to be captured immediately, precisely, and, to a large extent, perfectly—or the opportunity was forever lost.

I showed Greg the 170 photos that I had taken on that first visit to Beidian. He looked through them silently and called them a good start.

"Start?" I asked. I thought I could put together the photo essay with what I had.

Greg patiently explained that, in order to give the project more depth, I needed to go back at different times of the day, on different days of the week. I needed more examples of what people did on daily routines. I nodded grudgingly, realizing it was exactly the same thing I would do if this were a story I was writing instead of putting together visually.

A week later, I returned to Beidian to wander around a bigger area with Cheng Ayi. We met two more women, both with fine-boned, lightly freckled faces, who had secured jobs as housekeepers in Beijing to support their families at home. They had come with their husbands, who became laborers at the city's innumerous construction sites. It was an existence vastly different from the farm life they knew—and not quite the promised land that they had wanted.

"Sure, we make a little more money here, but it's also more expensive," said thirty-seven-year-old Shi Ayi, who had lived in Beijing for a decade. "In the end, the benefits aren't that great, but we have no choice. There are still more opportunities in the city than where I'm from."

Wang Ayi, five years older, described the roads of her village near Hefei as "mud, all mud. We would be up to our knees in mud in winter. It's miserable. Here it's a little more civilized. But it's still hard to make ends meet."

They usually worked six days a week, and on Sundays they took it easy with their friends. There were still chores to be done, but the highlight was a speedy Anhui-style version of mahjong, the game of strategy and luck. The noise of tiles rattling together as they were shuffled or "washed" filled their Sunday afternoons. The sense of camaraderie made them feel—almost—like they had never left home.

Cheng Ayi, the women said, was the most diligent of the lot. "While everyone takes weekends off, she works all the time," Shi Ayi said. "She saves money and doesn't waste it like us."

Cheng Ayi laughed awkwardly and shushed them. Animated, the women chattered to each other in their dialect as they shared *laobing*, an unleavened flatbread. White lilies sat in a vase, brightening the room, which, like the others I had seen, was furnished simply. A fist-sized slab of cured pork hanging by a wire from a nail, like a surreal still-life, was riveting.

Keeping a sharp eye for quotidian life, I snapped close-ups of pots of chives growing in the courtyard, stacks of giant pucks of coal, and piles of peeled turnips drying in the cold air. As we walked to the wet market—the opposite direction from where we had gone the last time—I shot photos of brick walls, garbage piles, and even the dirt on the road.

Within five minutes, we had come to a drearier part of the village, paths littered with debris and trash, buildings more run-down. But it was also a gateway to a wide variety of interesting edibles. Simple, hearty fare abounded almost every few feet, starting at a shop with a giant wall of wooden boards out front painted with a sky blue background, its menu items written helter-skelter in red paint: breakfast lamb noodles, hand-cut noodles, dumplings, dough crullers, porridge, egg soup, wontons, and soy milk. Next to it stood a tiny stall that had a display case with characters advertising *shaobing* with fillings like red bean paste or chopped scallions.

China has countless variations of *bing*, which translates to cake, but is usually a savory staple made from wheat flour. They can be round or oval and flat like a pancake, stuffed and solid like hockey pucks, or rolled like a crepe. In *congyoubing*, finely chopped green onions provide the main flavoring, and there were *jianbing*, the Chinese breakfast burrito, and *laobing*, which looked a lot like *roti prata*, the Singaporean version of the Indian flatbread *paratha*. *Heyebing* wrapped slices of Peking Duck, and *shaobing*, studded with sesame seeds, sometimes accompanied hot pot meals.

I said hello to the stall owners, watching as one of them rolled out balls of dough with a small wooden dowel. Cluttering the work area were plastic basins of a flour-and-water mixture, empty bottles of cooking oil, pots, pans, and a variety of kitchen utensils, from tongs to spatulas and pastry brushes.

The flattened rounds of dough, fillings encased, browned on what looked like a well-greased giant pancake griddle. Brushed with oil and sprinkled with sesame seeds, they were then further crisped in a row under a grill. I inhaled deeply to catch the earthy fragrance of toasting sesame. The vendors worked quietly and quickly, cramming a third of the display case with fresh *shaobing* within minutes. I paid a few cents for two stuffed with minced pork and cabbage and munched happily as I looked for Cheng Ayi and her friends. They had wandered away, bored, as I photographed the *bing* makers.

On a nearby brick building, a large green billboard that said HOT FOOD caught my eye. A Plexiglas pane, the storefront had two windows and was covered with red cut-outs of characters that said SELF-SERVE COOKED FOOD. A woman stood behind the partition in front of trays of what looked like smoked meats and preserved vegetables; I couldn't really tell from the assortment of shapes, sizes, and colors. But what caught my interest were the contents of a big metal bowl steaming away over an old paint can filled with heated coal. A man stood over the setup with a pair of large tongs, moving around palm-sized slices of something slick and cartilaginous. They almost looked like pig's trotters in a standard soy-based braising liquid, but each had a crab claw–shaped protrusion. A rich, meaty smell wafted over.

"*Nihao!*" I said. "What's in there?"

"Pig's ears," said the man, holding up a floppy piece with the tongs. It was a little ragged and curled at the edges. "Want some?"

"No," I said. "Thank you." While I enjoyed the gelatinous mess of pig's feet, nibbling on ears was inexplicably beyond my threshold.

Farther along the road lay a shop selling jackets, with samples hanging off a clothesline strung from the main door. Fleece vests in pastel colors hung next to raincoats in primary hues. A woman out front was selling *bingtanghulu*, candied haw on sticks, from the back of her bike. The fruit from the hawthorn tree looked a little like red ping-pong balls, squeezed seven to a skewer, shiny with a caramel-colored glaze. Parked a few feet away stood a small truck with whole heads of garlic, their papery skins tinged with purple, piled in the back bed. A gaggle of older women surrounded the vehicle, scooping up handfuls and filling plastic bags to take home. Others picked tiny, sweet clementines from five blue plastic crates set up near the front wheels. They cost 1.5 yuan per *jin*, about 20 cents per pound.

Popcorn strewed the ground on the opposite side of the street by a wire basket and giant plastic sacks of puffed corn. Next to the display a man was sitting on a tiny stool in front of a stack of bricks, working a metal contraption that looked like a pot-bellied pig on a spit over another paint can of hot coals. I had never seen anything like this before; friends laughed at my sense of wonder when I excitedly told them about it. Turns out it was the dying art of making popcorn the traditional Chinese way.

The process involved a bellows, a length of iron pipe, a portable stove, and the "pig," a pressurized container made of cast iron containing corn kernels sweetened either by sugar or saccharin. While the mechanics were beyond me, it appeared that a crank rotated the sealed pot in both directions as the flames, fanned by the bellows controlled by the other hand, roared underneath, sometimes engulfing the entire vessel. The kernels slowly roasted and popped, and after a few minutes the pot was lifted off the fire. One end tipped into a large bag or basket, and the pipe released the lid with an explosive bang and hiss, accompanied by a cloud of steam and dust.

The Beidian vendor, his hands black with coal dust, was still rotating the iron container when I saw him, but I didn't stick around for the explosive finish. Bundled in several layers of clothing, his cheeks chapped from the cold, he eyed the camera warily, gave me a small smile, and kept working. I did, however, get a bag of the puffed corn, airy and slightly sweet.

By late afternoon, the streets had filled with shoppers buying food for dinner and the week ahead. Many came on foot, their hands tucked deep into pockets to keep warm while others pushed bicycles loaded with bags as they browsed the offerings. I finally caught up with Cheng, Shi, and Wang Ayi, who were buying chicken wings in the open-air market. Different parts of the bird were laid out on trays, from leg quarters to breasts to splayed feet.

Behind me, some two dozen shadowy forms made a loud splash, crowded in a bathtub at another stand with a sign that said VARIOUS LIVE FISH. A heavy thump preceded a scratchy sound as the fishmonger killed and scaled a specimen, sending a shower of glittering silver disks into the air. Crimson drops of blood patterned his workstation. All around, people were placing orders and haggling.

Farther in, more stalls huddled under a corrugated tin roof, one displaying an impressive array of crates filled with sweet snacks like cookies, baked dough twists, slices of Swiss roll, and cookies covered in powdered sugar. They looked tempting, but experience had taught me that many Chinese baked goods didn't taste as delicious as they appeared, often lacking the richness of eggs and butter that are standard in the West.

One seller not only had parts of pig body—from the inside and out—on the counter, but a pair of whole hog heads serenely resting, face-up, on plastic bags. Their faces were smooth and hairless, their eyes closed as if napping. Their snouts—I was so close I could see the pores—looked rubbery, and their ears were disproportionately huge, bat-like. At least a dozen cloven-hoofed feet were stacked daintily next to the heads.

Outside, a man was presiding over sacks and open crates bursting with dried fruit, crackers, spices, nuts, and flavored sunflower seeds roasted on the premises in an old-fashioned furnace with an interior that spun around like a front-loading washing machine. When he saw me taking pictures, he tried to help me out with an "action" shot, using a ladle almost two feet long to reach across his wares and pretend to scoop up some seeds. I laughed, and he seemed very pleased by my reaction.

Pockets of fluorescent, neon, and yellow lights from naked bulbs flickered on as the sun set. It was getting dark, and Cheng

Ayi said it was time to head back. The other two said they would start dinner as Cheng Ayi and I took a small detour to see just a little more of the village. We passed hair salons, mom-and-pop grocery stores, small restaurants, and the requisite sex shop, a common sight in China, marked by characters that translate literally to "adult health care." More street vendors selling food had popped up because it was close to dinnertime. Several carts had small pans of oil set up for deep-frying a variety of skewered snacks, from fishballs to sausages to tofu. Others cooked the skewers in a broth based on chili and Sichuan peppers.

Shi Ayi was cooking up a storm when we got back. The smell of ginger, garlic, dried chilies, and spring onions perfumed her home. Joining us for dinner were Wang Ayi, Shi Ayi's husband, and Cheng Ayi's son. It was another tasty spread to welcome me: stir-fried spinach, the wings, spicy tofu slices with fresh shiitake mushrooms, soybeans and eggplant with dried chilies, garlic bolts with cured pork slices, deep-fried pork cutlet, and a steamed egg custard with chopped chives.

"This is almost like our Chinese New Year dinner!" exclaimed Shi Ayi as everyone dug in. It was her way of underscoring that this was a far cry from what they normally ate. The meal had strong, simple flavors—the smokiness of the cured pork, the spice of the tofu sauce, and a hint of licorice in the chicken—and textures that witnessed the freshness of the ingredients. The egg custard was warm, soft, and comforting. Spoonfuls slurped from the bowl slid down my throat.

Cheng Ayi's son smiled his way through the meal, visibly happy about the bounty. There was very little chatter. Soon, almost all the plates were empty, and piles of chicken bones lay by everyone's bowls. The leftovers were carefully put away. For dessert there were bananas and clementines.

As I was getting ready to leave, Shi Ayi asked if I could take pictures of the group and give them prints as a way to remember the occasion.

"Of course," I said. "It's the least I can do."

Even now, as I look at the shots, I can't help but laugh. A handful featured Wang and Shi Ayi, their heads close and arms around each other like sisters. Shi Ayi and her husband agreed to one in which they stood awkwardly apart. When I urged them to be more intimate, she leaned her head on his shoulder. I took three of Cheng Ayi and her son with the lilies in the background. The last two were group shots, with the four women standing in the back and the two men sitting on stools in front. Shi Ayi was hugging Cheng Ayi, who had her hand on her son's shoulder. It was a moment of natural affection, contentment, and ease. Of the 397 photos I took that day, that last is my favorite.

器

My final trip to Beidian took place on a cold, gray morning a few days later. The blue and white sign with the village's name welcomed me yet again, but I felt more like an outsider without Cheng Ayi by my side.

Because it was a weekday, everything seemed sleepier since most people had gone into the city to work. Men stood around a ping-pong table, playing not the well-loved sport but rounds of Chinese chess. A small hairdressing salon was steamy and cluttered with a television sounding softly from a corner of the ceiling. One man sat staring off into space in his chair, black dye running down his scalp. Rubber caps covered his ears, protection against staining. From what I had seen of the Chinese leadership, it was quite common for older men to keep gray out of their hair by artificial means. Another man was lying almost prone, at the tail-end of an old-fashioned shave, a white smear of shaving cream on his chin.

As always, there was plenty of food, from a truck piled high with Napa cabbage, carrots, and potatoes, to half a dozen kinds of dried beans displayed in linen sacks on the ground. A man in a small silver van opened the back of his vehicle, pulled out a large, shallow metal box, put it on the ground, and filled it with live fish that he scooped out with a green net from a plastic container. The fish, bright silver with reddish-pink markings and fins, writhed and flopped, attracting the attention of passersby.

Later the sky turned blue, and the afternoon sun cast a warm light. It helped make a nice silhouette of a woman strolling down an alley and the yellow walls behind a vendor repairing a bicycle wheel even brighter. By the end of the afternoon, I had 471 photos on my memory card—enough to start work on the project.

※

Within months of my visit, developers razed the entire village as part of the capital's here-today-gone-tomorrow construction. I had no idea until I saw Cheng Ayi again in June 2010, when I visited Beijing after a fellowship in Boston. In the year I had been gone, she had moved twice because she had been having trouble finding a place as affordable that didn't involve an even longer bus ride.

From Beidian, Cheng Ayi and her husband, Mr. Liang, relocated to a residential district about five miles away. It wasn't much farther out, but the distance more than doubled Ayi's commute to four or five hours because traffic was so bad. Her clients began to complain about her showing up late. She rose every day at 3:30 a.m. to make breakfast before heading out to work half an hour later with her husband. Sometimes Mr. Liang, who still worked odd construction jobs, didn't come home until 8:00 or 9:00 p.m. If he arrived first, he cooked dinner. After nine exhausting months, the schedule proved too grueling. They found another room closer.

Cheng Ayi invited me for dinner at their new home. I picked her up in a taxi from her last job of the day, waving wildly as I spotted her from the car window. She looked the same, perhaps a little thinner. She said the same of me. We caught up during the ride, which took almost an hour because of rush-hour traffic. By the time we arrived, it was already dark, and I couldn't see the surroundings very well. But the narrow alleys and bustling crowds reminded me of Beidian.

Because it was so far out of the city, I told the taxi driver that I would pay him a flat fee if he waited for me. He asked me to name a price and actually bargained *down* because he said I was offering too much. I cocked an eyebrow in surprise; I realized first that living in America had made me lose my haggling abilities and secondly that I had met perhaps the only driver in Beijing with integrity. Cheng Ayi invited him to dinner, but he declined, saying that he would find something in the area.

I hadn't met Mr. Liang before but had heard about him through Ayi. He had moved to Beijing about five or six years after she had settled in, returning once to Anhui to help with repairs on their house after heavy rains had damaged it. He was wearing a blue mock turtleneck T-shirt, a gray fleece vest, and jeans. He was shorter than I am, a touch taller than Ayi, with a stocky build, a mess of dark hair, and a toothy grin that never left his good-natured face. Mr. Liang greeted me like a long-lost relative. "Welcome! Welcome!" he said, holding up a gauzy, azure curtain so I could walk through the door. "We're really glad you can come over."

Because their son was living on his own now, the room was smaller than the space in Beidian, but it was still crammed with their belongings. In one corner, cardboard boxes piled to the ceiling. There was a white television set at the foot of the bed next to a shelf of cooking condiments: salt, Sichuan peppercorns, chili paste, and even a half-full bottle of Tabasco sauce. Spotting a black-and-white clock from my apartment gave me a pleasant shock of recognition; I had forgotten that I had given it to Cheng Ayi. Thick wires were strung around the room, from which hung clothes, drying towels, an umbrella, purses, and gloves.

"Let's eat," Cheng Ayi said.

We sat around a small table pushed against a wall with a map of the world tacked to it. I hadn't noticed before that it was already set with food.

"I made sure my husband cooked tonight so dinner would be ready when we got home," she said. Liang's smile broadened even more.

She had asked him to make my favorites—braised pork ribs and braised chicken wings, both meats glistening with oil and stained a deep caramel. There was a plate of stir-fried greens with garlic and what looked like a dangerously spicy bowl of egg drop soup with tomatoes and tofu. Cheng Ayi scooped out steamed rice, and we started the meal. Mr. Liang's food was almost as good as his wife's.

It was obvious they had been together a long time. The couple grew up just 650 feet apart in Baobei village outside Hefei. The families were so close that Ayi's younger brother married Mr. Liang's younger sister. "We played together from when we were children. We always played after dinner," Mr. Liang said with a small smile as he recalled the memories.

They were completely at ease around each other but not afraid to give each other a hard time. "You should go back and tell Anita and Scott and the rest how short my husband is. You're going to tell them, aren't you?" Cheng Ayi said to me, laughing.

Mr. Liang, his sense of humor lubricated with liquor made of dates and wine lees, grinned and launched into a story about how Anita had asked him to stand in line for baseball tickets for the Beijing Olympics. Cheng Ayi nudged him and clucked her tongue in disapproval because she felt that his story was rambling on with no point.

I asked them about life in Anhui, where the couple and their families tended paddies of rice and fields of wheat. Their relatives took over the crops when they left. "There's no money in the land," Mr. Liang said, serious for the first time. "I labored bitterly. It was so hard to make a living."

Like their friends in Beidian, they talked about how everything in Beijing was expensive.

When it was time to leave, the couple saw me out to the waiting taxi, waving and smiling. Over the years, many people had shown me such kindness and made me feel a part of their family, but it never failed to tug at my heartstrings. It was always harder when I didn't know when we would meet again.

Breakfast of Champions

For centuries, incarnations of Peking Duck have whetted the appetites of emperors, inspired poets, nourished diplomatic deals, and won the hearts of Olympians.

Roasted whole, either over a blazing fire of fruit-tree wood or slow-cooked by radiant heat in a closed oven, the finished fowl, skin crackling and flesh succulent, is usually carved in front of diners into between 108 and 120 wafer-thin, pinkie-length crescents. A piece, or two at a time, is rolled along with julienned scallions, a couple of cucumber sticks, maybe some sugar or a dab of sweet, dark sauce into a papery *heyebing*—lotus leaf pancake—made of flour.

Some restaurants use the carcass as the base for duck soup, a translucent white broth usually served at the end of the meal. Bits of the remaining meat can be stir-fried with thumbs of ginger and green onion over a high flame, the brown sauce caramelizing into a fragrant, gooey mess. The bird's wings, webbed feet, gizzard, liver, heart, and pancreas are offered up in a variety of ways: brined, boiled, dry-stewed, sliced, shredded, fried, or flavored with chili, Sichuan peppercorns, wine, or mustard.

Like many dishes, the origins of Peking Duck—China's unofficial dish, known simply as *kaoya*, or roast duck—remain somewhat murky. Some accounts say a version appeared around AD 400. Another references broiled or roasted duck peddled in the streets of Hangzhou as mentioned in *Mengliang lu*, a book detailing the splendors of night markets during the Southern Song dynasty more than seven centuries later. But duck done that way didn't catch on in imperial circles until the next dynasty, the Yuan.

A favorite dish in imperial and more humble circles for centuries, Peking Duck is the country's unofficial national dish. The Chinese believe that, besides being delicious, duck can clear the lungs, nourish the blood, and help alleviate bruises, headaches, insomnia, coughs, and fevers. Australian swimmer Libby Trickett reportedly fueled her 2008 hundred-meter butterfly gold medal by having it at breakfast, lunch, and dinner, and Henry Kissinger famously said, "After a dinner of Peking Duck, I'll sign anything."

That rendition, simply called *shao yazi*, "roast duck," appeared in a book called *Principles of Correct Diet*, written in 1330 by Hu Sihui, a court physician and dietician who focused on nutrition, seasonal eating, and hygiene. It was made by pulling out the innards of the duck before stuffing it with a mixture of sheep's stomach, cilantro, scallions, and salt. The whole bird was speared on a fork and roasted over a charcoal fire.

When the capital of the Ming dynasty, which followed the Yuan, moved from Nanjing to Beijing—Nanking and Peking in pre-pinyin spellings of those cities—the dish still featured prominently on court menus. Local lore has it that top chefs from all over the country traveled to the imperial kitchen to cook for the emperor, and this was when Peking Duck as we know it today was created and crafted to perfection. Royal recipes smuggled out of the palace kitchens meant that imperial dishes—including the roast duck—became available to the palates of the masses.

In another telling, a man surnamed Wang began roasting chickens and ducks in a tiny workshop in one of Beijing's alleyways during the Ming dynasty. Instead of hanging the birds from hooks and cooking them over a flame, he fueled the ovens with sorghum stalks until the walls were super heated before putting them inside. This *menlu* style made for beautifully browned and crispy skin and guaranteed tender flesh. Because the owner was particular about the process and the results were fresh, tasty, and cheap, the shop soon became a favorite among distinguished officials.

One day, a military official embroiled in political intrigue rushed into the alley in a fit of anger and stopped short when the aroma of food reached his nostrils. He feasted on roast duck, wine, and a variety of other dishes, but when it was time to pay he was surprised at how inexpensive the meal was.

"What is the name of this place?" he asked.

"This shop's main goal is to be convenient (*fangbian*) and pleasant (*yiren*)," the proprietor said. "There is no name."

Because the eatery had dispelled the anguish and unhappiness in his heart, the official asked for a brush, ink, and paper and wrote three characters in bold strokes—"*bian*," "*yi*," "*fang*"—which roughly captured the essence of the shopkeeper's sentiment. The words were meticulously hung on a board above the shop's doors and the capital's first roast duck restaurant was officially launched. From that day on, its reputation was known far and wide, and Bianyifang was acknowledged as the originator of Peking Duck.

By the 1700s, the mahogany-colored roasted birds—whether from Bianyifang or elsewhere—had become a favorite of the upper classes, *de rigueur* at banquets, and inspiring mention as one of the most coveted delicacies of the time. Yuan Mei, a famous poet in the Qing dynasty, China's last, put together a cookbook in which she mentions roasting a duckling on a fork.

In addition to being flavorful, duck meat is packed with protein, phosphorus, thiamin, iron, copper, zinc, and other trace elements and vitamins and, the Chinese believe, can help relieve a slew of ailments. Because the meat falls on the "cold" side of the yin-yang scale, it can clear out the lungs and nourish the blood and help with bruises, headaches, insomnia, coughs, and fevers. The accompanying cucumbers and scallions supposedly can help with sore throats and conjunctivitis, promote digestion, prevent colds, and nourish the skin.

The famed fowl has also played a part in boosting the health of international relations. While on trips to Beijing in 1971 to work on details for President Richard Nixon's upcoming historic visit, National Security Adviser Henry Kissinger wrote about two banquets featuring Peking Duck. The first came during a contentious segment of talks about the Shanghai Communique that served as a basis for American policy on Taiwan and normalizing US-China relations.

"I suggest rest now and relaxation," Premier Zhou Enlai said as Kissinger was about to jump into another involved point. "Otherwise you will be under tension and the duck will be cold."

"That would be calamitous," Kissinger responded. "Tension we can take."

During the meal, comprising twelve dishes with the duck as the marquee offering, Zhou selected a choice piece of meat and wrapped it in a lotus pancake to show the American envoy how to enjoy the duck.

The second banquet came months later. "After stuffing us with roast duck," Kissinger said, Beijing presented a communique draft where China took an uncompromising stance on a host of issues. "It left blank pages for our position, which was assumed to be contrary." It appeared that the banquet was meant either to dull the Americans' negotiating edge or tease out some goodwill before Beijing took a hard line.

In 1972, Nixon arrived in China accompanied by his wife and officials, including Kissinger. According to CIA reports, Kissinger toasted with the notorious Maotai brand of distilled sorghum-based liquor—but only after feasting on duck, which he seemed to find more intoxicating.

"After a dinner of Peking Duck," he said, "I'll sign anything."

Duck diplomacy aside, almost every major Peking Duck restaurant has photos of famous customers hanging on their walls, from movie stars to foreign dignitaries including Fidel Castro and Helmut Kohl. But it's not just famous people who are daffy for it. Along with the Great Wall, the Forbidden City, and designer knockoffs, the dish ranks high on almost every visitor's to-do list. My friend Darius, as serious about food as he is about biking, had a list of thirteen must-try restaurants. The top three showcased Peking Duck—but he was open to other suggestions.

So where to go? This issue polarizes locals, especially when just about every other eatery in the capital city serves its interpretation of the classic. Beijingers are picky and fiercely loyal about where they satisfy their cravings and won't stand for any substitutions.

"Bianyifang. Nowhere else," Xu Jinhuan, a sixty-four-year-old retiree told me when I interviewed her for a duck story I was writing days before the start of the 2008 Beijing Olympics. The old restaurant that claims to have been first to peddle roast duck in the capital is long gone, but a handful of branches remain.

"The skin is very thin and very crispy. Their sauce is not too salty or too sweet. One bite and the oily duck juice spurts into your mouth," Xu said with a gleeful grin as she enjoyed the sunshine with three other friends outside the National Stadium. "I like the soup afterward. Or I bring the carcass home, and I tear off the rest of the flesh and enjoy it with the sauce. It's another dish. I eat every part—the neck, the web, or the liver. . . . It's the best representation of our country. You have to climb the Great Wall, you have to go to a *hutong*, you have to buy silk—and you have to eat Beijing *kaoya*!"

For Sun Aili, the restaurant of choice is Quanjude, a historic chain favored by the Chinese government. "It's the most authentic. The skin is crunchy, and the flesh is tender. Its taste is different from all the others," she said as she ate lunch (not duck) with her family a few feet away from Xu. But the Olympians shouldn't overindulge on the fatty fowl, she warned with a laugh: "They won't be able to move."

Sun was responding to Chinese media reports of how Peking Duck, in its plump and lacquered glory, had won legions of new fans in the Olympic athletes. "The famed Beijing duck is a hot gold medal contender for the most popular food in the host city of the ongoing Olympic Games," Xinhua News Agency crowed.

Deng Yaping, China's four-time Olympic gold medalist in table tennis and deputy director of the Athletes' Village, said the dish was so beloved that officials had doubled the number of ducks on hand from three hundred to six hundred a day. Australian swimmer Libby Trickett reportedly fueled her hundred-meter butterfly gold medal by having it at breakfast, lunch, and dinner. "Is Peking Duck the superspeed food? It could be," her husband, Luke, told Australia's *Daily Telegraph*. Coach David McGowan of the Dutch rowing team said he had eaten duck every day. "I think I had it for breakfast the other day. So it's good."

At a counter serving roast duck from Quanjude, the official supplier of the delicacy for the Games, workers dressed in chefs' whites and matching toques stood in a loose assembly line, slicing the bird and turning the meat and flour pancake into one of the desired duck rolls. "It's sold out every day," said one of the duck distributors. "We've been asking them to get more. When people are here, they want to eat Peking Duck."

Above them hung a giant yellow sign with a bird browned to glistening perfection. BEIJING ROAST DUCK CONTAINS 16% TO 25% PROTEIN, VITAMINS, MINERAL SUBSTANCE, AMINO ACID AND 7.5% FAT, MOST OF WHICH IS UNSATURATED AND LOW CARBON FATTY ACID. DUCK FAT CONTAINS LOWER CHOLESTEROL THAN OTHER ANIMAL FAT, it said.

In August 1966, shortly after the start of the Cultural Revolution, Red Guards from some of Beijing's middle schools overran the Quanjude branch in the historic Qianmen area. Employees were goaded into smashing the restaurant's seventy-year-old signboard and replacing it with a newly painted sign that said BEIJING ROAST DUCK RESTAURANT. It was the birth of a new revolutionized eatery, which sold dishes barely costing a few cents, and welcomed workers, peasants, and soldiers. I am, however, not a fan of Quanjude. I have sampled my fair share, from the chain with the grandiose name of Duck King to Duck de Chine, an upscale establishment with Hong Kong and French influences. I have been to Da Dong and Made in China, two glitzy and ritzy options, as well as Xiaowangfu and Xiheyaju, mid-range alternatives popular among my journalist friends. But when it comes down to it, I have enjoyed two places with far more modest surroundings. These were the ones to which I brought visitors over and over again.

The first was a no-frills eatery a five-minute walk from my old office in the diplomatic area that, like so many other places in the city, was torn down to make way for a mall. The characters for roast duck in red neon on the window lured many customers despite the mismatched tables and stools, fluorescent lights, and surly staff that banged down teapots and shuffled around in slippers.

When friends came to town, I ordered a duck, prepared on the premises by a man who for hours on end cheerfully hauled fowl—hung by their necks on giant metal hooks—between oven and chopping board. The meat, sauce, and condiments were served on chipped porcelain plates, and the pancakes were piled willy-nilly. But one bite of the crisp skin was enough to forget everything—and at about a third of the price of other places.

The other Peking Duck restaurant I liked was an unabashed tourist haunt, but I enjoyed going there because it was housed in a traditional, albeit run-down and slightly grimy Chinese court-yard home tucked in a *hutong*—a labyrinth of narrow alleyways—south of the Forbidden City. The place had character, the duck was always tasty, and we could always indulge in another of their specialties: a paper-thin omelet, rolled and stuffed with shred-ded vegetables before being sliced into pinwheels.

When I lived in Beijing, directions to the Li Qun Roast Duck Restaurant went something like this (caveat: some vendors may have moved): Take a right at the southern mouth of *Beixiangfeng hutong*, the first left after the reeking public restrooms and the roasted sunflower seed sellers. Veer right at the fruit stand so you're heading down the lane that starts with a newspaper seller. Take the first left, walk about fifty yards. At some point, you will see pictures of ducks, arrows, and the Li Qun name hand-painted on the walls of other courtyard homes to guide the lost. (Locals who live in the area point foreigners in the right direction even before they ask.) Finally, Mecca. You can't miss the white sign with red lettering painted on the wall next to the restaurant's entrance which is almost obscured by piles of chopped wood: LIQUN ROAST DUCK RESTAURANT. WELCOME OVERSEAS GUESTS. ENJOYING TRADITIONAL CUISINE IN OLD CHINESE COURTYARD.

Many a first-time customer, grouchy and starving after meandering unsuccessfully through the warren of alleys, has been pacified as soon as they walk through the door and catch a glimpse of a string of ducks burnished to the color of molasses over a roaring fruit-wood fire. The sense of well-being often intensifies with the aroma of fat and meat and the sight of framed photos of famous faces, from Al Gore to Hong Kong movie star Simon Yam. Daredevil celebrity chef Anthony Bourdain filmed an episode of *No Reservations* here. It was all worth the trek.

The restaurant is a jumble of tables and chairs, cartons of beer and ice chests, all under fluorescent lighting. Zhang Liqun, the kindly owner, smiles so much there is a fine network of wrinkles around his eyes. He built the family business with the help of his wife and daughter. The staff consists mostly of the children of friends he made during the Cultural Revolution, who asked Zhang to help them make some spending money.

Zhang says his birds are the Beijing *tianya*—literally "stuffed duck"—the northern Chinese breed said to be reared exclusively for the dish and consumed throughout the country. Like their goose cousins whose livers are fattened for foie gras, the *tianya* are plumped through force-feedings.

The ducks are no older than fifty days and are about thirteen pounds each before cooking. They are prepared the traditional way—air pumped to separate the skin from the body, scalded with boiling water, brushed with a sugar-water mixture for color while cooking, and hung out to dry for about a day.

The prepped birds, heads attached, are hung by their necks on metal hooks and roasted for forty minutes over date, peach, apricot and pear wood–fueled flames in the restaurant's huge brick oven. It has no door to facilitate easy access to ducks, which are moved and rotated by hand to ensure even cooking. The whole bird is served on a metal tray and swiftly carved on a sideboard. Several small plates of scallion, cucumber, and plummy sauce accompany platters of crispy skin.

One customer at a table with three other friends slowly folded a pancake and held it ceremoniously aloft before taking a huge bite.

"Now this," he said, face flushed from beer and meat, "is a good meal."

Though the younger generation tends to prefer Western-style beverages, tea has steeped in thousands of years of Chinese history. I drank it every day, hot and straight, watching the brittle leaves slowly soften, unfurl, and settle after the initial scalding pour of water.

5

Have Some Tea

One afternoon, I brought a vacuum-sealed pouch of early harvest jasmine tea leaves to the office and opened it in the kitchen, inhaling deeply with my nose in the bag. The scent never failed to lighten my heart, at once clean and sweet, sultry and innocent.

I offered some to Xi Yue, one of our Chinese researchers eating his lunch at a table by the window. In his twenties, Xi Yue wore funky rectangular maroon glasses and was a sweet-natured but tenacious news gatherer. He politely declined, saying he didn't drink tea.

I couldn't believe my ears.

"Not at all?" I asked. "*Really?*"

He shook his head.

"What do you drink then?"

"Cola, fruit juice," he said sheepishly.

Zhao Liang, another researcher also in his twenties, walked in, and I offered him a sample. He, too, said no as he filled his cup with water from the cooler.

"You're kidding me," I said, half-laughing. "We're in *China*, guys!"

They told me that people of their generation rarely drank tea anymore except when with older relatives.

Suddenly, I felt ancient.

"I suppose in their day," said Zhao Liang, "tea was one of the few choices one had for drinking at one's leisure, apart from alcohol. Nowadays, people have too many other choices. They drink cola, juice, and coffee. Those are faster and more convenient to buy. As for tea, I know very few people of about my age having a particular taste for tea. They see tea as either something for the older generation, or a luxury" because of the cost and time involved in spending time at a teahouse.

If he and his friends did indulge, Zhao Liang added, it was a bottled, usually sweetened, brew that cost a few American cents and left the original flavor and culture of tea behind.

Xi Yue later told me more about growing up in Xi'an, the former northern capital best known now for its famous terra-cotta warriors.

"I think I got my first taste of Coke back in the early '90s, when I was seven or eight. I still remember at the time there were vendors in the street selling *dawancha* or 'large bowl tea' during summertime, effectively quelling your thirst. But for young people, I guess once you got a taste for Coke or juice, the next time you feel thirsty you just automatically think of these drinks instead of tea or water.

"I also remember when I was really young and Coke was still a luxury for my family, I once read something from a magazine saying a US family consumed dozens of cans of Coke or something like that. And I said to my mom, 'I want our family to be like that!'"

Xi Yue's and Zhao Liang's unenthusiastic responses initially disheartened the tea-lover in me, but, despite the changing tastes of new generations and fierce competition from other beverages, tea still played very much a key role in daily life for many in China. As the saying goes: Better to be deprived of food for three days than tea for one.

Throughout Beijing, small eateries plonk down pots of cheap, hot tea when you sit down at a table, while fancier restaurants charge for a more premium variety. I learned to do the finger tap to thank the person who poured the tea. The practice stems from the legend of the Qing dynasty emperor Qianlong, who traveled his kingdom in disguise to see how his subjects lived and to mingle with them.

In one version of the story, he was at a teahouse with his companions and decided to take his turn pouring the tea for them, an unthinkable honor. Custom mandated that people bow before the emperor, and, because he had served them there was an even greater imperative to show their gratitude. But in doing so, the emperor would no longer be incognito. He told them instead to tap their middle three fingers on the table to represent the bow—the middle finger signifying the head and the other two, the prostrate arms. Sometimes, people used just one or two fingers. Every time I did it, it reminded me of being at a blackjack table and asking the dealer for another card.

Tea was the beverage of choice for taxi drivers, who usually had a tumblerful next to them, right by the gearshift, regardless of the season. A mile-long stretch in southwest Beijing features shops and entire malls devoted to the leaf. Teahouses are everywhere, although I never took the time to spend an afternoon in one. While they were rarely bustling, it was becoming trendier to conduct business deals over a pot or two.

In the foreign community in Beijing and other big cities, however, teahouses were often associated with a common scam, in which English-speaking students would chat up tourists at famous landmarks to "practice" the language and eventually invite them for a drink at a teahouse. The unwitting visitors would enjoy a few samples and maybe even buy some of the product—then get hit with an exorbitant charge, sometimes running thousands of dollars.

Steeped in thousands of years of history, the beverage is so ingrained in Chinese identity and culture that it also signifies myriad other things: hospitality, a cure, respect, status, a threat, an apology, or simply one of life's essentials. Chairman Mao refused to brush his teeth, reflecting his peasant upbringing, preferring instead to rinse his mouth with tea.

It is drunk or offered to ancestors during funerals, Chinese New Year, and other festivals. One of them, *Qingming Jie*, or Tomb Sweeping Day, honors ancestors by visiting their burial sites, bringing food offerings, and cleaning their graves. It's also the time of the first tea harvests. Leaves picked before the festival are labeled *mingqian*, considered superior, with a subtle, fresh green-ness to the taste.

In ancient China, terms for a trousseau, engagement, and acceptance of a proposal had the character for "tea" in them. In a traditional marriage, the bride and groom knelt and served tea to show gratitude and respect for their parents. In return, the parents sipped the tea—sometimes enhanced with dried longans, peanuts, dates, and lotus seeds for added prosperity—and gave the couple a red envelope filled with money. This is still widely practiced even if followed by a more Western-style ceremony.

Most importantly, even today it is served to welcome guests, to foster a sense of togetherness among friends and family, or to show respect for elders or someone in a higher position. The host is supposed to pour until the teacup is seven-tenths full. The rest is to be filled with friendship and affection.

Like all China-related numbers, tea statistics are over-whelming. The government says there are twenty tea-producing regions in the country that employ some eighty million people in the industry. The country has overtaken India to become the world's top producer of tea, contributing to about a third of the global total. In 2010, that amounted to close to 1.45 million tons, an increase of 6.4 percent from the previous year. Tea exports reached more than one hundred countries and regions, with top buyers being America, Russia, Japan, Morocco, and Uzbekistan.

Domestic consumption has doubled since 2001, with Chinese drinking more than 1.1 million tons in 2011. The sweetened, bot-tled incarnations Zhao Liang talked about appeared everywhere, from newspaper stands to mom-and-pop stores to supermarket chains.

I enjoyed tea every day, hot and straight. I loved watching the brittle leaves slowly soften, unfurl, and settle after the initial scalding pour of water into a clear glass. It was comforting to feel the aromatic steam warm the tip of my nose before I took the first sip and let the taste slowly pool then expand in my mouth, dark as a mood or fresh like young jade, depending on the type of tea.

At work, the ritual of a five-finger pinch of leaves in a mug plus water from the dispenser got me through the day. The habit was one I truly enjoyed after twelve years of feeling marginalized and uncool in coffee-obsessed Seattle and New York. I was now living in a nation where, aside from major urban hubs, the dark bean brew held next to no pull. In China, the words for espresso translate simply to "coffee concentrate," while coffee and latte were transliterated to *kafei* (kah-fay) and *natie* (nah-tee-eh).

While Starbucks had more than five hundred stores throughout China and planned to start its own coffee bean plantation in the nation's tea heartland, it still had a way to go before achieving full conquest. Luring consumption was one thing—the company's China coffee sales amount to hundreds of millions of dollars a year—but overcoming cultural roots was another story. Until a few years ago, there was an outlet on the grounds of Beijing's Forbidden City, former home of imperial rulers and now one of the country's top tourist destinations, but an online campaign protesting the trampling of Chinese identity gathered support, igniting rabid protests online, and forced it to shut in 2007.

Another cafe opened in its place a couple of months later. "With wooden tables, wooden chairs, and pictures featuring Chinese culture, the Forbidden City Café serves not only coffee but traditional Chinese beverages such as tea," the Xinhua News Agency said in a short dispatch to announce the new venture.

One of the AP drivers introduced me to my "supplier." "Tea Lady Liu," as I called her, had a tiny shop in the basement of one of the fur complexes on Yabaolu, the heart of the Russian district where I lived. Tea sets and metal and glass canisters filled mostly with the harvests of her home province of Fujian, where my ancestors were from, lined three of its walls.

An indication of her clientele, English, Chinese, and Cyrillic labels adorned the canisters. Some stools and a low table topped with a tray filled with paraphernalia for a tea ceremony blocked the entryway. In one corner were two toads—one with a coin in its mouth for extra good fortune—and a fat cross-legged Buddha, all made of *zisha*, literally "purple sand," a fine, mineral-rich, often reddish-brown clay from Jiangsu province. She poured the extra tea during each step of the process over the clay forms to "nurture" their texture and color, she said, adding that every teashop did this for good luck.

Palm-sized teapots made of *zisha* are considered ideal for brewing because they can withstand sudden differences in temperature, maintain heat, and are porous and unglazed, which means they absorb the essence of a tea's flavor and become seasoned over time. If possible, one should have a different teapot for each variety of tea leaf to protect the integrity of its taste.

Tea Lady Liu had arranged on other parts of the tray a variety of strainers, a trio of lidded porcelain teacups, and tongs for picking up 1.5-ounce teacups—which hold the equivalent of a civilized slurp—soaking in hot water in a big basin next to her.

On my first visit, she asked me what type of tea I liked.

"Jasmine," I answered without hesitation.

She nodded, picking out a couple of different leaves from the canisters before beginning the ceremony by pouring heated water from an electric kettle into a big teacup filled with the leaves, then straining the contents into a *zisha* funnel sitting over a glass teapot, said to be better for the more delicate green teas. She used the first brew—considered undrinkable—to rinse out the smaller cups before repeating the process and filling them with the second and the third and so on. They were a little like shots of espresso, to be savored slowly.

Liu worked quickly, surely, with very little showmanship. She explained how the teas would taste at different stages. The sampling and refills lasted more than an hour as I tried several grades of jasmine, a white tea, and some *tieguanyin* (Iron Goddess of Mercy) from Fujian. When steeped, the colors varied from pale amber to light chartreuse, while the tastes ranged from the potent green of fresh-cut grass to a deeply verdant bass note.

Liu broke down the huge array of teas into a handful of categories: green, white, yellow, oolong, black, red, and floral.

Oxidation and the length of fermentation—if fermented at all—or which flowers were smoked with the leaves determined the type. In between varieties, I snacked on green tea–flavored melon seeds that magically enhanced the flavor of what I was drinking.

"Don't think that the teas that taste *jing* and bitter are good. Those are low-grade ones," she warned.

"What's '*jing*'?" I asked.

"That means a strong flavor. The moment you drink it, it tastes astringent and bitter," she said. "The better grades, when you brew them, they taste clear and soft. When you drink it, there's a sweet aftertaste. That's good."

At the end of every visit, she always gave me a little present. Once it was a fat packet of melon seeds. Another time it was a dainty glass teapot that contained enough to fill a couple of thimbles. "Come back again" she always said, "and we'll try something new."

※

The origins of the tea plant, *Camellia sinensis*, are unknown, but the two main varieties used to make the beverage are the large-leafed *assamica* and the small-leafed *sinensis*. The former is native to northeast India, although plants are also found in China. *Assamica* is the foundation for the Indian black tea industry as well as China's famous and pricey *pu'er* tea. Most Chinese teas are based on the *sinensis* variety, found mostly in the sub-tropical southwestern provinces of Guizhou, Sichuan, and Yunnan.

Tea was originally called *tu*, a catchall name for bitter vegetables, but eventually needed its own word because it had become such a fundamental part of life. The current Chinese character for it, "cha," poetically consists of the radical for "person" between those for "grass" and "wood," indicating harmony with nature while drinking it.

Legend credits ruler Shennong ("Divine Farmer") with teaching the Chinese agricultural practices like planting crops and plowing more than five thousand years ago when there was insufficient meat to feed everyone—and discovering tea. Just as there are many types of tea, there are also numerous Chinese versions of the genesis of the brew.

In one story, Shennong, also known as the Emperor of Five Grains, got his first taste when leaves from burning branches of tea shrubs were carried up from the fire by the hot air and landed in his pot of boiling water, changing its color and imparting their fragrance. In another account, Shennong, also regarded as the god of Chinese medicine, ingested and identified the properties of a vast number of herbs, including more than seventy poisonous ones in a day. Because of this, he suddenly fainted while walking through some mountains. When he awoke, he spotted an unfamiliar plant in the sun and, in a desperate move, tried its leaves. He felt better instantly and gathered handfuls to dry and brew so that he could drink it on his journeys.

The roles and uses of tea have changed over the centuries, although the specifics were often lost or muddied by overlapping eras or differences in styles of preparation, depending on the location, with the south usually being more advanced than the north. In ancient times, tea was used as a medicine, boiled with leaves, seeds, and bark to cure a host of ailments.

During the Zhou dynasty (1046–256 BC), practitioners of Confucianism and Daoism espoused the physical and spiritual health benefits of drinking the stimulating result of boiling the leaf in water. Through this association, tea-drinkers were usually well respected and considered of high standing in society because they were moral, educated, and principled.

The Qin and Han dynasties marked the beginning of tea being regarded as a beverage instead of medicine. At the time, tea leaves were pressed into balls before they were dried and stored. When prepared, they were crushed and boiled with orange peel, ginger, and sometimes even small onions.

Tea eventually became an imperial fad. It was the fashionable drink at ceremonies and banquets at the palace instead of liquor.

But it also found its way into the hearts of ordinary citizens, who were slowly learning to appreciate the refreshing qualities of tea over its healing properties. Soon it had firmly entrenched itself in everyday life.

By the Tang dynasty (618–907 AD), China's golden age of economic and diplomatic expansion, along with blossoming literature, arts, and culture, the country was ripe for a tea trade. Techniques in tea planting and processing advanced dramatically, and people started making tea in earnest. The emperor ordered that a special production base be established on Guzhu Mountain, home of the clean-tasting "purple bamboo shoot" green tea leaf that yielded a premium beverage for imperial consumption. The dynasty also saw the centralization of the tribute tea system, which began centuries before as a voluntary act but eventually became a form of mandatory tax.

Inspired by the rulers' love for tea and Buddhist monks who drank copious amounts to cultivate their moral character and develop their temperament, the masses indulged as well. Teashops mushroomed in the capital city of Chang'an—then the most populous city in the world, now known as Xi'an. Lured by the taste, merchants, moneylenders, and entrepreneurs from across Asia and parts of Europe also packed the city, situated in a key part of the Silk Road. They began buying the leaf in bulk as they headed west toward Central Asia and the Middle East.

During this time, the custom also spread to Tibet, Mongolia, and, thanks to Buddhist monks, Japan. Historians have described bricks of leaves and stalks of the tea plant, herbs, and ox blood—sometimes bound with yak dung—used as currency in ancient China. Manufactured in the country's south, the bricks were particularly prized by tea-deprived Siberia, Mongolia, and Tibet, which traded them for swords, horses, cattle, and wood.

Along with firewood, rice, oil, salt, soy sauce, and vinegar, tea became regarded as the seventh essential of everyday life. For the consumption of ordinary citizens, leaves were first steamed to make them more pliant, then pounded in a mortar, and compressed and baked into bricks bound with thin strips of reed or bamboo. To prepare, a piece was first broken or shaved from the brick and toasted over a fire—likely to get rid of insects or molds—but the flames gave the leaves a smoky flavor. The fragment was then coarsely ground and boiled in water.

It was during the Tang dynasty that Lu Yu, a writer and tea-lover, penned the *Cha Jing* or *The Classic of Tea*, a poetic ode to the leaf that remains relevant and revered to this day. The comprehensive manual took him two decades to complete but only contains a little over seven thousand characters. Lu, who honed his passion and skill under the guidance of a monk who adopted him as a child, was revered as the Tea Sage or sometimes even the Tea God for his work.

From the translation by Frances Ross Carpenter, "If one would merely slake his thirst, then he can drink rice and water. Should melancholy and sadness or anger strike, he can turn to wine to drink," Lu wrote. "But if one would dispel an evening's unproductive lassitude, the meaning of 'drink' is tea."

Written in the condensed and refined style of scholars and poets, the book has ten sections that cover everything from origins and harvesting to brewing apparatuses and famous areas that produce the best leaves.

The shoots should grow in rich, fertile, slightly stony soil. They should be picked when the dew is still cool and only on a clear day unmarred by rain or clouds. Lu identifies eight categories of tea leaf shapes, including those "that look like a Mongol's boot to those that are like a lotus flower killed by frost."

When brewing tea, the best water to use comes from slow-flowing mountain streams; well-water gives inferior results. He even poetically describes the exact moment to stop boiling the water:

"It must look like fishes' eyes and give off but a hint of sound. When at the edges it chatters like a bubbling spring and looks like pearls innumerable strung together, it has reached the second stage. When it leaps like breakers majestic and resounds like a swelling wave, it is at its peak. Any more and the water will be boiled out and should not be used."

Unlike his contemporaries, who still added orange peel and ginger among other accompaniments to their brew, Lu advocated a more elemental tea, unembellished except for a little salt in the water.

"The first cup should have a haunting flavor, strange and lasting. There are those who allow it to continue simmering to nourish the elegance and retain the froth even through a first, second, and third cup. After the third cup, one should not drink more than a fourth or fifth cup unless he is very thirsty."

In the Song dynasty that followed, tea appreciation elevated even further as refinements surrounding the beverage expanded. Accounts say that harvests became rituals in themselves, including sacrifices to mountain deities and tea picking to the rhythm of a drum or cymbals. The workers, usually young girls, had to keep their fingernails at a certain length so that the leaves didn't touch their skin. They couldn't eat pungent foods like garlic and onions so as not to taint the leaves with odors.

Cakes of compressed tea, bound and sweetened with plum juice, became all the rage, and it was also during the Song dynasty that brews were infused with flowers like jasmine. With the development of grinders, whipped tea became the latest incarnation of the beverage. It was made from boiled water poured onto a finely ground powder of leaves, steeped, then made frothy by a bamboo whisk. Tea competitions became a popular way to showcase this new method. Participants vied to produce the greenest, frothiest cup of tea, its vivid color highlighted by blue-black or dark brown glazed cups.

Mongol hordes overthrew the Song. Some say it was because rulers had been too obsessed with tea culture to worry about defenses. The invaders, fierce and foreign warriors with no interest in decadent tea ceremonies, were more open to the loose-leaf version with which the Song had been experimenting before they were conquered. A new way to process tea was discovered called *chaoqing*, literally "frying the green," in which the leaves slowly were withered in a pan over a small flame as the heat quickly vaporized the moisture, blocking the oxidation process and protecting the essence of the flavor.

During the Qing dynasty (1644–1911), China's last, tea reached Europe, Africa, and the rest of Asia. England, a nation of avid tea drinkers, became the most active traders in China. But they disliked the restraints that the Chinese placed on the business and were grappling with a potentially huge trade imbalance. They wanted to buy the silk, porcelain, and especially tea for which China was famous in exchange for British manufactured goods, such as textiles. But the Chinese expressed only tepid interest.

Later, the British started exporting opium grown in their colony of India and aggressively did all they could to increase business, including doling out free samples, bribing officials, and establishing elaborate smuggling schemes to ensure the narcotic penetrated deep into the country. The ploy worked: Millions of Chinese became addicts, turning the British trade deficit into a surplus. Chinese efforts to enforce laws against the import and sale of opium led to the First Opium War (1839–1842), which had disastrous consequences for China. Defeated by the British, the emperor had to accept British demands and sign a peace agreement. It ceded Hong Kong to Britain for 150 years and opened five new treaty ports, including Shanghai and Canton (now Guangzhou) to foreign trade. It was the first of what Chinese historians call "unequal treaties" that opened the country to the West and began an era of foreign exploitation.

樂

A cup of tea served as the gateway to some of my most memorable experiences while traveling the country. There is no better way to start an interview.

I sipped with soccer fans thrilled by a visit from Real Madrid and David Beckham, with villagers whose homes were weakened and waterlogged because of the Three Gorges hydroelectric dam project, and with a fifty-three-year-old farmer deep in debt living off apples and instant noodles while on a quest to find out why her son was executed for murder and what had happened to his body. At the height of the initial outbreak of SARS, pig and poultry farmers served cups of tea as I interviewed them in humid Guangdong, where the disease first emerged.

The horror of the 2008 Sichuan earthquake brought the country together in a way I had never seen—and tore lives apart in a way I would never forget. A couple in Beichuan, whose fifteen-year-old son had died in it, invited me into their home one year after the disaster for the anniversary story I was writing. Their smiles tentative, they worried that authorities would harass them for talking to me, but they still welcomed me with hot green tea brewed from leaves grown in the surrounding mountains. The surprisingly bright taste of the tea was a sad contrast to the dark story they told. Crying and interrupting each other, they recalled how they had heard their son calling for help from deep within the wreckage of his school but could not dig him out.

Twenty-four hours later—silence.

When I interviewed the couple, the wife was seven months pregnant, her belly hidden under a frilly, flowery, blue-gray smock.

"Perhaps you have some hope for the future now that you're with child again?" I asked.

"You can put it that way," she said with a small, mirthless laugh. Then as if feeling a wave of guilt and loss, she added: "But we will never forget the past."

"We will never forget our son," her husband said firmly.

My heart held a familiar heaviness when I left their home. Less than a dozen steps away, under four wooden poles supporting a square of corrugated tin roof, a woman was roasting tea leaves in a giant wok-like pan. It was hot and fragrant at her stall. Something about the motion of her ladle and the quiet efficiency with which she worked soothed me. I couldn't resist buying three sachets of cooled leaves, vacuum-sealed on the spot. It was ridiculously inadequate, but I wanted to give one to the couple as a way to thank them for sharing their story and, somehow, to convey my sympathies over what they had suffered. I knocked on their door. They were surprised to see me.

It's a small token of appreciation for your time and my good wishes for your future, I said. The wife was resting her hand on her belly as she smiled and thanked me.

For many months after, I brought those two other bags of tea with me through moves from Beijing to Massachusetts, California, Singapore, then back to California. I didn't open them, wanting to preserve the freshness of the memories they held.

It was a hot and sunny September afternoon in 2011 when I finally pulled open the silver package and inhaled deeply. The leaves still smelled fresh, nutty, and tempered by fire. Camouflage green, they were wrinkled and curved like a sliver of fingernail. The brew, however, was nothing like how I remembered it, tasting rough and slightly bitter. Maybe it was better this way, a fitting tribute to the parents of Sichuan.

藥

Strangest of all were the cups of tea served by police officers who had detained me and spent hours questioning and sometimes lecturing me about my activities and interviews. I could never figure out if the gesture was the antithesis of the friendship and hospitality that the beverage was supposed to represent or if it was a way to smooth over a tense situation. Or was it simply a courtesy so ingrained in the culture that no one gave it a second thought? For me, having the warm cup in my hand while facing police officers often brought a small measure of calm.

After bringing us either to a government office or police station, officials checked notebooks, deleted photos, and confiscated videotapes. But they very rarely laid a finger on us unprovoked. Our passports, by and large, protected us, unlike the people about whom we wrote. At worst, our visa status was threatened, or we were expelled from the country—and even that was extremely rare. Being roughed up on the scene while trying to cover the news was a different matter as many of my friends could attest, especially Han, the Singaporean AP photographer, often mistaken for a local reporter and beaten up like one. He has the scars to prove it.

In recent years, the term *hecha*, "drink tea," has taken on sinister connotations for dissidents. It refers to the practice of state security agents inviting people they consider subversive for a cup of tea but interrogating them instead and warning them against further activities. In Communist China, tea has become a form of punishment.

It's hard to explain to an outsider how little freedom there is to report within the strict—yet inconsistent—framework set up by the government. It rarely has the guts-and-glory drama or horror of war, but the toll can be just as profound. It's a slow burn. There's a relentlessness in the heartbeat of the country that keeps it moving onward and upward at any cost.

Our work often led us to the grittier side of life, the underbelly of the world's fastest-growing economy. Paranoia, frustration, cynicism, anger, and despair took root and festered, the consequences of regular run-ins with showy but opaque governance, blatant abuse of power, corruption, or adamant intimidation. These encounters belonged more to the people we wrote about, but they magnified the ugliness we felt while living where lawlessness seemed rampant. Some were more affected than others.

Said one reporter: "I felt like there were two or three Chinas—Official China, which I had anger and outrage towards from what I saw on the ground, like how they bullied people. Then the Ordinary People China, which had hardworking, hospitable, loving, and interesting citizens. I felt many times heartbreak and helplessness for them, especially the ones who got bullied. Also fear and anxiety for the ones who would get in trouble for sticking their necks out talking to foreign reporters."

Another friend talked about the secrecy and paranoia of the government that leaks into all of society. "Of course there are secrets everywhere. But that sense in China, despite all the freedom, that when it comes to important things, the government will know what you said. . . . Punishments are very irregular, so you never know if you will be the chicken killed to frighten the monkeys or the monkey who, for some reason, is allowed to run free.

"It's almost Cultural Revolution–like. They can listen to all phones, read all e-mails, have spies in every office. Or that's what you end up thinking. I really do think of us being wrapped up, blind, fighting to punch our way out of an impenetrable thing, this paranoia of no one wanting to talk."

We dealt with these emotions in a combination of ways that worked in the short term. Some partied with mindless abandon, while others took refuge in their families or in sports. We traveled outside the country every few months, seeking sanity and a temporary respite from our assignments. Many found refuge in alcohol, but I have a near-zero tolerance, so I picked up smoking instead. One friend found solace in gallows humor.

"You make jokes about it, like everything else that's serious. You play games with it," he said. "One thing's for sure, though, and that is that you can't take any of it seriously or you will burn out, go mad, or get kicked out."

Reporting rules loosened in 2007 for the Beijing Olympics the following year and the changes became permanent after the Games. Most important for us was that we could now interview any individual or organization as long as we had their permission. We were already doing that in practice, but now regulations specifically supported us. The problem was that the message hadn't trickled down to the cities, counties, towns, and villages. Or if it had, directives from local officials still won out, and those to whom we spoke were questioned or harassed, and we were detained.

For me, getting busted was frustrating and stressful because it meant lost time and being turned back even before I got any reporting done. I tried to be cooperative but firm about needing to do my job just like the police needed to do theirs. I didn't lie when caught—I never said I was a tourist—because that would just make the situation worse when our passports were checked and our journalist visas told the real story.

I had a few close calls, though. Once, I was walking by the front desk of my hotel in Xinjiang where an earthquake had hit when I heard a couple of men ask for the room number of "the AP reporter." This was the difficult part about staying at bigger places that required guests to show their visas at check-in. Those details were recorded in forms given to local police, who then paid us a visit if they didn't want us there. I had been about to ask for directions from one of the hotel employees but moved quickly outside to catch a taxi instead.

My first detainment happened in 2004, when Greg and I visited a village in central China after a traffic incident escalated into violent clashes between Muslim Chinese and non-Muslims. At least seven people died, and police had swarmed the area, but as always there were conflicting reports of what had happened. While China suffers occasional ethnic tensions, the level of violence is rarely clear because the government is eager to maintain its narrative of unity, routinely suppressing reports of social conflict.

The area in Henan, one of the country's poorest provinces, was flat and checkered with rows of cabbages and wheat. There were more donkey-drawn carriages and bicycles than cars. Villagers sat outside shabby brick houses beside piles of drying corn. Thousands of police lining the road into town and government minivans with loudspeakers strapped to their roofs broadcasting appeals for calm disrupted the otherwise rustic scene.

Greg and I, lucky for a while, managed to get through checkpoints without incident and split up to do our work during the day. A few hours later, we reunited, along with another reporter and photographer from Agence France-Presse, after police detained all four of us. I had been in a car with a driver slowly cruising down the village's main road as I called details in to the Beijing office for my story. Suddenly the driver stopped. An officer had spotted us and was demanding to know why we were there.

We followed the police car to a mom-and-pop grocery store, where I spotted Greg and the two AFP colleagues: Peter Harmsen, the reporter, a low-key Dane; and Peter Parks, the photographer, a Brit with a big heart and a wicked sense of humor who worked as hard as he played.

The officers told us we were going to be questioned in a room at the back of the shop. Greg went in first, then Parks. To burn off nervous energy, I walked around the store, about the size of a 7-Eleven, but much more bare-bones. Its shelves were stocked with biscuits, instant noodles, candy bars, and preserved meat. For once, I wasn't hungry.

My heart was beating fast when my turn came. I was determined to be polite and not lose my cool as I walked into the sparsely furnished, fluorescent-lit room and sat down in front of one of the officers. I don't remember much about him, but when someone poured me a paper cup of tea I thought: *This may not be so bad after all.*

Then the session began.

The officer looked at my passport. "You're from Singapore?" he asked in English.

"Uh-huh," I answered brightly.

"Do you speak Mandarin?" he said, switching languages. A female officer next to him was taking notes.

"Yes, but not very well," I said, also switching languages.

"What were you doing here?"

"I had heard there was a situation. I'm here to understand what happened."

"How long have you been in China?"

"About two years," I answered without thinking.

He pounced. "If that's the case," he said almost triumphantly, "you should know by now you are not supposed to report outside of Beijing without prior approval."

I hedged. "I'm just doing what my boss told me to. It's my job."

"But you should know the rules," he said.

"But it's my job," I repeated.

"But your boss should know the rules."

"But it's my job."

The exchange lasted a few more seconds, going nowhere. The female officer poured more hot water into my paper cup.

Eventually they asked me to write a statement in English explaining what I had been doing in town. They made me change the phrase "trying to get to the bottom of things" because they didn't understand what it meant and didn't believe my definition. I wrote instead "trying to understand the situation." I signed it, and we were done.

At one point, I heard hissing and popping noises outside, near the room's only window. The officers and I looked at one another, puzzled. Greg and Parks grinned mischievously at me when I emerged.

"Did you hear the firecrackers we set off outside your window?" they asked, barely able to contain their laughter. Bored and looking for something to do after their interviews, they had found some poppers in the store and lit them up to distract my interrogators.

❈

Tea is life for Tibetans, who are said to drink up to forty cups a day of a brew fortified with yak butter called *boeja*. The morning begins with at least three cups, enjoyed after a prayer of offering to the Buddhas. There are variations on how the beverage is traditionally made. One way is to soak Darjeeling or any black tea leaves in hot water before boiling the leaves. After the liquid is strained, it's poured into a bamboo or pine churn that looks like a long wooden cylinder with a stick for a handle. Salt, heavy cream, and dollops of butter made from the milk of *dri* (female yaks), are added, and the mixture is vigorously churned and served in wooden cups or poured into kettles to be kept warm over fires. A simpler preparation I often saw involved hot tea being added to a cup already containing salt and a lump of butter.

Either way, the result is a hearty, milky-brown drink with a purplish tint and the consistency of broth. The richness provides important calories and nutrition to cope with the high altitudes. A cup or bowl filled to the brim is offered to guests to show welcome and respect. The host is expected to refill it as soon as a guest takes a sip.

When drinking, the film of butter on the surface is usually blown aside and later rubbed into the outside of the cup (if it's wooden) to keep it pliant and able to withstand the temperature changes. The warm fat is also considered an ideal moisturizer to keep faces, lips, and hands from being chapped. *Tsampa,* ground roasted barley flour, is usually mixed into the tea dregs until it is a doughy ball—a traditional Tibetan staple—and washed down with more tea. Tibetans also drink plain black tea and sweetened milk tea, or *ja ngarmo,* to which sugar and milk are added.

My first experience with yak butter tea was actually in Mongolia, where the beverage is also commonly served. My assignment was to cover a visit by the Dalai Lama, but I was out interviewing nomads who lived in the grasslands for a side story about a Mongolian weather phenomenon called *zud,* a combination of summer droughts and bitterly cold winters devastating to herds of livestock. As we went from *ger* to *ger,* the felt-lined tents in which nomads live, we were served steaming cups of the tea. At the first stop, I took a gulp, thinking it was regular milk tea, and gagged at the unexpectedly salty, rancid taste. The hosts also served a gray hunk of meat they had been boiling in water, and I chewed the gristle for almost five minutes, nodding politely, before I could swallow. I tried the tea a couple of times while in Lhasa but could never stomach the flavor.

Chinese historians say that tea came to Tibet during the Tang dynasty, when a Tibetan king married an imperial Chinese princess who brought the aromatic leaf with her. Other accounts say that the Tibetan military had conquered ethnic tribes in southwest China, so they were already familiar with teas from Yunnan and Sichuan, where tea plants are indigenous.

The leaves were not only made into tea but also eaten as a supplement to the meat and dairy diet the Tibetans ate, a result of the area's harsh climate and rugged terrain that made it difficult to grow anything green. A system of exchange evolved from mutual needs—the Chinese got the strong and powerful Tibetan war steeds they wanted to boost their military defenses in return for the currency of crude tea bricks made of leftovers from the quality stuff saved for imperial pleasure. Historic accounts say one horse fetched between forty-five and 120 pounds of tea, depending on the emperor.

Caravan routes developed to transport huge loads of tea on the backs of mules, yaks, and horses along mountain roads and passes that were treacherous in the best of conditions. The main one was called the Tea Horse Road, a network of paths that crossed often inhospitable terrain, wending hundreds of miles through the Ya'an tea-growing region in Sichuan province and the tropical lowlands of Xishuangbanna in Yunnan province, often ending in Lhasa, the capital of Tibet at an altitude of about twelve thousand feet.

In the early twentieth century along these caravan routes, men and women carried more than their weight in tea to eke out a living. The porters strapped up to fifteen packs on their backs, each weighing between thirteen and twenty pounds. The more they carried, the more they earned, one silver dollar or twenty pounds of grain for every pack of tea by one account. But the end gain was paltry, factoring in taxes and the cost of food and shelter.

It was an unimaginably arduous and dangerous journey they took, fortified with only meager amounts of grain that depleted quickly. They had only homemade straw sandals and iron-tipped walking sticks to help with balance. Stopping every few steps to catch their breath, they painstakingly traversed mountain passes through punishing weather, sometimes carefully teetering their way through paths so narrow only one person could fit. Many died on the journeys.

The Tea Horse Road operated for more than a thousand years until the Communists took over China in 1949 and built highways through the region, making the ancient network redundant. Today, tea comes into Tibet by trucks along paved roads.

Most of Tibet had effectively been independent for centuries until the eighteenth century, when it recognized the superior role of the Qing dynasty, especially in foreign affairs. It was incorporated into the mainland after Chinese Communist troops entered in 1950 and claimed sovereignty. Beijing did, however, grant it the status of an autonomous region, which in theory means it has more legislative rights.

In 1959, an unsuccessful uprising against Chinese rule ended with the Dalai Lama fleeing into exile in India. Since then much has changed under suffocating controls on Tibet's unique Buddhist culture, which permeates nearly every aspect of daily life. Beijing views devotion to the religion and the Dalai Lama as a threat to its supremacy. Under party guidelines, the numbers of monks in lamaseries are limited, and religious teachings are restricted. Since 1996, monks have been required to attend political classes and denounce the Dalai Lama. Chinese officials, however, deny that Tibetan Buddhism is being diluted.

In 2008, unrest began brewing as Buddhist monks started marching in Lhasa to mark the anniversary of the March 10, 1959 uprising and to demand the release of compatriots arrested the year before. Police took the monks into custody, and ordinary Tibetan citizens soon joined other monks in demanding their release. Over the next three days, their demands spiraled to include cries for Tibet's independence and turned violent when police tried to stop a new group of protesting monks. Pent-up grievances against Chinese rule exploded on March 14 in a stunning display of defiance as Tibetans directed their fury against the Chinese and their shops, hotels, and other businesses, burning, beating, and looting as they pleased. Mobs and fires spread through the city.

In one case, gasoline was poured over a person who was then set on fire and died, the Chinese-appointed governor of Tibet said. In another, the protesters "knocked out a police officer on patrol and then they used a knife to cut a piece of flesh from his buttocks the size of a fist."

Casualty numbers were hard to confirm. China said that twenty-two people died while Tibetan exile groups claimed at least 140 were killed. Because of Beijing's restrictions on access to Tibet for foreign journalists and the subsequent shutdown on news flowing out, it was difficult to verify any information. We worked fourteen- to sixteen-hour days, making calls and combing through blogs and social media sites for any details we could find.

It was the largest and fiercest challenge in nearly two decades to the authority of Beijing, which responded by imposing a strict curfew and dispatching armored carriers that rattled on mostly empty streets. Soldiers poured into the area, manning checkpoints. Several witnesses reported hearing occasional bursts of gunfire.

The government said the riots were engineered by supporters of the Dalai Lama, whose government-in-exile has been based in the Indian hillside town of Dharamsala since he fled. He is still the region's widely revered spiritual leader and one of the figures most reviled by China's Communist leadership, which had been striving for a trouble-free run-up to the Beijing Olympics in August. Instead, it was embarrassed by the chaos and the unwelcome international attention, especially from overseas human rights groups.

Preparing the public for tough measures, state-run television showed footage on the evening newscast of red-robed monks battering bus signs and Tibetans in street clothes hurling rocks and destroying shop windows as smoke billowed across the city. "The plot by an extremely small number of people to damage Tibet's stability and harmony is unpopular and doomed to failure," a narrator said as the footage played.

Even as Chinese forces appeared to reassert control in Lhasa, sympathy protests burst through strongly traditional communities in the Tibetan plateau where the provinces of Gansu, Sichuan, and Qinghai converge, home to Buddhist monasteries chafing under Chinese-imposed religious controls. Though many were small in scale, the widening scope of demonstrations forced security squads to mobilize across a broader expanse, suppressing protests while on the move in the country's vast western region where more than half of China's 5.4 million Tibetans live. Authorities expelled foreign reporters in those areas, claiming it was for their safety.

Less than a month after the violence, in early April, Han and I arrived in the region, a mountainous, arid, undeveloped area that has for centuries formed the blurry frontier between Tibet and China. During our travels, we realized that the barricade of police checkpoints and roadblocks, firmly in place only days before, had mostly disappeared. Smashed panes of glass in shops and government buildings had been replaced, and businesses were open again.

Despite the signs that life had resumed, jitters prevailed. Many of the towns resembled armed encampments, and residents worried about fresh violence. Monks said local authorities had stepped up their watch and warned them not to talk about what happened. Their furtive glances around and refusal to engage were equally telling. Others showed flashes of the defiance that fueled the latest unrest or spoke of great sadness that they would not or could not explain. Monks at three monasteries within a mile of each other said they had heard of recent violence—but either would not talk about it or said they had been ordered not to.

"Life is fine," said a monk at one monastery, where a picture of the Dalai Lama—an icon banned in central Tibet by the government since the mid-1990s—sat on an altar, draped with white and gold silk scarves. "It's hard to say why all this happened; it's complicated."

Han and I had slipped into town, somehow avoiding the dragnet of soldiers and police patrols. At dusk we walked through the grounds of the seven-hundred-year-old Rongwo monastery, renowned as a center for Tibetan arts, especially the embroidered paintings called *thangkas.* Glad for the cover of gathering darkness, we found a group of monks cooking their evening meal in a small room dimly lit with a single bulb. They offered us butter tea, *tsampa,* and porridge. I sat on the floor with them. They looked troubled.

A twenty-two-year-old monk and dozens of others had staged a peaceful protest, climbing a hill behind the monastery where they burned incense in a traditional Tibetan Buddhist ritual. That evening the rite became an act of defiance against authorities who had issued a directive not to gather in groups. "It is our right, our ritual," the monk said with a stubborn set to his jaw. The other monks nodded in agreement. Troops who had ringed the monastery had left, but plainclothes minders from the local government were keeping watch.

Our main goal was to spend time in Xiahe, a historic town whose Chinese name means "Summer River," where more than one thousand monks and lay Tibetans staged two days of protests, smashing windows in government buildings, burning Chinese flags, and displaying the snow lion flag representing Tibetan independence.

The checkpoint into Xiahe wasn't manned, and I breathed a sigh of relief when we passed it without incident I tensed up again moments later, though, when trucks with riot police carrying shields, batons, and five-foot-long wooden poles rumbled past us through the town's main drag, lined with two-story buildings. Official notices stamped in red ink and posted on shop fronts and walls urged people to surrender for taking part in the unrest.

Han and I headed right for Labrang, a sprawling eighteenth-century monastery that is one of the most revered centers of Tibetan Buddhism outside of Tibet. Walking toward the main compound, we separated to cover more ground. Like the other monasteries I had visited, Labrang filled me with a strong sense of cloistered peacefulness. The surroundings were dramatic, with mountains, valleys, and a fast-flowing river. The buildings were either simple—single-story, white-walled residences—or incredibly ornate, multistory temples with gold roofs and the bright primary colors of Tibetan designs.

All was quiet in the warren of alleyways housing the rooms where the monks lived. The echoing shouts of paramilitary police performing drills in the town square mingled in an odd counterpoint to the snatches of prayer chants I heard as I passed temples and schools. Monks walked briskly in the light snow in robes of crimson, fuchsia, and scarlet, fingering prayer beads or jostling each other playfully. Some met my eyes then glanced away, while others looked right through me. Those who stopped when I approached them said things were fine but shook their heads or walked away when asked about the March riots. No one wanted to talk to me, perhaps seeing me as a government spy. I identified myself as a journalist from Beijing, but that was probably just as bad—and it made me nervous because I wasn't sure if anyone would report my presence.

I asked a thirteen-year-old girl with pigtails and a wide smile for directions to the bathroom. She led me there instead, cheerily chatting the whole time. She told me there was a festival that morning that I should see and led me to a path snaking around several buildings and past the entrance of what looked like one of the major temples. Already hundreds of lay Tibetans—including elderly pilgrims and mothers clutching babies—had jammed the path that opened out into a courtyard. Many spilled over onto the slopes of the surrounding hills.

The snow had stopped, and the sun was shining as we waited in the cold. The girl told me what she had seen during the riots, her recollection coming haltingly, then in a rush of words: "On the first day, crowds of monks and others started gathering on the streets, holding pictures of the Dalai Lama. Armed police also amassed with rifles and lined the streets. I thought they would shoot but they didn't. The next day, the crowd swelled again, and they started marching. Some gathered in front of the middle school, and they started hurling rocks. One man was wielding a sword. . . . They broke the glass of a picture of [President] Hu

Jintao, pulled out the photo, and burned it. They took down the Chinese flag and put up the Tibetan flag. . . . I was so scared. My mother's hands were shaking so badly she couldn't pick up her chopsticks for the rest of the day."

Turning patriotic she asked: "What is the use of Tibetan independence? Under the government, our lives are so much better. I feel much safer with the armed police in place."

Close to noon, about ten monks emerged from the buildings holding clay bowls filled with blessed water from kettles that other monks were carrying. They took sips from the bowls and sprayed the liquid through their mouths onto the crowd as they walked past, a rite believed to heal physical ailments. Everyone raised their faces in anticipation, trying in any way to be spat on. Some opened their mouths to receive the blessing directly, while others reached out with used bottles, cans, and jars to beg for leftover water from the bowls. The ritual took me by surprise. I was glad I had chosen to stand near the back. I spotted Han in the distance, rapidly taking shot after shot of the colorful ceremony.

I lost track of the girl as the crowds surged forward then quickly dispersed after fifteen minutes, leaving Han and me alone. We decided to get lunch, a good way to interview residents and have time to assess the situation and plan our next move. It seemed like there were police or soldiers every few feet on the street, so we opted to find a place to eat on a second floor, hopefully farther away from a potentially bad situation.

Han loves food as much as I do, and he has a quiet, cheesy sense of humor. His calm demeanor, however, is so different from mine. Once, when I ran yelling after a rat leapt from the television set onto my bed in a low-rent motel we were staying at to avoid authorities, he simply said, "They are more afraid of you than you are of them." He offered me the spare bed in his room and remained unfazed even when two more rodents appeared, lurking near his windowsill and squeaking through the night.

The five-table restaurant we chose was empty except for two men slurping noodles. In the tiny kitchen, the Tibetan owner was steaming dumplings, one of the few items readily available on the menu. We ordered tea and noodles, which were thick and chewy, soaking in a thin broth with nothing much else. I picked at them but enjoyed the tea, which smelled and tasted like the green of the mountains around us. We chatted with the owner's nineteen-year-old daughter, who was shy at first but warmed up quickly.

"Not many people come in anymore," she said, apologizing for not having much food on hand, a consequence of the protests and ensuing police clampdown. "They are too scared to leave their homes much. What can I do? One or two customers are still better than none."

Still hungry, Han and I moved on to a nearby fifty-seat cafe that advertised Western fare. We got chicken burgers and fries, curious as to how they would turn out, which was better than we expected. I ordered more green tea. As we ate, small groups of monks came in for meals, many choosing the fried rice that seemed to be a local specialty.

We had a table by a window overlooking the back of the building and the "Big Xia" river after which the town is named. It was peaceful and sunny, and the cafe owner was friendly. Up there, it was easy to forget the violence.

A young monk whom Han had met while exploring the monastery grounds soon joined us. He politely refused food and my recommendation of the green tea, ordering yak butter tea instead, which he sipped for the next hour or so. At twenty, he was soft-spoken with high cheekbones and a dimpled chin, and had the slightly awkward mannerisms of someone just out of his teens. He laughed in short, nervous bursts and often looked down at his hands when he talked. He seemed more at ease with Han, whom he invited to play soccer in the surrounding grasslands with other monks in summer, when the weather warmed and the trees and flowers were in full bloom.

The conversation had many pauses, and we sometimes struggled to understand each other. He was more comfortable with

Tibetan, which neither Han nor I spoke. Both sides, however, were glad to have a chance to learn more about each other over some tea.

The restaurant's TV was playing what I had seen every time I switched on a television set in the past few days: a special report by CCTV showing scenes of monks overturning cars, storming government buildings, tearing down signs, and toppling brick walls. The narrator listed the names of the towns and how much damage was incurred. The Dalai Lama and his supporters masterminded the "beating, smashing, looting, and burning incidents," the report said.

"I've seen this already," the young monk said after watching a segment showing monks shouting as they swarmed the streets of Maqu, a town south of Xiahe. He was eager to switch over to another channel.

About twenty of his friends had asked him to march with them in Xiahe, but he declined because he was afraid of what would happen. In the end, security agents took away about four or five monks from Labrang. When pressed for more details, he said he didn't know much more.

"We can't talk about this," he said.

I asked what a monk's life was like. He paused for a long time and then told us about classes and prayers, with snatches of rest in between some of the longer, more taxing sessions.

"What are the lessons like? Do they include political topics?" I asked, thinking about reports of party guidelines that restricted religious teachings and required attendance of "patriotic education" classes that denounced the Dalai Lama.

He looked uncomfortable.

"I don't understand," he said, an answer he gave whenever he felt we were veering into sensitive areas.

"How is life different now, since the protests?" I asked.

"Life is fine," he said, but the abbots were more strictly enforcing an 8:30 p.m. curfew. Monks could no longer go to local Internet cafes, he said, which he had enjoyed doing. He liked using QQ, the mainland's hugely popular online messaging service, and watching movies while there.

"What movies?" I asked.

His answer surprised me: "Scary ones."

"Me too!" I exclaimed, amazed to find someone who enjoyed those kinds of films—particularly a monk.

As the sun slid down the mountains, he asked if we wanted to see his home. We jumped into a taxi, safer than walking on the streets. The monk had a small room enlivened by different kinds of fabric patterns in a riot of baby blue, orange, pink, and yellow. There was a small wooden chest and several photos of temples, a Buddha, and a group shot of other monks in the snow. He offered us bread and dough twists from a couple of plastic bags and, of course, more yak butter tea. His favorite food, he said, was potatoes. In any form, but especially stewed with beef, which his family used to make. He cooked very occasionally, simple vegetarian meals. Otherwise, he ate *tsampa* with yak butter tea and *momos*, Tibetan dumplings stuffed either with meat or vegetables before being steamed, and sometimes fried afterward.

We sat with him, sometimes in silence, enjoying the peace of the surroundings and the opportunity to receive his hospitality. Even though he didn't say much, the young monk liked spending time with people outside his world. Late in the afternoon he walked us out to say goodbye.

❀

Over the next few months, he occasionally called Han or me, just to say hello. I called him a couple of times to see if he was okay. We didn't speak many words during those exchanges, but we always remembered that afternoon conversation over tea.

6

Happy Country Home

It was the tail-end of a hot and sticky summer filled with bitter-sweet goodbyes. My mood grew dark with bad city traffic and an endless drive through curvy mountain roads filled with campy, theme-parked guesthouses, part of the growing industry of get-aways run by farmers.

Before I left Beijing for good, I stayed at Farmer Sun's home near a run-down but famously picturesque portion of the Great Wall. Five friends and I had rented a small van and a driver to take us there. Our chatter, initially animated, died down as he jerked his way through gridlock, his foot pumping the brake every few seconds. I opened the window and stared out, trying not to get carsick. Eventually, buildings and highways gave way to villages and farmland as we headed into the mountains. The trees grew closer together, and dogs lazed in the shade on the side of the road, a welcome breeze blowing through the van.

We arrived at the village and pulled up at Farmer Sun's home. The driver turned off the engine, and suddenly my ears were ringing with . . . silence. In front of his gray single-story home and its red roof stretched corn and lavender fields. I smelled the clean air and . . . had I just heard chickens? A smile tickled at my face as Farmer Sun, a rangy man with big ears and a wide grin, welcomed us with a hearty "*Nihao!*"

After exchanging pleasantries, we sat on shaky metal stools under a corrugated tin awning built over part of the vegetable garden. A light, cool rain began falling, and mist gathered in the distance. The silhouette of the Great Wall snaked along the tops of surrounding mountains, like a ridge on the humps of a dragon's back. It was perfect.

That weekend, we feasted on a variety of vegetables straight from the garden, coarse rice dotted with corn and mung beans, and homemade tofu and flatbread. The first night, Mrs. Sun brought out a wonderful omelet that I then requested at each meal. Golden and big as a Frisbee, it was light and flecked with scallions. Sun and his wife graciously accepted my profuse compliments, but why I loved the humble dish so much puzzled them. To be honest, I couldn't figure it out either.

Maybe it was the freshness of the eggs. When Mrs. Sun showed them to me, she had just come back from a visit to their forty-six free-range chickens on the hill behind their house; bits of grass still adhered to the shells. Or perhaps it was because the spring onions had been pulled from the garden minutes before, chopped, and then thrown into the beaten eggs, perfuming everything with their sharp greenness. The perfect amount of peanut oil used to fry the concoction may have had something to do with it, resulting in a puffy disk with beautifully browned spots and crisp edges. It wasn't a hearty American brunch omelet or a buttery, pale French one. It was the best of *jiachangcai*—home-style Chinese cooking—where simplicity, speed, and freshness were key.

Farmer Sun has lived in Xizhazi village at the base of the Jiankou segment of the wall all his life. In one hour, the sixty-three-year-old—one of the rare Chinese who has never smoked in his life—can hike up the steep face of the surrounding mountains to the outer edges of the wall, a feat, he said with small smile, that would take foreigners like me at least ninety minutes. "And that would be considered really fast," Sun added, breaking into a slow laugh.

He used to make his living solely by farming. "It was a lot more tiring—and you don't make any money," he said of the backbreaking grind. At that point, friends from the city, mostly amateur photographers, began flocking to the area to capture

166

Five friends and I stayed at Farmer Sun's nongjiale ("happy country home") near a run-down but picturesque section of the Great Wall. Farmer Sun is pointing to the omelet that Mrs. Sun prepared for me on our first night. It was so heavenly—golden, fluffy, and flecked with scallions—that I requested it for every meal.

the jagged, emerald beauty of the scenery. Sun, himself an avid picture-taker, opened his home—one large room and a series of smaller ones around a courtyard dominated by his garden patch.

Word traveled, and "one car, two cars, three cars . . . more and more people started coming." A business was born.

He charged between $3 and $7 a night for rooms, with meals costing another $3. The quarters were spare, small concrete rooms with single beds and no heating, and guests shared the one bathroom on the premises. But it was quiet and breathtakingly green as far as the eye could see.

We ate dinner the first night under the awning and dim fluorescent lights. A moment of sadness hit me when I realized it would be my last getaway with friends, but I shook it off, determined to enjoy the trip for what it was. After the meal, we lined up our chairs at the edge of the awning and peered into the darkness of the fields, luxuriating in the rural silence, real quiet unmarred by humans or machines, inhaling deeply to see if we could catch a faint fragrance of lavender from down the road. Above us fanned out an inky sky decorated with a scattering of winking stars, a sight rarely seen in Beijing.

As always in China, the peace broke within minutes—this time with a group of three middle-aged men also staying the weekend. They sat down at the table next to ours, drinking bottle after bottle of beer as they raucously chatted about business and love. Their voices rose and fell late into the night, their hearty laughs carrying in the cool air. The tips of their cigarettes glowed from their mouths long after the communal lights went dark.

The next morning, we breakfasted on pungent stalks of spring onions with a slightly sweet bean paste dip, stir-fried shredded potatoes and chilies, steamed buns, and rice porridge studded with red and green beans. Sated, we braved the climb to the Jiankou section of the wall, considered one of the wildest and most dangerous parts because so much of it lies in disrepair.

Built during the Ming dynasty (1368–1644), the section is famous for its white rocks that stand out in stark relief against their verdant surroundings and its uniquely narrow, almost vertical steps that stretch toward the heavens. We arrived at the top, sweaty and exhilarated, and began the scenic trudge along the winding length of the wall after paying an "entrance fee" of a couple of dollars to a villager perched on a rock, an unofficial watchman.

No matter how many times I've been to the wall, it never fails to take my breath away. It was a heady feeling to be on a virtually untouched part of it, gritty and uneven with rocks and dirt, imagining others who had trod the same path before us. The route was overgrown, and there were some dizzyingly steep bits—walls of gray rock so worn and smooth that it was nearly impossible to find a hand- or foothold—but we kept moving forward, propelled by a sense of freedom and exploration.

A couple of hours later, we saw the three men from the night before coming from the opposite direction. We nodded and exchanged hellos, stopping for a minute to sip from our bottles of water under the late-morning sun. Together we looked down and tried to find Sun's home but couldn't locate it in the maze of fields and trees of the villages below. My friends gave up and continued walking.

I didn't, though, suddenly pensive about what lay ahead during my fellowship in America. I was on the cusp of another big move in my life, filled with a familiar panic of not having done enough, understood enough, pushed myself enough. It hadn't seemed possible, but China had become my comfort zone—and I was bracing myself to leave. Even though I had lived in America before, I would still have to start over again in a new place and make new friends as I carved out a life that would last only one school year.

After that, the unknown.

Like so many of my last days in China I wanted to hold on to this moment, to freeze the view, the sunshine, the sound of the wind in a memory. I had begun feeling nostalgic about a country I was still living in.

Sun's family business is one of about 1.5 million small Chinese-style bed-and-breakfasts that have blossomed nationwide in the past fifteen or so years. The phenomenon, part of a thriving rural tourism trend, has become a crucial component in government efforts to spur the economy and social development in the countryside.

The government declared 2006 the year of rural tourism as part of its efforts to build a "New Socialist Countryside" for its eleventh Five-Year Plan. In other words, officials wanted to use tourism to improve the livelihood of farmers and help them reap the benefits of the country's economic boom, hoping to close the income gap between the affluent cities and the lagging countryside.

Shao Qiwei, the director of the China National Tourism Administration, said the development of rural tourism would not only increase the types of work and income-generating activities in rural areas, but also contribute to improvements in the quality of life. This improvement would come in tangible forms, such as the industrialization of agriculture, but also as the development of "character" and civilization that comes with the introduction of new ideas and concepts from the city. This new proximity, in turn, would yield an increased understanding between farmers and tourists. One caveat, though, was that the countryside still had to retain its innate and unique characteristics, and rural residents could not be forced to adopt tourism.

The government's encouragement added impetus to the enterprising spark already ignited soon after the economic reforms of the late 1970s, when farmers living near tourist attractions spontaneously started businesses to capitalize on visitors willing to spend money. The small businesses included inns, eateries, transportation, and photography services integrated into the larger framework of the state's tourism system.

The practice really took off as farmers realized the money-making potential of their own homes and threw their doors open to overnight guests for a small fee. They charged extra for meals, which added value to their produce and crops.

The Ministry of Agriculture said that in 2010, there were 1.5 million *nongjiale* in nineteen provinces that received a total of about four hundred million guests. *Nongjiale* has many cheery translations—happy country home, happy farmer home, the joy of farming, peasant household pleasure, happy days in farmers' homes—but they all embrace going back to basics and the promise of a quick getaway to a little-known location filled with gorgeous scenery and farm-fresh dishes.

Over the years, the phenomenon—said to have started in Chongqing municipality and the surrounding Sichuan province, areas renowned for beauty and a relaxed lifestyle—has expanded to include "happy fisherman's home" in coastal areas and homestays in the villages of ethnic minorities. Activities center around nature and the culture of the area such as fishing, fruit-picking, therapy using local herbs, rafting, and courses on folk customs and recipes. *Nongjiacai*, or country cooking, has also become a popular concept even in cities, where restaurants have developed this theme.

For the farmers, *nongjiale* builds on what they already had and involves relatively little extra capital. The ease with which they established guesthouses made it perfect for individual farming households to invest in and run them. For city folk, an economy growing in leaps and bounds and a change in government-structured public holidays meant more money and opportunity to focus on leisure activities. Time in the countryside made people nostalgic for their rural childhood. For those who grew up in cities, an escape from the concrete jungle held the romanticized appeal of lazy days, fresh air, and down-to-earth simplicity. Foreigners like us enjoyed the reprieve from the sweltering, smog-choked city and felt like we were experiencing the "real China."

Rural tourism has also helped absorb surplus countryside labor and redirects rural employment to nonagricultural sectors. It has created millions of jobs, including indirect and seasonal ones.

Because farmers have become tourism service providers, they have gained new insight into the rules and principles of the country's market economy, as well as increasing their ability to adapt to the development of rural areas. Some have learned how to speak Mandarin (in addition to their local dialects) or English and picked up computer skills. Rural tourism has also increased the awareness of, and helped preserve, heritage sites and significant aspects of Chinese culture.

But all is not rosy. While rural tourism has somewhat increased awareness of environmental protection, overall it has led to ecological degradation and damage. There's a lack of professional planning and development expertise to manage the hordes of people who swarm previously pristine areas. In Farmer Sun's village, noise, traffic, and other urban blights were starting to seep in. His village sends representatives to their section of the Great Wall to pick up trash left by hikers and other visitors. While they receive a small fee to do it, it's more important that they keep the landmark clean.

In the effort to keep up with demand and lure repeat customers, more construction—often garish and entirely at odds with the rural environment—is taking place in the face of fierce competition from neighbors and friends all doing exactly the same. Profitability and sustainability are suffering. Those who remain out of the loop resent the development. And as building continues, at a certain point it detracts from the very reason for its existence: a getaway that takes urbanites back to the comforting familiarity of village life or to a new experience of life in the country.

A year after that first visit, when I had finished my fellowship, I stopped in Beijing on my way back to Singapore. I quickly got back into the swing of things, deciding to drop by to see Farmer Sun with Emma Graham-Harrison, a loyal friend and fearless reporter who had gone on the initial trip.

We found a construction site around his home. The sound of hammering and the shouts of workers filled the air. Planks, window frames, and coils of wire lay piled under the garden shelter where we ate our meals the summer before. The rooms had been gutted, and debris—broken glass, old boxes, rusty wires—was strewn around knee-high mounds of sand.

"Renovations," said a worker, when I asked what was going on, dismayed and worried that Sun was no longer there.

Minutes later, he came back from the fields, his blue cotton pants rolled up to the knee and a straw hat on his head. "I'm doing things up!" he said cheerily.

He told us about his plans to add two more rooms, en suite bathrooms, and other modern amenities to make it "more comfortable, more what foreigners are used to." In winter, the floors would be heated with firewood. "Give me a call before you come, and I will make sure the floor is warm for you," Sun said. "You can enjoy it for yourselves."

He walked us around the compound. His old family room, once dominated by a huge *kang*—a sleeping platform heated underneath by a coal fire, common in northern China—and framed photos of the Great Wall that he had taken, was now an empty shell.

"We couldn't live here anymore," Sun said. "There were leaks. I'm also getting up there in years, so I had to change the living conditions."

Like his neighbors, he too wanted to capitalize on the country's prosperity. "Everyone is opening *nongjiayuan* to survive, to make money. To make use of the natural environment to attract some guests to come eat and stay here and spend some money."

Sun offered us tea, and we sat down in the room set aside for living while the renovations were ongoing. We started talking about my favorite subject—food.

When Sun was young, provisions were scarce and variety limited. "There was only corn—corn noodles, corn porridge, buns made from corn flour. At that time, meat was so rare. The economy was not developed. There was no money to buy meat. We also ate a lot of big white radishes then. There was no cabbage at the time because cabbages need a lot of water, and there was a shortage because we had a serious drought."

He described the ways the root vegetable was prepared, often braised, sometimes softened in soup and other times chopped finely to be used as a filling for hearty dumplings or buns. Only a pinch of MSG and a few drops of oil were used in the cooking. Now, both he and his wife loved cabbage along with potatoes, either stir-fried or braised with mung bean noodles, or stewed with a little meat.

"Food is the most important thing to Chinese people. Grain is the number one priority, number two is vegetables. Without them, there is no way to survive," Sun said. "The farmers of China do not rely on buying or selling. They mainly rely on their own hard work on the land."

The quality of meals naturally depended on the economy. "Of course everyone wants to eat good food. In the past, about thirty years ago, everyone wanted to be warm and full, they wanted their bellies to be full. Now it's about elevating the food culture. People now want to eat better, more nutritious food. This will benefit your health. If you keep eating bad food, of course it's not good for you. In the past, you were content if you were full. Now you're content if you eat well."

Sun didn't think he was in a position to have a true understanding of China's eating culture because his meals were simple—like traditional porridge with salted vegetables for breakfast. But from his experience, eating well wasn't about having abundant meat or a plethora of dishes at each meal. It was about having an intimate knowledge of the supply chain from land to table.

"It's best to eat things right after they are picked," he said. "In the city, the food is so different, there's a big difference. It's not that the food in the city is no good. But it's all shipped, imported, whereas what we eat is fresh. We pick it from our backyards, we cook it, and then we eat it. There are no additives or chemical fertilizers."

Autumn usually brought a harvest of cucumbers, yardlong beans, pumpkins, potatoes, chives, chilies, and all sorts of green vegetables, all of which are supposed to last through winter and spring. Staples like noodles and buns were homemade. The only things Sun's family bought were cooking oil and small amounts of meat. "We don't have a real love for meat. We don't think it's healthy to eat too much of it. But if we do, it's pork, lamb, chicken, or fish cut into slices then stewed." Sun thought for a bit. "No beef because we are not used to eating it. And no dog or frog."

Mr. and Mrs. Sun grew up in Xizhazi and married young. They had two sons and were very proud that both had steady jobs outside the village. The elder, in his forties now, worked in a bank in Huairou, a district in the northern outskirts of Beijing, and the younger had a job at a cement factory. Neither wanted to be a farmer.

Short and sturdy with ruddy cheeks and cropped graying hair, Mrs. Sun had slightly crooked teeth that she revealed with her shy smile. Her fingers and nails had blackened with the earth she worked. Unlike her gregarious husband, she was retiring and a little awkward, but she had a good memory for faces. As soon as she saw me, she gave me a huge hello and a pat on the arm, saying that she remembered me from the year before.

The Suns shared cooking duties, but that day it was Mrs. Sun who headed first to the kitchen, a small room with concrete floors, tiled walls, and windows that overlooked the garden. On the way, she pointed out neat flourishing rows of lettuce, cabbage, sweet potato, and pumpkin. She spoke in a clipped manner, and both she and Sun had a slightly rolling, slurring local accent that I found hard to understand.

Against the kitchen walls: a metal shelf packed with a jumble of boxes, seasonings, and pots; a stove with a propane gas tank attached; and a wooden chest bearing a rice cooker and some dried red chilies. Plastic bottles of peanut oil and a large thermos flask sat on the floor. The woks were black and oily—indicating that they were much used and well seasoned.

Mrs. Sun generously offered to cook us anything we wanted, then asked us to take home some mushrooms that she had picked from the surrounding mountains. She excitedly brought out a white plastic bag filled to the brim with caps and curls of dried fungi in varying shades of brown. When we refused, telling her that she should enjoy the fruits of her own labor, she switched tactics, pouring out several handfuls into a large bowl to be reconstituted in hot water and served at dinner.

When I asked her what she liked to eat, she immediately answered "hot pot" with a broad grin. When I asked her for the recipe, she looked confused. Like Cheng Ayi, she cooked without thinking or using measurements. *"Yidian'er"*—just a little bit—was the best she could do.

To make the stock, she added water, green onions, oil, a little soy sauce, and some small, white cabbages—"Just tear them up," she said—in a pot. Then add mung bean noodles, potatoes, and fresh tofu. "You can add whatever you like, actually. You can put meat in, but I don't like meat much." As soon as the liquid boils, the dish is ready. "It's delicious," she smacked her lips in delight.

She also loved shredded potatoes stir-fried in a touch of peanut oil with fresh green chilies, a splash of vinegar, and salt. Red chilies, she firmly instructed, should be paired with shredded white radish. For carnivorous guests, she sometimes made a dish of her own creation—pork belly stewed in a pressure cooker and flavored with dark soy sauce, onions, ginger, and garlic.

When making dumplings, Mrs. Sun favored a cabbage filling with ginger, scallions, and garlic—the holy trinity of Chinese cooking, just like the *mirepoix* of chopped carrots, onions, and celery forms the basis of many traditional French dishes. Pepper, she said, was the one ingredient she didn't use. "I don't like it. If I don't like it, I don't add it to my food."

As the day settled into twilight, the drilling and hammering from the renovations stopped, and we could hear a patter of rain on the leaves. Mrs. Sun started prepping for dinner, beginning with the flatbread that she and her husband often ate. She opened the wooden chest to reveal a huge sack of flour, a scoop of which she poured into a metal bowl and added water at intervals, briskly stirring the mixture with a chopstick until it turned lumpy and then formed a giant ball of dough.

Swinging around to the sink, she checked to make sure the mushrooms were soaking properly before briskly peeling a pile of potatoes and shredding them on a plastic mandoline. I caught a whiff of their earthy and raw flavor. Next, she sliced green chilies into thin strips and cut tofu into uniform squares. Farmer Sun walked in with five grass-speckled eggs, which he cracked carefully into a bowl. My eyes had a greedy gleam as I spied the start of my omelet.

Mrs. Sun moved into another room to set up an old wooden board, a wooden dowel, a metal scoop of flour, and an electric *bing* cooker. She used a chopstick to move a portion of the sticky dough onto the board, which was sprinkled with flour, then kneaded and pressed it out into a thin circle, and added a few drops of oil before rolling it into a long sausage shape and curling it into a coil. After a few minutes, she rolled out the dough again and put a section of it into the *bing* cooker, which looked like a waffle-iron made of black plastic with a smooth interior. When she lifted the lid, the pancake was browned and steaming. She pulled it off with a wooden spatula and chopped it into quarters.

Meanwhile, Farmer Sun was working fast in the warm and fragrant kitchen. He had already fried the potatoes as well as a glistening mound of mushrooms and chilies. Emma and I silently watched him wield his metal ladle as he prepared the next dish— homemade tofu with a spicy sauce.

When he finished that, he picked up the bowl of beaten eggs to which he had added a pinch of salt, chopped scallions, and smashed garlic. He whisked the mixture using wooden chopsticks one more time before slowly pouring it into the hot wok filled with a few tablespoons of oil. Immediately the edges bubbled and frothed and puffed while the middle remained a pool of uncooked egg and green onions. He waited a couple of minutes, blinking at the pan, before using a slotted metal spatula to flip the omelet. Its cooked side was perfectly golden. I jumped up and down in anticipation, and he laughed at me.

They piled the food high on small white plates decorated with red flowers along the border, and laid them out on a little table atop the *kang* in the other room, where Mrs. Sun made the bread. There was a watery gruel made of a variety of beans, a can of beer, and a bottle of *baijiu*, sorghum liquor.

We dug in. Everything was lightly seasoned and fresh with textures—the meatiness of the mushrooms, the firmness of the tofu, the slight crunch of the shredded potatoes. And of course, the pillowy omelet, of which Mrs. Sun kept urging me to eat more.

With a couple of shots of *baijiu* in him, Farmer Sun talked freely, calling me *Xiao Hong*—Little Hong, a diminutive of my name in Chinese—to show me that we were friends. He talked about dropping out of high school one year before graduation because his family couldn't afford his books or fees.

Until a few years ago, it was a common story for many of China's rural citizens. While government-funded, free, compulsory education has been the country's goal for about a century, lack of funding—because of wars and social and economic problems—has kept it just out of reach. Children in the countryside have it especially hard because governments in poorer regions often lacked the necessary money. In 2005, Premier Wen Jiabao pledged that the central government would eliminate charges to all rural students for nine years of schooling—though in practice, cash-strapped officials still levied fees. "If I could've received a free education, I wouldn't have become a farmer," Sun said with a sad laugh.

He talked about the Great Leap Forward, Mao Zedong's brutal campaign that began in 1958 to propel the country into an industrial power by galvanizing farm and factory output through labor-intensive methods of industrialization and collectivization. The goal of overtaking Britain and America in the production of steel, grain, cotton, and other products in fifteen years was shortened yet further, leading to a frenzy of activity as peasants were forced to mobilize and local officials competed to have the most fruitful results. They wildly over-reported their harvests to Beijing—even though fields often went untended and rotted because people were focusing on producing iron and steel and working on massive building projects. What was thought to be surplus grain was sold abroad.

Chaos ensued as agricultural reserves were exhausted and the Great Famine took its terrible toll as the worst catastrophe in China's history. An estimated thirty-five to forty-five million peasants died from starvation and in crackdowns in which people were executed for not falling in line with the experiment or deprived of food because they were too weak or too inefficient—or simply disliked by someone with more power. Some people ate the dead of their own families to survive.

"Over here, no one starved to death," Sun said. "There were things in the mountains to help with the hunger."

"How many meals did you have a day?" I asked.

"It's not how many meals a day that counts but what you had for each meal. We ate leaves."

"We ate wild vegetables," Mrs. Sun added. "We had eight in the family at the time, including his mother and other relatives. But the eight of us couldn't cobble together more than three *wen*," an old form of currency.

Sun shushed her, saying I wouldn't understand, then continued. "There was a lot of claiming there was this much food when there wasn't. Central party members couldn't come down here to check on all the people. Some did, some didn't. There was exaggeration. Those below bluffed those on top. . . . In the end, the common people went hungry."

Mrs. Sun pointed at my barely touched portion of bean gruel. "Do you not like it?"

I didn't—but saying so would have been impolite given the conversation. "I'm just full."

"If you're not going to eat it, give it to me," Mrs. Sun said, reaching for the bowl.

"But it's already cold," I said, feeling even more awkward that she wanted to eat my leftovers.

"It's fine, it's fine," Farmer Sun said. He pondered a question I had posed earlier. "You asked me about the significance of the saying 'To the people, food is heaven' . . . China traditionally is an agricultural nation. It's not like Western nations that are industrialized. If farmers don't work the land, what would they eat? No matter what fate befalls me, so long as I have my land, I'll have food."

We offered to pay for dinner, but they refused, telling us to come back for a longer stay when the renovations were complete.

"We'll have rooms for you, and it will be even better than before," Farmer Sun said. "And we will cook you the omelet as many times as you want."

幡

Just under half of the country's 1.3 billion people call rural China home. It's where millions starved and perished during the Great Leap Forward and millions more are still struggling in spite of the central government's ongoing efforts to relieve the situation.

The drive first began in the 1980s in the form of poverty alleviation through tourism. The program focused on areas where hundreds of millions of farmers were living far below the international threshold for poverty of around a dollar a day. China's rapid modernization had transformed cities but bypassed rural residents almost entirely.

In 1985, the country's poverty line stood at an annual per capita income of about 200 yuan or $68 at the time. The limit increased periodically, and the number of people living below that line appeared to fall. The government touted the change as the dramatic result of years of programs and policies centered on regional development, subsidies, improving infrastructure, and tax reforms—including the abolition of the 2,600-year-old agricultural tax. But experts from the World Bank and Chinese think tanks urged the government to raise the threshold to include more poor rural residents.

China's definition of poverty has caused controversy because some experts say it has been kept artificially low to magnify the leadership's achievements in alleviating the problem. It has also touched a nerve with critics of China's human rights record who say that those in power insist that providing basic necessities like food and shelter are the foundation for the most fundamental of rights and trump everything else.

At the end of 2011, the government raised the poverty line to 2,300 yuan a year, still about a dollar a day, but that move represented an 80 percent increase from 2010 for a total of 128 million rural residents who were officially poor and qualified for assistance. The new standard, however, still sat lower than the $1.25 set by the United Nations and World Bank, but it brought China closer to international norms and better reflected the country's higher standards of living overall.

By comparison, about 15 percent of Americans were considered poor in 2010, according to Census Bureau standards of $61 a day in income for a family of four, or $15.25 per person.

For centuries, the unequal distribution of land and the resulting destitution has acted as a main cause of China's political and social instability. History has begun to repeat itself as unhappy peasants mobilize over corruption and tough living conditions. Economic reforms introduced in 1978 propelled China into white-hot growth in its cities but also widened the urban-rural gap in all areas of life. Those living in the countryside lag not only in income—making less than a third of what their counterparts in cities earn—but are also significantly less educated and less healthy, and they die younger.

At the center of their existence is the earth that they till and harvest to squeeze out a living. Only 15 percent of the country's land is arable. Of that, a little over 1 percent supports permanent crops. Farmers toil daily on small plots, bent under sun and rain as they tend to paddy, wheat, corn, and potatoes. Nature, compounded by despoliation, throws them annual floods and droughts, while human threats come in the form of land grabs by local cadres and outside contractors who want to turn fields into moneymaking developments.

The land issue was fundamental to the Communist revolutionaries spearheaded by Mao Zedong, the son of a prosperous farmer, who nonetheless won the fervent support of peasants through his theories on agrarian Marxism. The Communists, guided by the Agrarian Reform Law of 1950, gave land back to farmers who had suffered through onerous conditions under a feudal system run by warlords. Millions of acres were confiscated from the rich and redistributed to the poor, but the campaign was a bloody one in which people branded as landlords and rich peasants were executed or killed in state-sanctioned violence.

With full private ownership and the security to invest, the results were impressive: Grain production increased by 70 percent between 1949 and 1956, and average farm income rose by 85 percent.

Then Mao, inspired by Marxist goals of social equality—the Soviet model led by Stalin—and very likely, the desire for control over the countryside to exact agricultural surplus to support modern industrialization programs, began pushing in earnest his initial leanings toward collective farming. Collectivization began on a small-scale family level but broadened in scope rapidly—surpassing even Mao's expectations—until nearly all farms belonged to giant communes by 1958.

A frenzy of excess and waste, violence and starvation that characterized the Great Leap Forward and the subsequent famine fell over the country in the next four years. In 1962, the leadership backpedaled, moderating rural policies and scaling down the sizes of the massive communes back to village-level collectives. Production eventually picked up again—but nowhere near the heights of 1956.

In 1978, the Party introduced the household responsibility system under which land was contracted to individual households, giving them the right to use and develop the plots as long as they met government produce quotas. It led to the eradication of collective farms and was credited as the key to China's economic reform as the concept of a "contract" spread to areas outside of agriculture.

Researchers from Landesa, a Seattle-based organization that has worked with the Chinese government on land reform issues since 1987, found that farmers were also eating much better as a result.

"Now, they have solid rice, not gruel, and as many bowls as they want, three times a day. They eat meat once or twice a week or even more; vegetables all the time," said Roy Prosterman, founder of the Rural Development Institute, which became Landesa.

But there was an unforeseen drawback: the lack of land security because local cadres were allowed to "readjust" the distribution of the land according to population change to maintain absolute equality under the system. While farmers were doing their best to ensure successful harvests annually, they resisted making long-term improvements to their infrastructure or methods. After all, they didn't own their own land. For example, if in a handful of years the population of a village increased from 200 to 250, the cadre would have to reconfigure the amount of land for which each family was responsible, meaning they got less. Absolute equality also had the effect of absolute insecurity. Peasants never knew when readjustments would take place.

When the central government realized that farmers had frozen investment, officials slowly began working on a solution. In 1998, as part of a new land management law, farmers universally received thirty-year rights on the land and had provisions that strictly limited readjustments. The move marked a real beginning of the modern era of land reform in Communist China.

Today, land rights are enshrined in laws that also deal in detail with documentation, transactions, and violations. Farmers can contract their land rights to another as long as the transaction is voluntary and consensual.

At the same time, two new sources of instability have coalesced, putting the leadership's drive for social harmony in a potentially precarious position. The first is the problem of land grabs by local officials, which have given rise to grievances, lawsuits, and mass incidents—the Chinese term for protests or demonstrations—over inadequate compensation and unsatisfactory resettlement conditions.

According to a 2010 survey by Landesa of about 1,500 villages, about 37 percent had experienced the problem. In almost a third of the cases, the farmers were not notified in advance and more than half had not been consulted on compensation rates. Of the fraction that decided to pursue redress, fewer than one in five received anything for their efforts.

The other problem centers on the issue of land sales to developers, companies, or powerful individuals with the help of corrupt local officials. While farmers have the right to lease their land, the law mandates that such contractual arrangements be voluntary and consensual. In reality, that's not always the case. Sometimes farmers are pressured or coerced into the deals. In a third of surveyed cases, at least some of the land was used subsequently in a commercial project rather than agriculture, which is illegal.

Seething anger against official corruption has regularly erupted in violent episodes. One of the most serious backlashes exploded at the end of 2011 in Wukan, a fishing village of about thirteen thousand in Guangdong province, where land seizures by the government triggered an unusually sustained revolt by residents. Officials sold farmland to developers either without locals' consent or adequate compensation. The practice has been going on for years in Wukan but finally became unbearable because of the rising cost of living and the impossibility of making ends meet through fishing alone.

Fed up and furious, hundreds went on a rampage that September, smashing buildings, overturning cars, and clashing with police. They ran the longtime Wukan Communist Party secretary out of a government office building.

In the aftermath, the mayor promised to investigate the allegations of illegal land sales, and villagers were allowed to choose a dozen representatives for negotiations. Thousands still gathered almost every day to shout slogans for the return of their land as they pumped their fists in the air, but the situation didn't escalate.

The uneasy peace broke down when a group of men in vehicles without license plates entered the village and snatched away five of the people's representatives. When hundreds of armed police returned a day later, the villagers were ready. They had blocked the roads with fallen trees and armed themselves with sticks, clubs, hoes, and other farm tools. Officers fired water cannons and tear gas but couldn't break the cordon of people. The police retreated to set up blockades to trap villagers and prevent food supplies from entering the town.

Then Wukan residents heard that butcher Xue Jinbo, one of their abducted representatives, had died in police custody. The official version was that he had suffered a heart attack. But family members who saw his body said it was covered with cuts, bruises, caked blood, and open wounds consistent with a vicious beating. Authorities refused to release his body.

The standoff ended after provincial officials and a village representative finally agreed to hold talks almost two weeks later. The officials agreed to the demands of the villagers, including freeing the detained men, investigating Xue's death, and returning his body. The land sale issue remained unresolved.

❀

I had reported on similar unrest in 2005 in another village nearby. In that case, violence followed inadequate compensation for farmland used in the construction of a wind power plant. A furious protest by farmers armed with knives, spears, and explosives ended in a skirmish with armed police and reports of between three and twenty villagers fatally shot as security forces opened fire on the crowd. It was the deadliest use of force by authorities since the crackdown on demonstrators around Tiananmen Square in 1989.

Toting guns and shields, hundreds of riot police sealed off Dongzhou village. Our driver said he knew where the checkpoints were and had heard of a way around them, via small side roads. It worked.

We cruised slowly through town on dusty roads past red and white propaganda banners that read OBEYING THE LAW IS EVERY CITIZEN'S DUTY AND RESPONSIBILITY and STRIKE AT LAW-BREAKERS, MAINTAIN SOCIAL STABILITY. A cluster of people was kneeling on the sidewalk, wailing and crying, a couple with white fabric tied around their heads in a sign of mourning. Two appeared to have passed out with grief.

At a distance stood a roadblock consisting of a police truck and van. All the residents with whom I spoke were deeply upset. Many didn't want to be identified for fear of retribution. The situation there remained unresolved as well. Two years later, clashes and arrests still occurred periodically.

❀

The countryside seemed familiar no matter where I was. There was always a span of well-tended crops, small wood-and-brick or concrete homes with bare-bones furnishings, dusty roads running through townships that, no matter how small, always had room for an Internet cafe. There were pigs, chickens, ducks, or cows around homesteads, which often smelled of animal dung, old cooking oil, or burning coal.

Villagers were often very young or very old because those in between were trying to make a living in towns or cities and sending money home to support their families. If they stayed behind, they farmed, walking slowly as if bent under an invisible weight, with sun-toasted skin and teeth yellow or missing from neglect.

They were cautious at first; I was, after all a stranger from Beijing and worked for an American company with a strange name. Then they warmed up, welcoming me with a cup of tea or hot water, treating me like a long-lost relative when I explained that I was from Singapore and that my ancestors had come from the mainland.

It was also just as normal for villagers to surround me seconds after I identified myself as a reporter, clamoring for my attention. Very few could speak Mandarin, so they shouted their grievances in their local dialect. If I said I didn't understand, they yelled louder, eager to make their point. Their claims were often confusing, filled with references and complaints of regulations that only someone living there would understand.

Their attitude mixed aggression, frustration, and submission. *Meibanfa* over and over again. Nothing can be done. In these instances, the phrase embodied hopelessness and fatalism rather than stoicism. It was the antithesis of the English saying "Where there's a will, there's a way."

For a while I wondered why there wasn't more of a fight, but over time I began to understand their numbing sense of futility. Even if unhappiness was escalating and convulsing the countryside, uprisings as in Dongzhou and Wukan were rare. Even more unusual were fair and just resolutions.

There are many Chinese sayings tailor-made for what rural residents face. *Wunengweili* describes a sense of powerlessness and helplessness, while *shushouwuce* is to be at your wits' end. The David-and-Goliath battle against hardship and corruption is captured in *pifuhandashu*, ants trying to topple a tree, and *tangbidangche*, literally a praying mantis's arm stopping a running horse-drawn carriage.

But I like to think of the struggle in terms of *yugongyishan*, a fable about perseverance in which an old man is determined—many say foolishly—to move two mountains blocking the path to his house. Waving aside his wife's doubts and the difficulties of working without tools, the old man begins the task with the help of his children and grandchildren, dumping baskets of stones and earth into the sea. One day a wise man chances upon the laboring family and asks how the old man expected to complete the task in his waning years.

His reply went something like: "I may be old and will soon die. But I have children, and when they die I have my grandchildren. As my family grows bigger, the mountains will get smaller. Our determination will make it possible."

They worked through seasons and years with the gods watching from the heavens. The gods were so moved by the old man's resolve that they sent two immortals to the earth to take the mountains away.

The story made me wonder what would happen to the mountainous burdens of China's peasants as they chipped away at them. I could only hope that someday, somehow, those too would disappear.

Parade of Feasts
in the Hermit Kingdom

I gained weight in a country where famine has killed hundreds of thousands and left countless more ravenous, foraging for grass, acorns, bracken—anything remotely edible.

It wasn't much—a pound at most—but enough for me to feel pangs of guilt that I had consumed more than my fair share.

A Russian professor based in South Korea helped broker the five-day trip to the North during the 2005 celebrations for the six-tieth anniversary of the founding of the ruling Korean Workers' Party. Organizers told my international group of academics and journalists to say that we were affiliated with an Australian orga-nization: all part of the rigmarole of making travel arrangements to a notoriously unpredictable regime.

In North Korea, with active nuclear and missile programs, one of the most brutal regimes on earth rules an impoverished country of twenty-five million. The stories I had written from China offered a bleak reflection: unsuccessful six-nation efforts to end Pyongyang's nuclear ambitions, dire U.N. reports on recurring food crises, and, saddest of all, a series of desperate attempts by North Koreans fleeing starvation and repression to seek asylum in embassies, schools, and other foreign offices in Beijing or Shanghai.

Short, carefully scripted jaunts to the so-called Hermit Kingdom, the world's only Communist monarchy, only pro-vided a tiny surface to scratch. Even so the shiny visa in my passport gave me a shot at going beyond—even by just a hair—militant state media propaganda and the infamous North Korean shroud of secrecy. I would get to see for myself the mass-produced reverence for the North's late founder "Great Leader"

189

A couple in Pyongyang poses in front of the Kimilsungia and Kimjongilia hybrid orchids and a portrait of Great Leader and Dear Leader, after which the flowers were named. Their devotion to the Kims' cult of personality echoed throughout the North Korean capital, which I visited in 2005. We sat through a procession of feasts that gave us pangs of guilt in a country where famine has killed hundreds of thousands and left countless more ravenous.

Kim Il Sung and his son, "Dear Leader" Kim Jong Il, the latter's birth, according to official myth, heralded by a bright star over a sacred mountain and a double rainbow. I would actually get to interact with North Koreans instead of merely identifying them from afar by their mandatory Kim Il Sung lapel pins. It was unlikely that I would meet the rotund, bouffant-haired, platform heel–wearing younger Kim, who succeeded his father in 1994, but just being in Pyongyang, a showpiece to impress foreign visitors, brought me closer than most people ever got in a lifetime.

Aid workers, diplomats, businessmen, and also defectors—very few of whom speak on the record for fear of their lives or the lives of people who remain behind—provide the most revealing details, patched together, about the isolated state. Accounts have emerged of gastronomic excesses by the reclusive Kim that seemed especially odious given the suffering of his people.

In a memoir published in 2003 under the pen-name Kenji Fujimoto, a Japanese man, one of Dear Leader's former personal chefs, says that Kim has an exceptionally discriminating palate and could tell if a dish had been prepared with just a touch more of one ingredient than the day before. Kim's kitchen staff inspected each grain of rice before cooking it and removed all defective ones. Piles of money acquired massive quantities of quality foods procured, all expenses paid, by Fujimoto from around the world. They included pork from Denmark, caviar from Iran, and tuna and squid from Japan. Many purchases were made on a whim, when Kim heard that something was delicious or if he was curious to try a new dish. Shark fin and dog regularly appeared on the menu.

The Japanese chef described Kim as an avid karaoke singer, equestrian, and jet skier who hated to lose. He had a penchant for menthol cigarettes and expensive liquor, and an entourage of young women danced and performed for him, naked on at least one occasion. Fujimoto said he left North Korea under the pretext of buying sea urchins for a dish that Kim wanted to try.

Konstantin Pulikovsky, a Russian emissary who traveled by train across Russia with Kim in 2001, describes hours-long banquets, a daily ration of live lobsters eaten with silver chopsticks, and copious amounts of French wine imported from Paris. Three years later, Italian chef Ermanno Furlanis recounted how he was flown to North Korea in 1997—when 80,000 children were in immediate danger of dying of starvation or disease—to give lessons to three army officers on how to make pizza. They took copious notes and even asked how far apart to place olives on each pie. Furlanis was later taken to cook aboard a luxury liner where, he says, Kim made an appearance, his presence alone whipping the entire kitchen into a frenzy. One chef said he felt as if he had seen God.

Only a few of those details were rattling around in my head on the day we boarded the Russian-made red, white, and blue Air Koryo plane. Its interior showcased a time warp of earth tones and open baggage racks hearkening from the '60s or '70s. But the two-hour flight was pleasantly bright, clean, and airy, with a relentless soundtrack of patriotic music. Immaculately made-up flight attendants, hair drawn back in neat chignons, cheerily offered beverages from a cart. Our meal, served in two containers stacked one on top of the other, had hearty portions of meat, both fried and smoked, pickles, rice, and dessert, all compartmentalized bento box–style. The parade of feasts was just beginning.

It was a crisp and sunny autumn afternoon, the unpolluted air so unlike Beijing's choking smog. When we landed, we grudgingly surrendered our voice recorders and cellphones, a mandatory requirement for all visitors. While it was disconcerting to part with the tools of my trade, at least we could keep our notebooks and cameras. Our government handlers, two fresh-faced girls barely in their twenties and Mr. Choe Jong Hun, an officer from the Cultural Exchange Department, greeted us with wide smiles.

After quick introductions and awkward small talk, we boarded a rickety old metal bus, immediately sticking our heads and camera hands out the windows, eager to record everything the vehicle passed. Our minders firmly but politely told us to stop. Unauthorized photos were not allowed. Distracted by fields of freshly harvested hay, kids swimming in a river, and people on bicycles, we only half-listened to Mr. Choe's welcome speech.

The capital felt like a Soviet-era throwback, with run-down, boxy apartment blocks and looming official buildings and monuments. Flags and colorful propaganda posters with bold exclamatory slogans punctuated the drabness of the scenery. LONG LIVE THE NORTH KOREAN PEOPLE! LET US FOLLOW THE REVOLUTIONARY IDEAS OF THE GREAT LEADER! A third, depicting a giant fist crushing an American soldier, needed no translation.

Citizens, dressed mostly in simple Western-style clothing, looked relatively healthy and well fed. Given three days off for the holiday, many people were strolling on sidewalks, lounging in parks eating ice cream, or chatting in groups. Then again, only the country's elite lived in Pyongyang, which included senior officials from the Workers' Party, the military, and the government. Despite a series of traffic lights, few cars plied the roads, and life moved at an idyllic pace, devoid of congested traffic and the bustle of other Asian capitals. We were told, though, that power shortages were common, leaving much of the city dark at night.

In 2002, Kim's regime announced tentative economic reforms, but the results barely registered three years later. Visitors had reported seeing a restaurant styled after a Western fast-food joint, with fixed plastic seating and hamburger meals. Others spotted a pizza parlor and a cafe with an espresso machine. On "Restaurant Street," people tucking in and singing karaoke crowded a neon-bathed row of eateries.

A growing number of roadside vendors were engaging in open trade, which a few years before wasn't tolerated. The snacks they sold included a variety of homemade morsels like fried dough filled with red bean paste, battered green vegetables, and roasted sweet potatoes, the delicious perfume of which filled the city's air. Under the watchful eyes of my minders, it was impossible for me to sample—or even see—the offerings myself, though I did spy some ice cream sellers and happy customers licking what looked like pearly white sorbet on a Popsicle stick. The same minders did, however, treat us to a succession of feasts designed to show outsiders (falsely) that there's plenty to go around.

The traditional cornerstone of Korean cuisine is rice, accompanied by several dishes of vegetables and meat or seafood seasoned with distinctive and complex flavors that include *doenjang* (fermented bean paste), *gochujang* (fermented chili paste), and sesame oil. Taste, ingredients, and presentation differ, depending on where a dish originated, although the general rule is that offerings from the south are saltier and spicier.

Before this trip, my knowledge of Korean food mostly consisted of dishes widely found in South Korea, like *bulgogi*, thin-sliced beef marinated in soy sauce, sugar, garlic, green onions, and sesame oil, then grilled on an open flame; and *dolsot bibimbap*, a rice dish traditionally topped with a bright array of vegetables, meat, and a raw egg that cooks in the heat of the hot stone bowl in which it's served. The best part is the crisp, brown crust that forms at the bottom.

In Pyongyang, we experienced a very different cuisine showcasing a variety of meats, a luxury unimaginable to the majority of the country's citizens. We ate our way through steaming platters of cumin-spiced grilled goat, fried chicken drumsticks, crunchy breaded pork cutlets, and mini meatballs with a savory glaze. My first dinner was a peppery slab of pounded beef garnished with a small sprig of parsley, thick cut potatoes, cabbage slaw, and slabs of soft white bread—an awkward stab at Western food—reminiscent of the 1950s. Breakfast was an omelet decorated with a delicate flower made from carrot shavings. Accompaniments included New Zealand butter and Swiss jam.

Each meal provided a battleground for our conscience. On one hand, overwhelmed, we were grateful for the huge quantity and variety we received, but guilt wracked us whenever we left something uneaten on our plates. After all, we'd read and written so many stories about malnourished North Koreans that the abundance and waste felt downright criminal.

Outside the capital, families ate insubstantial and infrequent meals cobbled together from scavenged scraps: mountain greens boiled with salt, grains of corn, painstakingly split, and mixed with potatoes to make porridge, or a watery stew of grass cooked with a handful of cornmeal. When cornmeal ran out, there was just grass. Sometimes, the gruel was so thin and there was so little of it, that people were basically drinking warm water rather than swallowing solid food. Foraged odds-and-ends—mushrooms, the stalks and roots of random plants—sometimes proved poisonous, causing swelling, diarrhea, and vomiting. Children subsisted on water, not milk.

During the 1990s, hundreds of thousands of people died of starvation—some say as many as two million—in a famine known as the Arduous March that resulted from a combination of the loss of Soviet subsidies, cataclysmic flooding, and the collapse of the agricultural sector and the Public Distribution System, a state-run mechanism established to deliver staples to the major- ity of the North.

State media trumpeted the benefits of having two meals daily instead of three and gave citizens recipes for boiling grasses, but the situation eventually grew so severe that people went for days without food and had to eat pig swill or bark stripped from pine trees and boiled with corn powder—if they were lucky. Potato peels and cabbage roots became luxury foods. One survivor detailed how she ground up an entire ear of corn and made por- ridge from it to celebrate her eldest daughter's birthday. Other children in the family got half a bowl each while the birthday girl got a whole one.

With that in mind, I forced myself to finish every morsel on my plate. But the procession of dishes served to us never ended: whole fish bathed in sweet-and-sour sauce, squid sizzling on hot plates, and ginseng root with caramel coating, all artfully presented. We had several variations of a fragrant pancake made up of shredded cabbage and bits of seafood crisped in a pan. Slick buckwheat noodles in cold broth decorated with thin slices of boiled beef, egg, julienned vegetables, and Asian pear—Pyongyang's signature dish, called *naengmyeon*—ended each meal.

"It is the most delicious national folk dish," said Yon Ok Ju, my twenty-year-old handler. It was clear from the beginning that she, born into the North's elite class, existed in an alternate reality where favorite treats like *yakgwa* (honey cookies) and *mandu* (dumplings) easily and completely sated her hunger. She grinned as she spoke of her father's shared love for dumplings, an obsession her mother fed every day in steaming bowls of soup.

Like our other twenty-year-old minder, Paek Su Ryon, Yon, was gracious, engaging, and occasionally still a gawkish teen. The pair often sat together speaking softly in Korean but switched to English whenever we were around. While somber utilitarian fashions dominated the capital, they brightened their black skirt suits in their own way. Yon wore a green-and-navy striped sweater one day, while the more girlish Paek always held back her hair with a powder-blue barrette, wore a beige trench coat, and carried a pink plastic purse. She checked her compact mirror often and worried about being overweight.

"I'm 164 centimeters [5'4"] and should be under fifty kilos [110 pounds]," Paek confided one day after barely touching her lunch. Her parents were pressuring her to be thinner. "I've tried all sorts of diets, but nothing has worked."

A third-year student at the Pyongyang University of Foreign Studies, Paek was studying English, spoke it fluently, and was assigned, along with Yon, to translate for the group at the official stops. Both skillfully spouted the party line and negotiated the direct, sometimes sensitive questions we asked. Because they were our only access to North Koreans who spoke our language, we hounded them constantly. Sitting next to them at a meal gave us a chance to pin them down for a length of time and observe how they acted in everyday situations. On the bus, one person would ask them about their lives, and the pack of us would swoop in, pens poised over notebooks.

Paek had read *Jane Eyre* and *Romeo and Juliet* ("It's a love story, a sad story") and professed a liking for Harry Potter, but her favorite book was a novel by Kang Kyong Ae, the title of which she translated as *The Problem of Human Beings*. She could play the theme song from James Cameron's *Titanic* on the piano, but she also liked the Pochonbo Electronic Ensemble, North Korea's version of a pop music group named after a Japanese-occupied town that Kim Il Sung and his guerrilla troops raided in 1937.

The young women revealed other clues to their privileged upbringings when they described a wholesome, old-fashioned existence for their circle of young friends more akin to America in the '50s: school, homework at the library, time with family, bowling, ice-skating, tennis, and ping-pong.

"I like Pyongyang," Yon said. "I wouldn't want to live anywhere else."

In spring and fall, they spent up to a month helping to plant corn and beans and harvesting in the countryside. They made no mention of the plight of the masses—it was never clear how much they knew of the country's situation—but spoke of long days and how they wielded sickles in the fields.

"I like it a lot," Yon said. "It's good exercise."

Her family usually gathered around assortments of sweets and savories during holidays, when even average North Koreans get a rare chance to indulge. Defectors have described tables piled high with a variety of rice cakes, boiled pork, rice steeped in broth, and steamed pollock skin stuffed with ground fish and tofu.

On Kim Jong Il's birthday one year, one of Pyongyang's most famous restaurants put snapping turtle on its menu in honor of the occasion. The creations included turtle soup; raw dishes made of turtle heart, liver, and roe; and turtle porridge. The Korean Central News Agency said that Dear Leader himself provided "meticulous instructions" on how to breed and cook turtles, which Asians consider a symbol of longevity and a nutritious delicacy.

Another key holiday is April 15, Kim Il Sung's birthday, when defectors in Seoul sometimes recreate special dishes from their hometowns, unfamiliar treats to the southern palate. They include ostrich egg casserole, served and cooked in the shell and topped with the raw yolk, and steamed seven-spice chicken, stuffed with pine nuts, cinnamon, chestnuts, ginger, ginkgo nuts, jujubes, and roots. Spring herbs and an iced vinegar sauce infuse a northern version of kimchee.

The pungent signature dish in Korean cuisine, kimchee has over a hundred varieties, although its best-known incarnation consists of spicy, fermented Napa cabbage. Yon's family has their own special recipe, but she neatly dodged when asked to reveal how theirs is unique.

"Every recipe is different," she said, smiling, ever the diplomat.

❈

North Korea is in a war without end with the South. In 1950, the North invaded its neighbor to try to reunify the nation, a liberated Japanese colony cleft in two by America and the Soviet Union after World War II. At first, the North almost ran a weak joint South Korean–US force off the peninsula, but American reinforcements poured in, driving the northerners back. American air raids decimated North Korean cities and villages. Then Communist troops from China, repaying their debt to North Korea for help during the Chinese civil war, pushed the fighting back to the middle of the peninsula, where, in a grim echo of World War I, soldiers fought over bits of ground for two years.

Also like World War I, the losses were tremendous. Political executions eliminated tens of thousands of Koreans on both sides. The official US death toll for those killed in battle stands at 33,686. By a United Nations estimate, almost a million Chinese troops perished. Beijing gives a much lower number. Fighting devastated infrastructure on a massive scale, wiping out homes, factories, schools, railroads, ports, bridges, and dams. Some ten million South Koreans today are separated from family in the North, enduring invisible psychological scars. The war halted in a cease-fire—not a peace treaty—in 1953 that remains in tenuous effect to this day.

After the devastation, the two Koreas rebuilt their econo- mies, with the North emerging as an authoritarian one-party state obsessed with the ideology of *juche*, self-reliance. The South embraced capitalism and a civilian democracy. Today, the fraught DMZ—a 150-mile-long, 2.5-mile-wide strip of land on the 38th Parallel strewn with mines and laced with barbed wire—sepa- rates the two nations. Almost two million troops face each other on ready alert for resumed war, some twenty-seven thousand of them from the US military, making it one of the most heavily guarded areas in the world.

Everyone was excited about the scheduled trip to the DMZ. It was immediately apparent how events have played out for both sides since the armistice. From our vantage point off a viewing balcony on the North side, we saw a gargantuan, modern glass- and-tile building mounted with security cameras and a tradi- tional pagoda off one side representing the South's outpost. About ten soldiers in smart, forest green uniforms and white hel- mets congregated and milled, watching us watch them. One even looked like he was snapping photos.

On our side stood an austere, Soviet-style building where tourists gawked and also took pictures. The North Korean sol- diers looked a little shabbier, their olive-green uniforms a touch too big on their slight frames. Over the years, the military has had to lower its height requirements for new troops to just under five feet because the country's children were so malnourished they were growing up stunted.

In between the two sides sat three squat, light blue build- ings that looked like contractor shacks on a construction site:

the venues for joint meetings and administrative duties. They lay squarely on the military demarcation line—the actual boundary that separates the two territories. Pebbled concrete paved the South's side; the North's had a stretch of fine yellow sand.

In the years since the armistice, Pyongyang has threatened the South with destruction, though it has never followed through with an all-out military assault. It has, however, earned a reputation as a rogue state through a number of brash acts, from the 1968 seizure of the US Navy spy ship *Pueblo*, to the 2010 sinking of a South Korean warship that killed forty-six sailors, to its ongoing missile and atomic tests. In the deadliest attack, a bomb smuggled aboard a Korean Air flight exploded over the Andaman Sea in 1987, killing all 115 people on board. A North Korean agent captured in connection with the plot said that Kim Jong Il had masterminded it. Pyongyang has never admitted to the attacks, nor has Seoul retaliated, mindful of the price of another war on the Korean peninsula.

Often photographed in giant sunglasses and olive or khaki '70s-style leisure suits, Kim Jong Il was believed to have suffered a stroke in 2008. To bolster his physical well-being, Kim reportedly spent hundreds of thousands of dollars on rare and sometimes-outlawed remedies from Beijing, such as rhino's horn, musk pods from the male musk deer, and the bile of bear gall bladder, all prized for treating strokes. Folk medicine—widely used across Asia, sometimes in conjunction with Western treatments—remains popular in North Korea, particularly since the nation's medical system collapsed in the mid-1990s.

More sobering assessments by diplomats and world leaders who met Dear Leader temper the extreme, almost clownish, stories about him. Former secretary of state Madeleine Albright said in a 2003 interview on PBS's *Frontline* that he was "not delusional." He was someone "who is isolated, but not uninformed, who has operated in his own system where he is deified and, at the same time, wants to be in the outside world where nobody will pay any attention to him."

Kim Jong Il died of a heart attack on December 17, 2011, marking the end of an era for North Korea, which has known only Kim and his father as leaders. The North now falls under the leadership of Kim Jong Il's son, Kim Jong Un, a stocky twenty-something who bears an eerie resemblance to his grandfather. Like his father, he also appears to enjoy food, having spent hours at one of Pyongyang's showcase shops that sells kielbasa, frozen quail, and whale meat. The world knows very little else about him or in which direction he will take Pyongyang.

Unlike Kim Jong Il, groomed for two decades to lead, Kim Jong Un emerged as the anointed successor only in 2010 after he became a four-star general and took up an appointment as vice chairman of the Central Military Commission of the Workers' Party. The transition was smooth and faster than anticipated. Some worried that Kim Jong Il's sudden death would trigger instability and a power struggle. Beijing in particular feared that chaos, along with a flood of refugees from a collapsed North Korea, could spill across the two nations' shared border.

North Koreans have remained mostly ignorant of the world beyond that border. Only the elite have cellphones and Internet access beyond an internal network, though films and videos smuggled from China are slowly conveying a trickle of information. Every word printed or aired is weighed for ideological purity; shortwave foreign radio broadcasts are banned, and there is only one official source of television news. Until a few years ago, dispatches from the Korean Central News Agency still railed against American hegemony IN ALL CAPS. I loved reading those reports.

One of the most stunning examples of the tireless propaganda machine is the massive dance and gymnastic performance known as the Arirang Festival, which we watched on our first night. Named after a traditional Korean love song, the show typically features tens of thousands of gymnasts, who have endured unrelenting training from a very young age, in synchronized maneuvers and elaborate, giant mosaics formed by children turning pieces of colored paper in perfect unison. The performances focus on themes of self-reliance, social development, and the revolutionary exploits of Kim Il Sung. On our way to the May Day stadium, many parts of the normally dark Pyongyang were lit up for the holiday.

When we arrived, the excitement around us was palpable. As soon we stepped off the bus, we were hit with the glare of flood-lights and the distant roar of children practicing their songs. Spectators pushed past us, clutching plastic bags of snacks as they chatted to each other. It reminded me of the crackle of antici-pation before a massive rock concert or Baptist prayer meeting. Packed, the arena rippled with rumors that Kim was in atten-dance. We stretched our necks and scanned the crowds, but we never spotted him. The show was nothing short of a rousing spectacle, filled with bombastic music, fluid choreography, and symbolism I barely grasped.

The most moving scene, however, came near the end, when the performers illustrated the division between the north and the south with a border separated by barbed wire. The written characters for "National unification is the dying instruction of Kim Il Sung" and "Let us open the door of reunification with our hands" appeared on the giant mosaic in the background. A group of South Koreans sitting near us spontaneously stood up and erupted into fervent applause and flag-waving, some of them overwhelmed and weeping. It was a reminder of the pain of sepa-ration ordinary Koreans carry in their hearts.

Despite rattling against it, foreign aid has offered a lifeline to most North Koreans since the government disclosed in the mid-1990s the catastrophic collapse of its state-run farms, finally admitting that its people were starving. Moves toward economic reforms since then have proved largely underwhelming, includ-ing attempts at market liberalization in 2002 and sweeping cur-rency reforms that effectively wiped out personal savings and reportedly triggered rare unrest.

Famine remains a chronic problem aggravated by annual floods. Some horrific reports cite cannibalism as one means to stave off starvation. Even relatively well-fed military leaders in a state built around a "military-first" policy reportedly have been going hungry in recent years. Citing Kim Il Sung's ideology of self-reliance, the regime regularly waffles on accepting food aid from organizations like the World Food Program, which provides nutrition, like fortified biscuits and cereal milk blends, to vulnerable populations like the elderly and lactating mothers. International sanctions tightened in the wake of Pyongyang's recent and ongoing atomic tests have strained food supplies even further.

Its last major ally, neighboring China represents the biggest provider of aid and diplomatic support. Beijing's position, however, delicately see-saws between old loyalties to the North and its desire to be seen as a legitimate world power that has influence over global issues—like Pyongyang's nuclear disarmament. For the Chinese tourists whom I encountered, politics didn't play much into their desire to visit North Korea so much as a sense of curiosity and kinship did. After all, China had suffered widespread famine and millions of deaths that resulted from Mao's Great Leap Forward.

"Our countries have similar points, and we have some differences," said Sunny Wu, a Chinese businessman who had visited Pyongyang twice. "China is opening up, progressing. . . . North Korea is taking the path China took twenty years ago. What they are going through now—their economic, social, political problems—we understand because we've been through them."

Our tour group stopped briefly at the Yanggakdo, a hotel on its own small island, favored by the Chinese. A restaurant revolved at its top, but we never made it up there, spending time instead in the basement, where the nearly empty Casino Pyongyang—brainchild of Macau billionaire Stanley Ho—offered a few subdued craps among mahjong tables. I walked around once before succumbing to blackjack, my weakness, and promptly losing 100 yuan, about $13 at the time.

At my table sat a man named Ma smoking and drinking with a group of friends. "We're gambling here because in China it's illegal. My impressions of this place are bad. They are controlled to death here. I've been here twice, and I will not come back." After a drag of his cigarette, he had second thoughts and hedged his bets, though. "Change will come slowly to this country. I may come back depending on how it turns out."

The hotel's Chinese and Korean restaurants sat empty, as silent as tombs.

On our last night in town, we went to a large, drafty banquet hall reserved just for us. A photo shows Han and me smiling at a table covered with beer bottles and plates of deep-fried food—chicken wings, calamari—and beef with potatoes. That evening, our head handler, Mr. Choe, red-faced from alcohol and relieved that the ordeal of chaperoning us was coming to an end, turned on the room's karaoke machine and crooned a few Korean ballads. We cheered him on, delighted to see him let his guard down.

At the airport the next day, I asked Mr. Choe about North Korea's food security.

"During the Arduous March, people ate grass from mountains. But now, we have enough food. Not completely, but enough that we are no longer starving. We have entered a prosperous march."

When I asked him how hard life was during the Arduous March, he didn't answer at first. He said, after a thoughtful delay: "I cannot express it in words. Please use your imagination."

7

Poisoned Heaven and Legacy Garden

I once offered to cut off my arm in exchange for a tour of an illegal noodle-making operation.

I reached this peak of desperation in 2007 while on assignment in the southern port of Xiamen trying to capture the clandestine nature of China's countless unregulated manufacturers—many of them out to make a quick buck regardless of public health—who lay at the heart of recurring problems with food and drug safety. Regular mass poisonings or horror stories of money-saving measures to manufacture edible products or medications reminded the world that counterfeit goods can extend beyond pirated DVDs and designer knockoffs.

Despite continued crackdowns, the nation had many tiny mom-and-pop operations struggling to find a foothold in a long, ill-defined, often anonymous chain of suppliers trying to turn quick profits. Overall, the risk of getting caught was small, but the payoff was potentially big. Most of them sold to consumers within the immediate vicinity, but some made components of products that ended up in much bigger markets, including overseas.

It was blisteringly hot. Han and I had been walking and driving for two days around villages on the edges of Xiamen, a hilly mix of banana and coconut trees and chimney stacks of cement and car factories. A jumble of metal workshops, car showrooms, and vegetable fields lined the muddy or dusty roads. I needed a lead, a way to get into the story of the challenges of regulating food production in China.

We knew illegal operations existed, but because they were unlicensed they would be next to impossible to uncover on our own. Everyone whom we approached said they had seen those kinds of setups or had heard of them, but no one would or could give us usable information on how to find one, for fear of getting someone—or themselves—in trouble.

It was mid-afternoon in an industrial village jammed with small warehouses, workshops, residences, and eateries. We walked by shops selling strong-smelling chemicals or packed with rows of workers hunched over sewing machines. We got countless run-arounds and even the slip from a neighborhood tofu maker doing brisk business at a makeshift stand in a small alleyway when I greeted her. She told us to come back later for a "real" look at how she made a living—then shut down her stall and disappeared. I hadn't been gullible enough to believe that she would return, but I also didn't feel aggressive enough to pursue her.

On an unpaved road on the outer rim of the area sat rows of squat concrete buildings. Everything looked shuttered, and the place was deserted. Just when we were about to slink back to our taxi in defeat, a little girl with a strand of noodle on her head appeared from one alley and turned down another.

I did a double-take and motioned frantically to Han. We followed her, transfixed by that noodle. Her mother was standing next to an open door of a run-down building. Peering inside, we saw four workers sitting on tiny footstools grabbing handfuls of white noodles from washtubs and stuffing them into plastic bags sitting on the wet, flour-caked floor. A mangy dog wandered through the makeshift workshop.

Jackpot.

The woman's guarded manner exploded into angry panic when Han started snapping photos of the premises after we said hello. I hated this part of the job. The husband—a portly, shirtless man with a terrifying five-inch scar on his belly—emerged from the building shouting at us. The couple demanded that we erase the pictures and leave the premises.

Han grudgingly deleted his work as I introduced us as reporters and tried to explain that I wanted to talk to them and see their

Dai Jianjun, owner of Dragon Well Manor, the Chinese equivalent of Chez Panisse, where he serves seasonal, farm-to-table feasts in line with a Daoist back-to-basics tradition. Dai is laughing here before we sit down to lunch with Farmer Jin, one of his fish suppliers. Dishes included braised pig's trotters; chicken with a soy dipping sauce; fresh shrimp boiled with ginger and wine; and a huge, firm-fleshed braised fish.

workshop so I could understand what things were like for small producers. Manufacturing in China is a complicated situation, I said. "Maybe you could tell me your story?"

"No!" the woman answered fiercely. "We don't want people to know about what we do." She and her husband were suspicious. There was no way reporters could have found them coincidentally, they said. Journalists were bad enough, but they worried that we were health inspectors or officials from Beijing. I argued and pleaded and tried to stay calm. If I lost this opportunity, I was going to lose the story.

The couple called their friends for advice. I invited them to the waiting taxi and asked our driver to show them his running meter as proof that we had been driving around all day in a fruitless search. They still didn't believe that we had just stumbled onto their operations. I told them that the noodle on their daughter's head had led us to them. They looked at me like I was crazy.

The discussion moved back and forth, up and down. During a lull, the couple finally admitted their setup was illegal and could be shut down if anyone knew about it. They spoke of high costs and low profits, of having to struggle daily to make ends meet.

Slowly the wife opened up. I let her talk, fearful that questions might rile her. In a mix of her local dialect and Mandarin, she told me how her family, which had moved from the neighboring province of Guangdong, slept in a room above the workshop and barely managed to eke out enough money to pay 1,000 yuan ($155) a month for rent.

It was a rare glimpse, albeit reluctantly given, into the other side of the problem, in which producers, too, struggled to scrape together a living. It didn't justify the means, but it humanized the faceless supply chain and showed a different angle of the product safety issue. For some, it wasn't about making money; it was about making ends meet. The situation also underscored why it was virtually impossible to regulate these operations—people worked out of their homes.

"Life is so hard. We earn 8 *mao* per *jin* of noodles"—about 1 cent per pound—"that we sell, but we spend 1.4 *yuan*"—18 cents— "per *jin* on raw materials," the woman said. "Doing this kind of business is really difficult."

"I don't know how to make anything else," her husband added with a touch of resignation.

After half an hour of negotiations under a blazing sun for a quick glimpse of their workshop, I offered to cut off my right arm as a token of our goodwill. I have no idea why; the heat had gotten to me. I stammered through the proposal in a rush of words, waving my left arm to emphasize the point.

Again, they looked at me as if I had escaped from a mental institution. Han stifled a laugh. Shortly after, however, the couple relented, perhaps realizing it was the only way they were going to get rid of us. Five minutes and no photos, they warned.

In the end, I got two minutes, and Han stayed outside. But it was enough to take in the dimness of the room, the hum of the rickety machines oozing dough, heat fans drying noodles, flies buzzing around piles of finished product, workers sweating as they kept their heads low in stifling heat while filling bags. One picked his nose and used the same hand to pack a bag.

I had the start of a story.

In 2007, the world lost its faith in Chinese-made goods, seriously risking the country's position as a global factory. The product safety problems, long a troubling issue within the country and of sporadic concern internationally, exploded into the headlines after tests revealed an unpalatable array of deadly toxins and dangerously high levels of chemicals in exports ranging from frozen fish to juice and tires. The discoveries didn't come all at once, but, with governments becoming hyper-vigilant, awareness of the problem soared.

Kidney failure in dogs and cats in North America and South Africa, fatal in some instances, triggered the crisis, leading to the discovery of melamine—an inexpensive coal-derived additive—in Chinese-manufactured wheat, corn, and rice gluten, standard ingredients in pet feed.

The mildly toxic chemical, which has no nutritional value and is prohibited in any form in American food, is used in the manufacture of plastics and fertilizers and is rich in nitrogen. Food-quality tests for protein measure nitrogen levels. The sellers of the gluten were tracked back to China, where it's common to boost feed with melamine. One of the companies avoided inspections, according to American regulators, partly because it listed the gluten as a non-food item.

A couple of months after the melamine story broke, import bans and health alerts were issued in Asia, Africa, and North and South America against toothpaste made in China following reports that diethylene glycol, a potentially deadly toxin in antifreeze, had been used as a low-cost sweetener. In Panama, at least 138 people had died or been disabled in 2006 after consuming cough syrup laced with the chemical. Experts traced the cough medicine to a Chinese company not certified to sell pharmaceutical ingredients.

New Zealand launched an urgent investigation after children's clothes imported from China were found to contain dangerous levels of formaldehyde, an embalming fluid. Mattel recalled millions of Chinese-made items including dolls, cars, and action figures. Some were contaminated with lead paint while others had small magnets that children might swallow. American safety officials said the drastic measure was to prevent potential injuries; none was reported.

But the recalls kept coming. The resulting international furor brought China's long-running problems with domestic product safety under renewed scrutiny. In 2007, one of the country's quality watchdogs said almost 20 percent of products made for consumption within the country were found to be substandard. Canned and preserved fruit and dried fish were the most problematic because of excessive bacteria and additives.

The government initially played down the crisis. But then gradually—perhaps grudgingly—officials began to focus efforts on burnishing the country's reputation and stanching economic losses. The 2008 Beijing Olympics were only months away, and the last thing the government needed was the specter of top athletes poisoned by its food and products.

Zheng Xiaoyu, former head of China's food and drug administration who became a symbol of its wide-ranging problems, was executed for, among other offenses, taking bribes to approve an antibiotic blamed for at least ten deaths in the country and other substandard medicines.

The appointment of its top problem solver, then–vice premier Wu Yi, to head a cabinet-level panel overseeing a four-month initiative to overhaul safety controls and enforcement and to clamp down on the small, illegal enterprises that had thrived under the radar for years underscored the seriousness with which the government took the issue.

A stern-looking sixty-nine-year-old known as the "Iron Lady," Wu had shepherded China's difficult entry into the World Trade Organization and took over as health minister during the SARS epidemic. A month into the campaign, which she declared a "special war to uphold the health, life, and interests of the people and to uphold the reputation of Chinese products and its national image," she set out randomly to inspect shops and restaurants in the eastern province of Zhejiang.

It was an extraordinary, perhaps unprecedented, step in a country where no move by top leaders goes unscripted. State media didn't accompany her. She went with no itinerary and told no one in advance, ordering her driver to stop at her whim. In the sticky September heat, she examined business licenses and employee health certificates at a two-table dumpling shop, scrutinizing the kitchen and refrigerator to see whether ingredients were fresh. She gave it her seal of approval. At her next stop, she condemned a chain restaurant for not having the required employee health certificates.

The campaign—the fastest moving and most extensive unleashed since the SARS epidemic—resulted in an avalanche of activity. Authorities announced the closures of hundreds of thousands of unlicensed food producers and retailers, many of them with fewer than ten employees, for selling fake or low-quality products. In some cases inspectors found formaldehyde, illegal dyes, and industrial wax in the production and processing of candy, pickles, crackers, and seafood.

Teams of inspectors fanned out across the country, and labels showing that the quality of export food products had been checked became mandatory. Drug advertisements by celebrities and five kinds of pesticides were banned. Rigorous inspections delayed toy shipments. Along with the crackdown came a propaganda effort, with state television debuting a weeklong series defending Chinese goods with a ninety-minute episode titled "Believe in 'Made in China.'" The government also planned to unveil its first food safety law to address the weak points in food production, processing, delivery, storage, and sales.

But while state officials went into public relations overdrive, local authorities and individual companies remained leery about any kind of attention from the foreign press. There were almost daily public announcements from various levels of government, but several of China's quality watchdogs told us that foreign media were not welcome at their press briefings. They never gave a reason, but I'm sure they didn't want to face questions they couldn't or wouldn't answer.

While the food safety scandals created a watershed in crisis and safety management, the question remained as to how permanent the changes would be—and how much of it would actually alleviate ongoing problems not just with exports but also with the food eaten within China. Some obstacles: the country's convoluted bureaucracy, the tendency of local leaders to ignore edicts from the top, and the lack of traditional consumer watchdogs like a free press and independent civic groups that could monitor the situation.

The most distinguishing feature of the country's central food-safety regulatory system was that there wasn't one. Although there was a State Food and Drug Administration, in reality responsibility was divided among at least six agencies, including those that handled health, agriculture, and commerce. Lines of authority were murky, and different bodies oversaw different laws. Rampant corruption added to the problem. Officials could be bribed, and, instead of shutting down illegal operations, many regulators imposed fines so they could collect more money in the future.

As a result, eating in China was a little like playing Russian roulette with food. You never knew when you were going to get hit with something lethal. There were regular reports of mass poisonings at schools, restaurants, and even wedding banquets. The list was long and alarming: beans treated with banned pesticides, cooking oil recycled from gutters, soy sauce made with an amino acid–based liquid distilled from human hair and animal fur, egg yolks tinged with cancer-causing red dye, watermelons exploding after being boosted by growth accelerators, and pork passed off as beef after being soaked in a detergent additive.

One of the most widespread and gut-wrenching scandals was a cost-cutting scheme to boost infant formula that fell short of official standards on protein content with nitrogen-rich melamine, the same chemical that had killed North American and South African pets. Six babies died, and more than three hundred thousand were sickened as a result.

When the contamination came to light in September 2008, rumors spread that the government had prevented the news from breaking until after the August Olympic Games had ended, another example of officials' attempts to obfuscate and orchestrate even as they were trying to get a grip on the problem.

Dairy farmers and the middlemen involved in the scam conspired to increase profits by watering down milk and milk products before they sold it, fooling inspectors testing for protein content by adding melamine. Once the news started spreading and the outcry swelled, the government kicked into high gear, shaping the message to show how serious it was about product safety by meting out death sentences and other heavier-than-anticipated punishments to offenders. A dairy farmer and a milk salesman were executed.

The melamine formula scandal echoed what happened in Anhui province in 2004, when hundreds of infants suffered from and at least a dozen died from malnutrition after drinking substandard formula made mostly from flour, starch, and sugar. The formula had been on the market for at least two years before the link was made, so actual numbers are probably higher.

Poor families in village grocery stores on the outskirts of Fuyang mostly bought the fake milk powder. The sick children's limbs withered and their faces swelled, signs of edema, a buildup of fluid symptomatic of malnutrition. Investigators later found thousands of boxes of counterfeit formula nationwide.

Yet despite officials' efforts, the stomach-churning problems have persisted as authorities struggle to keep the food supply healthy. In 2011 alone, violations ranged from expired buns repackaged after being mixed with food coloring and sweeteners, to pork tainted with clenbuterol, a banned drug that produces leaner meat by speeding up the conversion of fat to muscle—but can also trigger muscle tremors and heart palpitations in people. "To the people, food is heaven," President Hu Jintao earnestly told the crowds around him during a visit to a product quality-inspection facility that year. "For food, safety is all-important."

鼚

On a trip to America in 2010, I stopped first in Beijing to see friends and then spent a couple of days in Hangzhou, the touristy but scenic and wealthy capital of Zhejiang province in the east, renowned for its lake and plantations of Longjing tea ("Dragon Well").

I wanted to have a meal at Dragon Well Manor, a restaurant in the outskirts of the city that many considered China's version of Chez Panisse, the legendary restaurant in Berkeley, California, credited with inspiring the American ideal of organic, sustainable, locally grown, seasonal eating.

I contacted Ji Chen, the news assistant in our Shanghai bureau, who grew up in the area, and asked her to come with me. I also invited Anita, my food-loving colleague from Beijing, to join us for dinner.

Organic food culture took root in China in 1990, when the Dutch certification agency SKAL certified green tea products from Zhejiang for export to the Netherlands. Since then, the movement has gained momentum, fueled by a growing network of young and educated Chinese who are joining or starting organic farms in an effort to control what goes into their bodies in the wake of the tainted food scandals. In a notable reversal of the rural-to-urban trend, those who become farmers have given up city jobs with lucrative paychecks to work the land for little, if any, profits, earning the comfort of peace of mind instead.

From 2005 to 2006, the amount of land under organic management jumped more than tenfold, from roughly 740,000 acres to almost 8.6 million acres. That made China, with 11 percent of the world total, second only to Australia in the amount of land set aside for organic farming. Of course, Chinese leaders and other elite party officials have their own secret supply of toxin-free, organic produce grown on tightly guarded farms, as well as specially commissioned sources of safe meat and fish.

Even so, there's still a long way to go before organic gains any real traction. There's a limited supply of high-cost, low-yield produce—much of which gets shipped overseas anyway—and, despite food safety concerns, a reluctant consumer base. On paper, the country has strict standards on what qualifies as organic, but in reality it's hard to enforce those standards or ensure that falsely certified products don't enter the supply chain. Chinese consumers are also leery about paying a lot more for food that looks imperfect and may not really be as organic as claimed.

So far, Dragon Well Manor has won a staunch following among well-to-do Chinese, officials and foreigners alike, with its promise of fresh, seasonal food untouched by anything but nature. Dai Jianjun, who opened the restaurant in 2004, hadn't heard of either Chez Panisse or Alice Waters until Western journalists like me made the comparison. For him, it's just a way to express his love for food and desire to be good to the land.

"Before I opened the restaurant, when I interacted with people from the villages, they would ask where I was from. When I told them I'm from Hangzhou, they would ask where the good food is to be found there. But when we actually became friends, they told me what we eat in the cities is stuff they wouldn't even feed their pigs," Dai said. "Every household in those villages has their own plot of land on which they don't use chemical fertilizers or pesticides. Pests always ravage the crops, but the farmers say they consider it 'sharing' the produce with the bugs. They tell me 'The bugs get to eat some, we get to eat some.' This is real harmony between man and nature, and this is what inspired me to open a restaurant like that. Plus, I love to eat."

With a slightly paunchy build, Dai had an easygoing personality and an expansive way with words, often peppering long, passionate conversational loops with idioms, bits of history, and nuggets of Daoist and Buddhist principles. He had the remarkable ability to be, at the same time, philosophical, earnest, and deadpan funny. It was sometimes hard to tell the difference between them until he cracked a sheepish smile. He arranged for us to go on a buying trip one morning, accompanying us even though he doesn't usually have the time to make the daily rounds. It was my favorite kind of outing, one that involved food and visiting farmers, whom I've always found to be especially welcoming.

A former district-level official and hotel worker in Hangzhou, Dai told us he had dressed up for the occasion, pointing to his cream-colored Mandarin-collared shirt made of thick linen, black trousers, black cloth shoes, and white socks. It looked like a cross between scholar and peasant chic, although he admitted later that he was just as comfortable barefoot and shirtless.

The day was hot and hazy as we set out in a small van. Every farmer we visited greeted him like a long-lost relative and called him "Ah Dai," a familiar, familial form of his name. He smoked and joked with the adults and carried the smallest of the children. As we drove to the first farm, an hour outside the heart of Hangzhou, we discussed the concept behind Dai's restaurant. At the equivalent of more than $200 per table—a seasonal meal of six cold dishes and twelve hot dishes for a table of eight, no a la carte—Dragon Well Manor still costs far too much for ordinary citizens.

His notion of going back to the basics—in line with a Daoist tradition called *fanpuguizhen*—began to form in 2000 after Dai read a pamphlet about how technological progress meant a bleak future for humanity's food supply.

"Nowadays, with large-scale industrialized methods of poultry farming—the chickens for KFC or McDonald's—you foment disease in the process. There are large amounts of antibiotics used in this farming process. This means when we fall sick we won't have any effective medication. This is a human tragedy. Humans are materialistic and satisfying their interest ahead of everything else. . . . Is technological progress ultimately good or bad? In my opinion, technological progress makes humanity lose its conscience."

He started laying the groundwork for the concept in 2002 by cultivating relationships with the farmers. He visited their villages—the ancestral homes of many of Dai's friends—and simply talked to them, gaining introductions to more people along the way. "When we speak with farmers, our best weapon is a cigarette. Once you tap his shoulder and offer him a light, he'll tell you all about authenticity. You can't do it without a cigarette."

From there, it was a matter of building on the foundation. "If a family has a newborn, you'll have to show up for dinner and offer a red packet [of money]. Only by doing things like this can you build up a relationship and trust so that they won't cheat you. You have to visit them when relatives pass away, or during the New Year. This way the relationship can be firm. Other restaurants can't do this, but we can. We're willing to forge such relation-ships, and understand them, and make friends with farmers."

Dragon Well Manor opened in May 2004 with only two seat-ings a day at its eight tables, each housed in a separate pavilion. At the time, there was only a pair of chefs, and the first meal treated friends who encouraged him to go all out for the project. By the time I met Dai, his kitchen staff had expanded to four chefs, a dozen sous chefs, and six procurers, each with a vehicle. He had established contracts with a network of about three thousand to five thousand farming households, although he saw most of them rarely because he had to wait for crops and animals to grow and be ready for sale.

"If each farmer rears two pigs, I'll need about 180 such farm-ers a year. As for ducks, they come in gaggles. Once I'm done with one gaggle, I'll find another farmer. Three years later, I'll come back to the first one. Once I go through a flock of chickens, I'll have to wait eighteen months before I can return to the supplier."

The rules were simple: No chemical fertilizers, pesticides, or hormones, and adhere to natural cycles by growing and har-vesting in accordance with the seasons. But it took many, many months before things fell into place.

"There were many painful processes. Some of them quit, some of them passed away, like the suppliers of *Guanyin doufu*. They used juices from leaves to make the product. It is greenish in color and extremely delicious. But the couple has passed away, and the technique has been lost."

Dai was willing to pay up to ten times more than market prices if farmers followed the rules, but greed motivated some of them, who bought produce elsewhere and tried to pass it off as their own. "Now our procurers can spot such tricks, but back then it was a price we paid for learning the lesson." Some farmers turned what they did for Dai into a sustainable small business, where they sold products to their neighbors.

Born in 1969, Dai was raised in Hangzhou by his grandmother, who fed him well and taught him the simple truth that the key to good food is using good ingredients. To be considered cuisine, he said, the dishes have to be made with the best ingredients in an authentic way to preserve the original flavors. "Cucumber should taste like cucumber . . . fish should taste like fish, and chickens should taste like chickens."

He promised to show us what he meant during dinner, invoking his grandmother's culinary tradition of steaming a fish whole, seasoned with nothing more than a touch of salt and two slices of ham. "Once you've had some, you'll ask if you can have it again. . . . If you ask me to bring this food to Shanghai or Singapore, I can't. This is a local fish."

I asked Dai what he thought of the saying "To the people, food is heaven." His answer was thought-provoking.

"It is the biggest need in life. It comes back to another saying, *shisexingye*, which means the desire for food and sex is human nature. . . . Once a child is born, it will seek its mother's milk. It doesn't have to be taught; it's instinct. This instinct is an inherent quality to learn from and understand the world. Of this, the most basic desire is that for food, an appetite. Therefore, 'To the people, food is heaven.' Eating sustains life. Only then can we have other desires—for truth, kindness, beauty."

He paused.

"We say *qiuzhen*, which means to seek the truth. But when even food isn't authentic anymore, what truth can you seek? As we look for the true essence of our lives, we can't resolve the issue of the meaning of our existence, but we can resolve issues about how we live. There are philosophical aspects that we don't explore, but, as to how we live, we should at least seek authenticity in that. To find the essence of our existence, we should at least start with consuming authentic food.

"The chicken you eat, its gestation period is just three weeks, twenty-one days. For the chicken soup you brew for pregnant women, you've got to get a hen of at least eight months of age before you can consider it a tonic. But now there aren't any old hens. In Hangzhou, there's a businessman who specializes in rearing and selling old ducks. But now he can't afford to raise his ducks until they're old. His sales volumes are too high, and he can only wait a few weeks before he serves them up. The oldest we can get is three-year-old ducks. On principle we want them to be older than three years. Three-year-old ducks are old ducks now, ducks that are seven years or older are called 'immortal ducks.' The older the duck, the better for medicinal purposes, the more effective. You can't find such ducks anymore because we humans seek speed.

"We in China have a saying, *tianrentongle*, which means: Many joys in life are derived from Mother Nature. We should let things live their lives to their intended purposes. There are so many things now that we cannot enjoy in their true state."

糶

At our first stop, a farm in Lijiaqiao village, its well-tended fields full of wheat and cilantro, we saw evidence of the point Dai was making. Set upon by bugs, many of the vegetables and plants bore jagged holes in their leaves, the trademark of greens untouched by pesticides. Several men and women worked in the dirt, under power lines that stretched for miles. One of them, a woman in a straw hat, flashed a huge grin at us, her eyes crinkling warmly, her smile as welcoming as the sun. Dai surveyed the crops and called out to me after a couple of minutes. He was brandishing what looked like a huge bunch of emerald leaves with a deeply ridged pattern. It was only when I got closer that I saw the thick, knobby base that looked like a broccoli stalk.

"Is this *wosun*?" I asked, referring to asparagus lettuce, one of my favorite vegetables in China. Often served as a cold dish, shredded and tossed with a variety of seasonings, from salt and sesame oil to mustard and chili oil, its stem has a delicate sweetness that belies a sassy crunch. Occasionally Cheng Ayi, my housekeeper, finely sliced the wosun stem and stir-fried it with shredded pork and a touch of garlic in a simple, homey dish that went perfectly with rice.

"Try it," Dai said, offering the stub of green left after he ripped off all the leaves. It was still cool from being in the ground and had an unexpectedly bitter taste. I winced; Dai laughed. He shouted something to one of the women, who then said something to a little boy of about eight or nine. He sped off and returned a minute later holding in each hand what looked like a purple bamboo pole twice his height with a tuft of long, grass-like leaves sprouting from the top.

"What's that?" I asked.

"Sugarcane!" Dai exclaimed, like he was performing a magic trick. I almost jumped for joy. In Singapore, I had only seen the green variety, mostly in manageable sections being pressed for juice at hawker stalls. It was the best way to beat the heat. Unbelievably sweet and refreshing, sugarcane juice is always served with plenty of ice and, sometimes, twists of lemon for added zing.

The boy put the stalks on the ground and used his bare feet as leverage to snap off the leaves with his hands. With a stamp of his foot, he broke off a section of the cane. Our driver took over with his hands until he had pieces a few inches long—the perfect snack. He gave Ji Chen and me two each. I took my cue from Dai, who used his teeth to rip off the tough outer layer. Underneath lay the fibrous core that yielded ambrosial goodness as soon as I bit into it. Juice ran down my chin and throat. The trick was to chew each mouthful until only the dry fibers were left, and then spit them out onto the ground. It was gloriously messy, and I couldn't stop smiling. I had eaten straight from the field so few times in my life that each occasion seemed like a new experience.

Before we left, one of the farmers, barefoot and pants rolled up, dug out about forty-five pounds of cilantro from the field and tied it into bundles with pink raffia. Dai bought it all for around $18—twice the going rate for the nonorganic product. His assistant snapped photos of the product and the sale, to be showcased in a purchasing diary at the restaurant as proof of freshness.

Next we visited one of Dai's fish suppliers in Dongtang village next to a reservoir called Sanbaitan, the waters of which lay in an environmentally protected area free of industrial pollution. Ji Chen and I followed Dai as he wound his way through backyards and narrow walkways along the shore, on which bobbed docked wooden boats, long and curved like blades of grass.

When we arrived at the fish supplier's home, a man was gutting and scaling the catch of the day in a spray of crimson and silver. He piled fillets in a straw basket while innards and unwanted bits fell to the wet floor next to him. Dai greeted Farmer Jin heartily and immediately offered him a cigarette from his stash of the premium Zhonghua brand. They lit up and chatted in the local dialect. After a few minutes, Farmer Jin invited me and Ji Chen onto his boat. As I sat at the prow ready for a ride, we traveled a few feet to retrieve a net fish trap. Then we pushed back to shore.

"That's it?" I asked, disappointed.

"There's more later," Farmer Jin said. He held up the trap to reveal all sorts of aquatic life wriggling within. He emptied it into a red plastic basin. I gasped involuntarily. It was a treasure trove of edibles: silver, black, and mud-colored fish that fit in my palm, dozens of translucent shrimp, and tiny water snails.

Dai, sitting on the steps in front of Farmer Jin's house, held an empty bowl into which he tossed six of the writhing shrimp. The driver filled it with scalding hot water from a thermos flask, and the shrimp turned bright orange almost immediately.

"Eat," Dai commanded.

I pulled one from the bowl, holding it by the antennae because it was so hot. After blowing on it, I pulled off its head, shelled it, and popped it into my mouth. Dai looked at me expectantly. It was amazing. Alive only moments before and cooked only in the briefest of hot water baths, the shrimp were firm and sweet. I reached for another.

"This is what I mean," Dai said, pleased. "You see how good it is when you eat it fresh?"

We went farther out in the boat and picked up more fish from a fisherman who had just pulled up his nets. By the time we returned to shore, it was past noon, and the sun was beating down fiercely. Farmer Jin called us to lunch in the kitchen, a huge, airy room with a bank of windows overlooking the lake. My stomach growled when I saw what been prepared for us.

In the center of a round table that could comfortably seat ten people sat a glass casserole dish filled with at least three dozen whole shrimp, boiled in water and flavored with salt, ginger, and cooking wine. Around that lay plates and bowls piled high with red-braised pig's feet with dried bamboo, stir-fried *wosun* with sliced pork, braised "fat head" fish garnished with chopped green onions, cucumber sticks with vinegar and sesame oil, stir-fried greens with garlic, and a whole chicken, boiled, chopped, and accompanied by a soy dipping sauce. Farmer Jin and his employees didn't eat this way every day. It was as much a treat for them as it was for us.

The food was so fresh and simply prepared that it was impossible not to devour it all with a big bowl of rice. I rarely got to eat pig's feet, which I loved. These were braised in dark soy and aromatic to perfection, a combination of meat, bone, tendon, cartilage, and fat. The fish, swimming around less than an hour before, was firm-fleshed and so big that, chopped up, it filled two serving bowls. Its braising liquid was a thick and wonderfully savory mixture of wine, dark soy, chicken stock, ginger, and a pinch of salt. The cucumbers, cool and crunchy, made the perfect vehicle for the vinegar and sesame oil, both powerful flavors.

Piles of shrimp shells and chicken and pork bones soon appeared on the table. Beer bottles and teacups sat empty, and cigarettes glowed. Back outside in the sun, Dai took off his shirt without ceremony, declaring: "I hate fakeness. I hate pretending. I'm always myself."

He talked about how his buyers had to go farther and farther out to get vegetables because development was eating up the land. I asked if he would eventually give up on his idea of eating locally and organically if the farms moved too far away. "I will persevere," he said. "As long as it's worth it to me, as long as my customers are happy, that makes it worth it."

Our final stop on the buying trip brought us to a village where Dai sourced his supply of persimmons, one of my favorite fruits. The variety I like is called fuyu, which looks like a tomato. At its peak, it has a burnt orange color, round and smooth with a star-shaped configuration of leaves around its navel. It tastes best to me when almost overripe, when it's soft and super sweet. In that state, it's easiest to make a little nick in the skin with your teeth, then suck out the pulpy goodness and slightly crunchy segments in one giant slurp and spit out the flat, black seeds.

The fruit was exactly at this sublime stage when we arrived at Dai's supplier's house. The farmer and his relatives ushered us to a big table where a basket full of persimmons was waiting, along with cups of Dragon Well tea. Ji Chen and I ate three persimmons in quick succession as Dai explained the reason for our trip. We headed out at a leisurely pace to see how the fruits were picked.

Villagers stopped to look at all nine of us—a huge group of mostly visitors—as we sauntered down the one road leading in and out of town, made up of two-story homes and shops. One of the farmers with us was holding a six-and-a-half-foot-long bamboo pole with a mesh net at the end—the special tool needed to pull the fruit down. A grandson of another farmer, no more than six or seven years old, tagged along, swinging a green basket to hold the persimmon harvest. We passed backyards and crossed fields. Then in front of us, flanked by less colorful plants, stood several gnarled trees with sparse leaves and bright amber fruit.

Persimmons!

The farmers immediately went to work, expertly wielding their bamboo poles and looping the fruit into their nets. The little boy transported handfuls to his basket, which he soon filled. On the way back to the village, Dai detoured to a farm that also supplied him with vegetables.

"All their crops are planted in night soil," he told Chen and me. I raised my eyebrows.

Night soil is an organic fertilizer, rich in nitrogen and nutrients, made from human and sometimes animal waste, a tradition in China for thousands of years because it resulted in lush and abundant produce. It also explained why the Chinese rarely ate raw vegetables and cooked almost everything over a roaring flame. The sludge, collected mostly at night, was often stored in open field pits of large earthenware jars. But because of potential health hazards and with the cheap and convenient alternative of chemical fertilizers, the use of night soil has decreased over the years. But, as with all of Dai's farmers, it was back to basics.

"Everything is grown in shit?" I asked Ji Chen. "Is that what he said?"

She nodded; we giggled uneasily. Dai, as always, was exuberantly calling something out to one of the farmers in the field. The farmer nodded and started digging into a patch of tousled green leaves. Within seconds, a pair of palm-sized white radishes emerged, and he handed one to Dai, who again had taken off his shirt.

"You have to try this!" Dai said. "It's fresh out of the ground and absolutely natural."

I looked at him, torn, and then shook my head. "No, thanks."

"What's the matter?" he asked. My unbridled enthusiasm had met everything he had offered—until now.

"Hmmmm. You try it," I said to Ji Chen.

She shook her head. "No, you try it."

"The night soil," I said to Dai. "I don't think I can do it."

"Come on!" he said, disappointed. "That's what's bugging you? Okay! I will clean it first!"

He walked over to a narrow ditch with murky water and washed the dirt off the radish. Then he used his fingernails to scrape off a layer of skin. "There. It's clean. You have to eat it now."

I looked at Chen and decided to bite the bullet, praying that if I got sick it happened before the dinner at Dai's restaurant—and didn't last long. After all, I reasoned, trying to psych myself up, I'm pretty sure I had eaten worse without knowing it.

I gingerly took a small bite of a freshly peeled section. It was spicy and burned my nose and throat in the way only horseradish can. Having done my duty, I handed the radish to Chen. She gamely took a bite, and in seconds the root vegetable was back in Dai's hands. He heartily bit into it and chewed with gusto.

Night soil aside, it was a beautiful day, and there was a certain romance to living off the land. One of the workers was hoeing purple yams, whose jewel-toned insides—exposed by one swoop of the tool—shone bright against the dirt. Fire engine–red beetroots nestled among worm-eaten leaves, proof again of the lack of pesticides.

It was time to head back to town so that the chefs at Dragon Well Manor could start work on the bounty we had accrued during the day. In addition to the basket of persimmons that Dai bought, the farmer also gave us a package of hand towels and a big blue tablecloth to take home. It was a heartfelt gift that the farmer must have paid a lot for. All of us were deeply moved.

❦

Hangzhou retains much of its natural beauty from when it was the capital of the Southern Song dynasty and named by Marco Polo as the finest and most splendid city in the world. The picturesque shores of the West Lake, lush environs ringed by mountains on three sides, have inspired centuries of paintings and poetry. There are temples, pagodas, and gardens to explore, and a strong tea culture thrives there, firmly rooted in the Dragon Well leaf's bracing, nutty flavor.

Dai's restaurant lies in the foothills of tea plantations just minutes away from the crowds of the downtown area. Its English name is Dragon Well Manor, but the name in Chinese, *Longjing Caotang*, refers to the tea leaf and a humble cottage made of straw, usually used to describe an intellectual's or scholar's home.

Dai was obviously proud of the beauty of his establishment, where even the parking lot was aesthetically pleasing, with granite slabs and an unparalleled view of mountains and bamboo. The early autumn light was fading to gold as the sun sank slowly behind the surrounding peaks. We walked through a stone archway painted with the characters representing "legacy" and "garden." Dai explained that it was a tribute to what the restaurant was before he developed the 4.5-acre plot—an abandoned nursery, a good place that had been forgotten.

We entered a paradise of weeping willows, lily pads, bridges, and streams. Ornately landscaped gardens—right down to carefully arranged rocks and wicker chairs—surrounded eight luxurious private pavilions decorated in the style of the Southern Song dynasty. The air was fresh, and the peace and quiet were precious, especially after the chaos of Hangzhou.

We sat down for a quick pre-dinner snack of persimmons, Hangzhou walnuts, four-cornered water chestnuts, and dried soybean pods accompanied by newly brewed Dragon Well tea. This must have been what life was like for the privileged in ancient China. Only the vicious mosquitoes marred my sense of goodwill.

The main building had a sloped tile roof and imposing wooden beams and columns, its interior furnished with scrolls and intricately carved furniture. Thick volumes of purchasing diaries contained numerous photos and catalogued the type of produce, the date it was bought, the length of time it would remain fresh, the name of the farmer, his address and phone number, and the name of the staff who made the sale.

I asked for a quick tour of the kitchen, the heart of the operation. Dai hesitated because it was peak dinner time and the chefs would be busy. I sensed that he also wanted to keep that part away from the public eye, but he relented with grace. As we approached the building, we saw one chef—white uniform and hat bright in the gloom of dusk—sitting on a stool and separating the leaves of an emerald green vegetable. He rose and smiled in response to Dai's hearty greeting. A wooden steamer was heating flour buns in the small entryway before the kitchen. Dai lifted the lid and handed us each one. We gobbled them up, enjoying their light softness.

All steel and tile and surprisingly small, the kitchen had a staff of about half a dozen working on prep and actual cooking in a practiced flurry. They manned stockpots, metal bowls, woks, and chopping boards with focused intensity. In one corner, a pair of boys barely out of their teens cleavered *wosun* into slices and pork belly into paper-thin rectangles. Nearby sat crates and trays of bright green snow peas, black curls of wood ear fungus, different cuts of freshly slaughtered pig—shank, ribs, tenderloin—and the fish we had bought, scaled and covered with deep slits. Every move was made with precision, and the work area was spotless.

On a metal table near the stove lay a cooked chive omelet, simply presented on a stemmed porcelain plate, and a clay casserole dish filled with what looked like a dark soy braising liquid with a giant knot of scallions. Two metal platters displayed the extraterrestrial forms of whole sea cucumbers, the rubbery, gray-brown, spiky creature the Chinese believe to be an aphrodisiac. On the other side of the table were peeled garlic, julienned red peppers and celery, thinly sliced pork, and piles of soybeans and shredded preserved cabbage.

Flames burned high and bright as the chefs shook and stirred and clanged their metal spoons and spatulas in a form of kung fu cooking. They reached for seasonings and strainers as pots bubbled and pans sizzled. The dishes plated before our eyes smelled heavenly.

"Now," Dai said after five minutes, "it's time to eat."

Zhejiang cuisine, another of the eight cooking traditions of China, epitomizes the bountiful "land of fish and rice," represented mainly by culinary styles from four cities—Hangzhou, Shaoxing, Ningbo, and Wenzhou. Its dishes embrace the qualities of freshness, tenderness, and fragrance.

Because Ningbo and Wenzhou lie near the ocean, seafood is often the main ingredient, usually carefully steamed, braised, or roasted to retain succulence and original juices. In Shaoxing, dishes focus more on freshwater fish, because of the prevalence of rivers and lakes, and poultry, with an emphasis on thick sauces and mild and light flavors. The area is also famous for its rice wine, often used in cooking.

Hangzhou's food involves more elaborate preparations finished off in sautés, stews, and stir-fries. It's home to the province's signature dishes such as West Lake Vinegar Fish, West Lake Beef Soup, Longjing Shrimp, and Beggar's Chicken, that according to legend was invented by a thief who stole a bird, wrapped it in clay, and baked it in a hole in the ground, some say, to keep the wonderful aroma a secret.

As the evening progressed, the glass lazy susan on the table in our pavilion slowly filled with a cornucopia of dishes, twenty-seven in all as a special treat for us, that Dai called "folk cuisine of the Zhejiang people." Meat, fish, and vegetables were steamed, braised, stir-fried, and boiled. Cooking times ranged from seconds to hours, which yielded the purest, most intensely flavored stocks and soups. Some dishes were light, others were cloaked in sweet and unctuous sauces, reductions of soy sauce, sugar, and Shaoxing wine. Most of the offerings were extraordinarily simple, relying on the snap-freshness of the main ingredient, and prepared with skill that showcased Dai's philosophy of seasonal, field-to-table eating. Presentation was rustic: neat piles of food on unadorned plates.

We started with two beverages, a jade-green glass of frothy, freshly pressed kiwi juice, tasty and tart, and a hot and comforting soy milk made on the premises. I sampled the rich, beany goodness on its own before adding the suggested condiments of tiny dried shrimp, preserved cabbage, chopped fried dough crullers, spring onions, and black vinegar, turning it into a savory soup. I eagerly sipped a second serving with just white sugar. When I asked for more, Dai cut me off, instructing me to save my appetite for what lay ahead.

Next came the cold dishes or appetizers: thinly sliced boiled beef with a five-spice dressing; an inverted cone of a pungent local green called *haocai*, boiled and sparingly flavored with salt and sesame oil; *kaofu*, wheat gluten, its spongy texture having soaked up the salty soy base in which it had been cooked; meaty dried shiitake mushrooms reconstituted in a rich chicken broth; finger lengths of cucumbers as the perfect palate cleanser; chunks of fish fried and coated with a clear, sweet-sour sauce; *doufugan*, pressed bean curd bathed in stock and topped with snipped chives; and grilled green chilies, at once sweet and smoky.

I was almost full when the hot dishes arrived, but I had to push on. It wasn't difficult when the staff uncovered a delicate porcelain casserole dish to reveal an entire duck half-submerged in its own stock. The skin and meat had melted off the bone. The resulting soup tasted so heady that I asked if they had added cognac to it.

Dai shook his head. "This is what happens when you cook a bird for four and a half hours." I sipped another mouthful and could almost feel the layers of flavors separate as they warmed my chest. Silence encircled the table.

The chive omelet, while delicious, was quickly overshadowed by the showiest dish of the night: sliced pork tenderloin cooked in broth. The meat arrived raw, in slices pressed together into palm-sized balls on individual leaves of spinach. A server cooked at a separate table topped with a pot of pork stock bubbling on an electric burner. She used chopsticks to separate each slice, putting it in a slotted spoon before patiently using another spoon to pour the stock over it until it changed color in a matter of seconds. She carefully laid the tenderloin in an individual serving bowl and filled it with the cooking liquid before serving it to us.

The duck was good—but this was sublime. The pig had been slaughtered that same day, and the meat was so tender that I barely had to chew. The soup held a deep, meaty essence cut by the last-minute addition of spinach leaves that quickly wilted in the heat. I yearned for more, but there was only enough for one serving each.

The next course also drew gasps: the tails of the fifty-five-pound fish procured earlier in the day, served on an enormous platter and covered with a thick brown sauce garnished with chopped green onions. Knobs of firm flesh above the fan of the tail had cooked beautifully in the braising liquid that included Shaoxing wine, soy sauce, sugar, onions, ginger, and garlic. I carefully scraped out the gelatinous bits between the tails' spines. Dai said they were the most coveted parts, but after a gummy mouthful I have to confess that I didn't see what the fuss was about.

Another casserole dish emerged, this one containing a whole chicken wrapped in a pig's stomach that had been steamed for three hours. The stomach was cut open to reveal the fowl curled in the lining, one eye half-open, peering out lazily. Despite our full bellies, we hungrily savored the elixir of concentrated flavors.

The next four dishes paid excellent tribute to vegetables, including something called *su dongporou*, a vegetarian version of braised pork belly, one of Zhejiang's signature concoctions named after Su Dongpo, a Song dynasty official, writer, and poet. According to one story, Su wanted to share gifts of wine and pork that he had received with laborers working on an irrigation project and told his family to cook the meat. They misunderstood and cooked the pork along with the alcohol, resulting in a delicious mistake.

"Guess what it's made of. You have to guess!" Dai said as we all took a bite.

"White radish?" I asked, not quite able to put my finger on what I was tasting.

"Wrong!" Dai said gleefully.

"Winter melon," Anita guessed correctly.

The mild-flavored gourd had been stewed for two hours and had taken on the glossy, mahogany sheen of the soy sauce–inflected stock in which it had been cooked. While it would never be mistaken for meat, it had a rich, surprisingly luxurious mouthfeel.

Then came the smaller fish we had brought back from Farmer Jin, steamed whole with wine and soy sauce, the juices blending in a salty broth.

Our eating had slowed markedly, but the dishes kept coming: lightly sautéed *baicai* hearts; stir-fried bamboo shoots with preserved cabbage and red peppers; and crunchy wood fungus in a chicken broth preceded Sichuan pickled vegetables and shredded pork, a beloved combination that my grandmother used to cook; matchstick-thin celery strips sautéed with bamboo and red peppers; shredded *wosun*; and a milky fish soup with bamboo pith, a type of mushroom with a silky netting.

Dragon Well Manor's head chef, Dong Jinmu, slipped into the room and joined us at the table. Dong spent a better part of four decades cooking at *Louwailou*, revered as Hangzhou's oldest and most famous restaurant. I asked him how the food at the two restaurants differed.

"We serve only seasonal dishes here. What you eat is what's available," Dong said. "I didn't have this concept at all when I started here. It was only after communicating with and learning from others that I gradually started to become interested in this. . . . As chefs, we have to be responsible to the boss as well as the customers. That's our job, and we have to act with our conscience.

"Right now, I don't think more people will adopt this philosophy because there are too many people and too little land. Only a small portion of land gets preserved. For him," Dong said, pointing to Dai, "regardless of the cost, he wants to keep the restaurant open. There are a lot of rich people now, and they want to eat well. So this is the right concept to adopt."

Two offerings came near the end that I couldn't stop eating despite my distended belly: a small bowl of *dongporou*, this time with real cubes of pork belly glistening seductively in a thick, salty-sweet sauce—Dai called it "a dish of mother's love"—and a plate piled high with stir-fried soybeans, cubes of bamboo shoot, red peppers, preserved vegetables, and pork. It was the freshest, most perfect marriage of contrasting textures and tastes.

Finally came the starches, usually served last in China. They included the buns we had sampled in the kitchen and steamed corn and yams. We also had sections of sugarcane and a local dessert made with hot water stirred into lotus root powder, which Dai had told us about earlier in the day.

"Have it for breakfast. In the past, we only prepared it for those who were ill. The powder now is all made by hand," he said as he first mixed a bowlful of the powder with a little cool water before adding hot water from a kettle and stirring vigorously. The result was a bland, lavender-brown goop with a pudding-like texture sweetened with a little sugar. It had the aftertaste of lotus root, which I loved, but not in this form.

Dai lit up a cigarette after dinner, and another chef, Guo Ming, joined us at the table. He spoke of the challenges of adapting to the philosophy behind Dragon Well Manor.

"The heavens decide what dishes we eat in accordance with the seasons. We don't make dishes if the ingredients are not in season, even if the customers ask for them. They can bring those things if they want, but we don't have it on the premises. The boss will get us if we do it! . . . This is a new start for us."

"Why do you want to work here?" I asked. "Is this way of cooking that much healthier?"

"That's for sure!" Guo said. "And we have familial ties here. We aren't doing this with outside acquaintances. We've known each other for twenty-something years. We do this in good conscience, bringing in good produce and preparing the dishes for the customers. . . . We make sure we bring in good stuff. Customers should trust us."

When the chefs returned to the kitchen, the rest of us sank into a food coma. Dai lit another cigarette and took a deep, contemplative breath before launching into another earnest monologue.

"China is in a difficult position. We're the workshop of the world. But all these pollutants, the Chinese didn't invent them—we're just more prolific users. We have 1.3 billion people, and we have too many burdens. It's difficult for us and for the government. I understand their problems. I've met with agricultural leaders and reported these issues to them. But our population is just too huge.

"We'll have problems if we don't change mindsets—we'll eat more and more and have all sorts of health problems as a result. We can't be poisoned to death. . . . All those chemicals in our system, we've developed antibodies," he said with sarcasm. "I really despise those who make fake medicine, fake wine, fake foods. They should be executed. But if we kill someone, outsiders will pressure us. But this is how it is in China. If we say we will kill someone who makes fake wine, then no one would do it."

He switched gears to tell us about a vendor of fermented tofu with whom he worked. "She sold the tofu to raise her sons. She's eighty-four years old now, but she still grows vegetables for us. Her sons are all grown now, and they work for big companies. We have a small mountaintop nearby, but her house is even bigger than that. It has a pond in the garden around which she rears ducks and geese, which she sells to us, too. Her sons object, but she says it's worth the effort because her grandchildren's favorite food is eggs from those ducks.

"When we went to Tonglu, there was an old man. He has thirty *mu* [five acres] of land but only cultivates two to three *mu* of the land. I asked him why. He said he has two daughters, two sons-in-law, a grandson, and a granddaughter. He said in his last years he'll just cultivate this little bit at small expense . . . to feed his children and grandchildren. That is his greatest wish.

"That encounter with him was my biggest lesson, and our interaction was the most carefree. He was once a state cadre but fell under these circumstances after he retired from his job. His spirit and actions really moved me. There are some who are willing to persist with this, but many are very old—in their seventies and eighties. The youngest farmer who supplies stuff to us started at thirty-eight. Now he's forty-four. . . . A few have passed away."

Lulled by good food and the long day of exploring, the conversation waned as the hour grew late, but Dai had one more point to make before we called it a night: "Villages are better than the city; we want to convey this idea, that the village is the true home. We Chinese people haven't learned this. We want to convey the voice within our hearts, expressed through our dishes. Chinese culture has a lot of media, but we just do it through our dishes. Preparing food is a process of seeking nature and returning to our essence."

He took one last puff of his cigarette.

I met Wang Wenying a month after the May 12, 2008, Sichuan earthquake that left almost ninety thousand people dead and missing. She was cooking dinner in a wok set on a fire built from cinder blocks and wood scraps from nearby ruined homes. Her concrete house had survived the catastrophe, but the walls had cracked. At the time of this photo, she was living in a tent with five relatives. "We still have to eat," she said. "We still have to survive."

8

Meals in the Quake Zone

Some moments will always haunt you.

For me, the 2008 Sichuan earthquake had too many of them. In a sweeping, blockbuster sort of way, it was the worst natural disaster in a generation, a milestone for China, and easily the most extraordinary, most difficult event I covered.

It was the first time I had seen the country truly united, top to bottom, with humanity that humbled me and with openness and spontaneity that surprised me. Hundreds of thousands of troops, police, and emergency personnel mobilized in a frantic scramble to save lives amid the almost unfathomable extent of death and destruction. Volunteers from across the country swarmed into the region, and donations poured in, unusual gestures of charity from a society still trying to climb into the middle class. For a time, there was also unprecedented media openness, with twenty-four-hour TV news coverage and rare freedom for journalists to travel and report without restrictions.

I am not a hardcore war correspondent or disaster veteran, but I have witnessed some remarkable events in my career. I've walked away elated, shocked, and saddened, but still very much a reporter, carefully and consciously distant from my subjects.

This tragedy was different. Nothing prepared me for how personal it would be, the tremendous highs and the ghastly lows of covering the story, or for the tears and the sleepless nights. At times it proved too much to bear, and I had to look away; I had never looked away. My heart broke inconsolably at the sight of how the 7.9 quake utterly destroyed not just physical structures but also families, lives, and souls. The people who died, those who survived and those who suffered, were my people—my blood, my ancestry.

After years of living in a country where I felt as if I would never quite belong or understand, it finally gelled: I was already immutably and unquestionably Chinese. It was that simple.

In Chinese, the characters for bearing hardship mean "eat bitterness." Along the jagged, 167-mile-long fissure that sliced through towns and villages—the monstrous scar that the quake left on Sichuan—so much pain and fear and sadness wrapped the bitterness of the tragedy that it seemed as though no one would ever stomach food again. Almost ninety thousand people died or were missing and presumed dead. Another five million were left homeless.

Yet life, as it always does, eventually pushed on, and I like to think that food served literally and metaphorically as the fuel. I like to believe that the recovery process began with the preparation and partaking of meals, that the routine created stability in the chaos of the aftermath.

In one of the most devastated towns, I came upon a woman making lunch in a temporary structure made of plastic sheets tied to metal poles. On a round wooden chopping board, she was using a cleaver to slice thinly several chunks of translucent preserved meat. The fat of the meat glistened on that hellishly hot afternoon. Concentrating on the task at hand, she refused to look at me or answer when I, at loss for more meaningful words, asked how she was doing. As I walked away, tears slid down her cheek.

It reminded me that food formed not only part of a daily ritual but also lay at the core of the Chinese spirit. Even when they had nothing to their names, people generously shared meager supplies and precious water with me and other reporters in the field. Volunteers dishing out rice and stews and stir-fries were also doling out hope and cheer.

"We still have to eat," said a woman sautéeing potatoes and beans in the middle of the ruins of her village, decisively clanging her metal spatula against the side of her wok. "We still have to survive."

Small, quiet, personal flashes of the aftermath's intensity still live in me. One crystallized in a sports field covered with dozens of corpses that didn't faze me until I had to describe the scene in detail over a tenuous phone line to Scott, my news editor, who was writing the story for me a world away in Beijing. I started crying—and couldn't stop. I tried to be coherent and professional, but all that came out were heaving sobs.

"Take your time," Scott said, worried and choking up himself. "Just breathe."

Because of space constraints, he distilled all of what I described into one paragraph in the story: "East of the epicenter in the town of Hanwang, the smell of incense hung over a crowd of sobbing relatives who walked among some 60 bodies wrapped in plastic, some covered with tributes of branches or flowers."

There wasn't room to depict how clusters of rescue workers and volunteers formed a gruesome assembly line to secure the bodies in comforters and whatever fabric they could find before placing them on wooden boards and winding what looked like a giant roll of plastic wrap around them. Rocks weighed down a second layer of plastic sheeting. Still, the tops of heads—hair covered in dust—and socked or sandaled feet remained heart-breakingly visible. The workers wore electric blue jumpsuits, white hardhats, and protective face masks. They completed their grim tasks quietly, efficiently, their heads bowed as they lifted, swathed, and tucked one body at a time.

Nor did the story include the shocked or deadened expressions of those who lived and had to identify their loved ones, or the gut-wrenching anxiety of those waiting to hear the fates of the missing. One man told me of how he had spent all day trying to pull his wife out of their destroyed apartment building, but he failed. And she died. The man and his son had to leave her broken body where it lay, trapped in an undignified grave. When he spoke, he didn't look me in the eye,

239

A couple of days later, I was walking on rubble several stories high, the remnants of the valley town of Beichuan. Only the epicenter town of Yingxiu was harder hit. Two photographers and I had been following the bright orange and yellow jumpsuits of rescue workers as they navigated the mounds of brown and gray wreckage. As I tried to keep my balance on the sea of unstable debris and not cut myself on rusted wires, nails, and jagged chunks of concrete, the afternoon sun was beating down on my head and shoulders. Then the air shifted, and the smell hit me—along with the realization.

With every step I took, I was walking on the remains of residents who couldn't escape the disaster, people trapped in offices, homes, shops, and schools as the earth engulfed the buildings and the surrounding mountains crumbled. They were fathers, mothers, and children, and they were decomposing as I scrambled over their unmarked graves.

Were survivors shouting for help? I stopped, straining my ears, but all I could hear was the silence of the valley and the occasional distant shouts of workers and villagers who had converged in the area. I didn't know how to capture the moment or process the sadness, calling out instead to my colleague Andy Wong, an AP photographer from Malaysia, about twenty feet ahead.

"Hey, Andy!" I said. "Can you take a picture of me?" He looked at me strangely but held up his camera and snapped. The image shows me in a black T-shirt and black pants, scrubbed hillside in the background, waist-high rubble in the foreground. My hands are on my hips, my face obscured by a stiff, white face mask. I look cocky, but my heart was painfully clenched.

One week after the quake, another photographer, Han, and I stayed past sunset in Beichuan. We had been monitoring two possible rescues, potential miracles that could offer much-needed morale boosts for the country after seven spiritually draining days. But it looked like efforts were going to go through the night, and, because we had deadlines to meet, we didn't have the luxury of waiting any longer. The other reporters had long gone. Twilight was fading fast when we headed away from the lights and workers to begin the thirty-minute walk back to the car. Darkness soon engulfed us, and we could barely make out the broken silhouettes of buildings only a few feet away.

In the eerie quiet, we occasionally heard unidentifiable scrabbles and flutters echoing through the ruins. We were literally walking through a ghost town. I stayed close to Han and wondered, of all the lost souls around us, whether they could possibly be at peace. I fought the urge to run. Suddenly, we heard a beep, a loud mechanical sound that we couldn't pinpoint but that seemed close by. Had we imagined it? It came again—and again.

Perhaps it was someone trying to signal to us. What would we do? Han, good at maintaining a Zen-like calm, said it was unlikely. He said there were many appliances and toys lying around; the noise was probably coming from something running low on batteries. But he too seemed unwilling to move, unwilling to let go. Eventually we started walking again, silent until we emerged from the darkness.

❖

When the quake struck at 2:28 p.m. on May 12, Greg and I were hundreds of miles east having lunch at a hotel in Fuyang, a city of over eight million in Anhui province where the children of poor families had died from consuming counterfeit formula. We were interviewing hospital officials there about an outbreak of hand, foot, and mouth disease, a common viral illness that had sickened thousands of children in Fuyang that spring. It was late, so we were the only customers, hungrily eating a simple lunch of beef soup and stir-fried greens—when the room heaved oddly, leaving the chandelier swinging.

The only other time I had been in an earthquake, I hadn't felt it. I asked Greg if he noticed anything strange. He said no.

"I swear the room moved," I said. "I think it's an earthquake. Look at the lights."

Greg looked up just as we felt another undulation. "I think you're right," he said.

"Cool," I replied, satisfied that I hadn't imagined the movement. I continued eating.

"Um," Greg said slowly, "maybe we should leave the building and stay outside, just to be safe?"

Common sense kicked in, and we scrambled out to the sidewalk. Around us, people looked rushed and panicked. I called Beijing to let my colleagues know there had been an earthquake. The phones rang a long time before Anita answered. She sounded harried, and I quickly told her what had happened in Fuyang.

"There's been an earthquake here. Not sure if it's worth a story yet, but I can give you a few lines of color," I said.

"It's in Sichuan. We felt it here in Beijing too. We've filed the news alert already," she said, referring to the one-line bulletin that the AP sends out when there's an urgent, breaking story. Around her, my colleagues were scrambling to make sense of what was happening as their thirty-story building swayed ominously. I found out later that our office on the twenty-second floor was forced to evacuate. Scott and Chris raced across the street to Scott's sixth-floor apartment to continue sending updates from there.

What Anita said finally hit me. Chengdu, the provincial capital—and the nearest major city to the epicenter—lay seven hundred miles from Fuyang. Beijing was even farther at more than a thousand miles. This was a big one.

Greg and I tried to catch the next flight to Chengdu, but we were too far away from the airport to make the last plane out and had to continue our original assignment. We met the hospital officials in front of the hotel where we had lunch and were supposed to spend the night—the Buckingham Palace. It had a British name, Greek columns, and a Chinese staff that stood nervously outside as water in an ornamental fishpond sloshed around during aftershocks. Tremors were felt as far away as Vietnam, Bangladesh, and Thailand.

Because I was in Anhui only for an overnight trip, I was far from prepared to be on assignment indefinitely in the disaster zone in northeastern Sichuan, where the worst-hit counties totaled the size of England. Besides my laptop and my phone, all I had were a notebook, one spare T-shirt, a tape recorder, and a small point-and-shoot camera. I had my chargers with me—but would there be electricity? Nerves wracked, I couldn't sleep that night, wondering what lay in store.

We caught the first flight out the next day, but the plane turned back halfway en route. No explanation was given, and I worried that the airport in Chengdu had been shut down. We waited on the same plane on the tarmac for almost an hour to give medical crews heading to Sichuan precedence. Back in the air again, I talked to passengers to see if they knew how things were on the ground, in their hometowns. Most knew nothing.

The saying in Chinese that Chengdu "has mountains and water" indicates that it is a place of great beauty. It has valleys, waterfalls, limestone caves, hot springs, and bamboo forests. The climate is sultry, the people are warm-hearted, and the food is spicy in a way that jolts your brain. I had been to Sichuan once before while doing a story on how China had made a successful business out of renting pandas to zoos around the world and had fond memories of the bustling capital and pristine mountains.

Chengdu, fifty miles southeast of the epicenter, hadn't suffered major damage from what we heard, unnervingly deserted even though it was mid-afternoon on a Tuesday. We hadn't expected shops to be shuttered. Our taxi driver didn't know the city, and we circled for a long time, looking for an ATM to stock up on cash and a place to buy provisions. We finally found a convenience store that was open and doing good business. Its shelves almost lay bare, but we managed to buy water, instant noodles, and an odd assortment of greasy and sugary snacks before meeting the AP's Beijing television crew and heading to the Crowne Plaza Hotel where other media were gathering. We needed to look at maps and figure out how to split up our resources.

Greg and the TV crew decided to try to head to the epicenter while I would go on my own to decimated areas north of the city. Two other writers from our bureau had arrived earlier that day and were making their way to other towns. The extent of the damage made for slow going. Greg and I said goodbye, disappointed that we had to part ways on such a big story. We had become close over the years, and it always felt better to be with someone you trusted on a breaking story. To make matters harder, it was pouring rain.

I tried to figure out the best way to remain under the radar. Renting a taxi would be the easiest and fastest option, but the bright green Chengdu cabs would stand out beyond the city and possibly make authorities in other areas suspicious. I assumed we wouldn't be welcome in the damaged sites, and the last thing I wanted was to be detained before I could get any reporting done.

In the end, I needed to get going, no matter what, and hopped into the next taxi that pulled up to the hotel entrance. Thankfully I got lucky. The young driver said we could use his personal car for the trip. Not only was I able to find an unmarked vehicle, but someone who grew up in the area was driving it and willing to explore the damage with me. We talked about what had happened. Driver Lei said he had heard that a town called Beichuan, nestled in a beautiful valley that he and his wife had visited the year before, had been completely destroyed.

"I need to go there," I said. "Let's go there tonight."

Lei laughed. "I'm not sure it's possible. Let's see how things go, but we can try. We can definitely try."

We picked up his car and his wife, who to my dismay was far less willing to make the trip. She kept saying how scared she was and how it was impossible to reach Beichuan. "We shouldn't even be going into the destroyed areas at all. We should be heading away from them!"

I tried to appease Mrs. Lei's fears, worried that she would dampen her husband's enthusiasm. But he seemed keen to continue the journey.

On the way, we stopped at a KFC, the only restaurant open for miles. It was going to be a long night, and we all needed to grab some food while we could. A KFC spicy chicken burger had become my default meal-on-the-run when traveling for work; it was tasty but, more importantly, there always seemed to be a *Kendeji*—a phonetic transliteration of "Kentucky"—around. Inside the Chengdu franchise, lines were long, and food was scarce. The cashier told the people ahead of us that they were out of just about everything. We left with their last two chicken wraps with sweet Peking Duck sauce.

To get to Beichuan, we had to drive through Mianyang, an industrial city of about 5 million people and home to the headquarters of China's nuclear weapons design industry. Traffic jammed the freeway, and the rain made it worse. I stared out the window, feeling helpless and impatient. Lei turned on an all-traffic radio station. For a while, it was little more than white noise to me—then words started filtering through to my consciousness. The broadcasters were reading text messages sent by survivors in stricken areas to let relatives know they were alive. My impatience turned to guilt. In my hurry to get there, to get the story, I had already failed to see the disaster in terms of people and lives lost. Thousands had died, and it hadn't registered. Had I really become that person?

In Mianyang, we found thronging temporary camps on its streets. Buildings were dark and deserted because officials had ordered residents to sleep outdoors for their own safety. There was no immediate sign of damage, but aftershocks were a worry; some as strong as magnitude-6.0 had been recorded. Security guards stood before apartment blocks to keep people out.

We drove slowly down the street, taking in the dismal scene. I was beginning to get an inkling of what the coming days would bring. The rain wasn't letting up, and many people huddled under makeshift tents made of striped plastic sheets strung between trees. Some had wrapped themselves in quilts and were eating by candlelight. At the railway station, a man was yelling through a megaphone, encouraging people with no food to grab a bowl of porridge. Beds from a hospital, also kept dry with plastic sheets, sat out on the sidewalk for people to sleep on. Clusters of residents camped under a viaduct. I spoke to a dozen people within a few feet of each other. With each story, my small window into the quake and how it had affected the survivors increased.

"I have not been able to sleep," said a man who had lined his bicycle cart with a quilt and was lying in it. "The ground shook for three minutes. I was so afraid. I felt it through my whole body. I was drinking tea at the time, and I thought a train was going by at first. Then I heard everyone screaming. I'm still so scared. I need to sleep but there's no place for me to go."

Nearby, a man clutched a blanket with a floral pattern around him as he tried to rest on two chairs pressed into service as a bed. I approached a cluster of tents where people were having a seemingly normal dinner. I didn't want to spoil their moment of peace but spoke to them anyway. "My family is still in a village, but I can't go home," said Wang Wanguang as he chewed on braised duck and dumplings. "There's nothing I can do." He and his family looked away, not wanting to talk to me any more. *Meibanfa.*

I called the office to check in, to give them the color and quotes that I had gathered. Charles, the bureau chief, sounded exhausted but grateful for the material.

At first, driver Lei and his wife waited in the car. But as I talked to more people, they got out with me and stood on the sidelines, listening. The wife seemed worried for her own safety and the possibility of aftershocks, but Lei was curious about the plight of the people I was talking to.

Despite Mrs. Lei's protests, we went next to the city's Jiuzhou Gymnasium, a mammoth sports arena where many thousands of displaced survivors were taking shelter. Lei and I walked through the vast openness of the parking lot, bathed in floodlights that illuminated the concrete magnitude of the facility. The sudden brightness was disconcerting after the relative dimness of streetlamps. The sense of loss and shock that I had seen on the streets magnified. It looked like a refugee camp in a war zone.

Hollow-eyed evacuees, dirty and dazed, sat fifteen to twenty deep under the eaves of the stadium on blankets and clothes, their belongings stuffed into bags held close by. On the ground lay empty water bottles, boxes of instant noodles, and cigarette cartons. The place was wet from rain and noisy with chatter despite the late hour. It smelled like chaos. Upstairs in the enclosed part of the building, more people crowded under bright fluorescent lights and posters of Arnold Schwarzenegger in his bodybuilding days. Children ran around, and adults stared into space or curled up trying to sleep, the lucky ones having commandeered one of the treadmills lined up against the windows. Others shouted into cellphones or smoked.

Lei, who spoke a Sichuan dialect, acted as a translator between me and villagers who didn't speak Mandarin. He and I took turns approaching people, but most didn't want to talk. Two boys wearing camouflage jackets were sitting on some stairs. They had been in class in Beichuan when rocks started rolling down from surrounding mountains. Terrified, they hid under their dormitory beds on the second floor, one hand holding the bed leg to keep it from shaking away, the other protecting his head. When it was over, the rubble had piled so high that they climbed over the second-floor balcony rails and walked straight out through clouds of dust.

We circled the area twice on foot and returned to the car. I tried broaching the subject of Beichuan again, but Lei's wife wouldn't hear of it. This time, he agreed with her. Instead, we drove around for almost an hour trying to find a place for me to spend the night—but nothing was open. They tried persuading me to go back to Chengdu, but I needed to stay in Mianyang and head out as early as I could the next day.

We finally found a hole-in-the-wall motel taking in customers. It had dim fluorescent lights and an hourly rate. They didn't ask for my identification when I checked in, which meant it was unlikely that I would have to deal with authorities that night—a blessing. I also got a room for Andy, the photographer, who was making his way to the motel and was going to travel with me the next day. Lei and his wife left, apologizing for not being able to stay. It was disappointing. Having a driver not only knowledgeable but also enterprising could prove crucial in situations like this.

As I navigated the narrow, winding stairs to my room, another aftershock threw me off balance. I briefly considered the wisdom of sleeping on the third floor, but I was too tired to care. My room had a double bed with a thin yellow blanket and no running water. I checked in with the bureau one more time before climbing under the sheets and falling asleep instantly.

Barely forty-eight hours after the earthquake, the death toll already stood at more than twelve thousand—certain to rise in the coming days and weeks.

The story was only just beginning.

❦

The next week became a blur of bumpy rides and sad tales, tragedy upon tragedy as we jumped into the heart of the disaster zone. Even survival accounts were tainted with wrenching loss, whether it was a man who lived but not his wife, or a child who escaped, but not before losing a limb.

Victims trapped under rubble experienced unthinkable suffering while praying for rescuers to find them. A concrete slab crushed one man to the floor of a collapsed office building, pinning him by the chest. For seventy-two hours, he could do nothing but take shallow, painful breaths of hot, dusty air. He willed himself to think about his wife and their ten-year-old daughter to keep calm. "I thought about everything that was precious to me," Yuan Jiang told me from his hospital bed, the cuts and gouges on his head and body exposed, his left ear rotting with infection.

Sleep-deprived and plagued with raging thirst, Yuan marked the agonizingly long days through the daily 8:00 a.m. alarm he had set on his mobile phone. Shortly after the stuttering beep sounded the third time, rescuers freed him. His daughter had survived. His wife did not.

Gong Tianxiu, a bank employee, whose husband died shielding her with his body, smashed her own trapped leg with a brick to slake her thirst with her own blood. When rescuers found her almost three days later, she amputated that leg with a saw that they passed to her so she could free herself. "I was desperate. I did it for my son," Gong told state media, which went wild with her story.

Every place we visited presented a post-apocalyptic scene that underscored the terrifying, relentless power of the quake. The first sight of destruction felt like a blow to the gut. At Hanwang, where I saw the plastic-wrapped corpses, apartment buildings had uprooted from their foundations or had literally been split in two, a cascade of furniture spilling out from the rupture. The town clock stood frozen at 2:28.

Elsewhere, windows looked like they had been punched out by a giant fist, which had also smashed down on rooftops. Streets were warped with cracks or clogged with slabs, chunks, coils, shards, and twists of every material imaginable. People walked around aimlessly with bags of belongings strapped to their backs. Many gas stations had run out of fuel. Lines at the few still doing business were long, and tempers were short.

Overwhelmed by the images, smells, sounds, and emotions, I went into autopilot and concentrated only on what the bureau in Beijing needed from me. It was easier than dealing with my own wash of feelings and reactions. But the professional need to get the story and meet deadlines pushed against my instinct to give people space to talk and grieve in their own time. That's what I would have wanted for myself. Instead, I was an emotional vulture, feeding off the loss of others. Every day I fought it, and every day I had to give in.

Each morning brought a new angle to tackle, an imminent crisis to look out for—strong aftershocks, dam damage, potential outbreaks of disease, dwindling hope for trapped survivors.

The issue that eventually dwarfed the rest and caused authorities abruptly to clamp down on the media was the growing anger over how thousands of children had died in shoddily built schools. The buildings—bitterly dubbed "tofu dregs schools" to underscore how flimsy they were—housed almost seven thousand collapsed classrooms. For months, the government remained silent on the number of students killed. For parents, the tragedy was doubly cruel because it not only shattered their lives but also robbed them of their sole offspring, the only hope for their future under China's one-child policy.

The matter became a contentious conflation of scientific evidence and anguished allegations of negligent and corrupt construction practices. Relatives who surveyed the wreckage pointed to poor design, a lack of steel rebar in the concrete, and the use of other substandard materials. American engineering experts who visited the quake site with Chinese counterparts said many of the school buildings were unreinforced structures—brick or block walls without steel—that had been outlawed after another massive earthquake near Beijing in 1976 killed many hundreds of thousands of people.

Yet He Xiaogang, an engineering expert from Tsinghua University, on a Chinese team of government investigators that visited quake sites, said the sheer power of the earthquake was to blame for the number of flattened schools. "We went to tens of thousands of schools, and almost all of them were up to national standards," he said.

Despite public outrage and media attention, parents had no recourse, no official acknowledgement, no local investigations. Most painful of all, they sometimes didn't even have a body over which to mourn and clung to what they had left: memories, photos, and the gnawing guilt of letting their child leave home that day, for failing to protect them.

Local officials and police often harassed and intimidated those who sought redress by trying to file lawsuits, gathering in protest, or talking to reporters. Others received financial compensation in exchange for their silence. Teachers, activists, and lawyers who took up the case were detained. On one of his many trips to the quake zone, police beat artist Ai Weiwei, who recruited people to help him compile the names of the dead children. He underwent neurosurgery in Germany.

Security measures, which included cordons around school rubble and restrictions on media reports, hammered home the government's resolve to control the post-quake message. After winning global praise for acting like an open society, authorities reverted to the habits of a Communist police state. Anything that distracted from the national—and natural—calamity was quashed and swept under the rug. The tactic stood in stark contrast to the transparency and relaxation of media restrictions that we saw in the very beginning.

The situation was particularly tense in Wufu, a farming village where about 130 children died when Fuxin No. 2 Primary School caved in while buildings around it remained intact. I was there for the first time around three weeks after the quake. Dozens of relatives—mostly rice farmers—had camped out at the remains of flattened classrooms, a poignant sea of concrete and tile threaded through with backpacks, pencil cases, and textbooks. They sat under the shade of trees, on wooden chairs and stools salvaged from a nearby kindergarten, trying to find some small measure of comfort and courage.

At first, they were cautious about opening up to me because they said they were being watched by authorities and had been warned not to complain to outsiders. But the stories soon came pouring out. "I have nothing left," said a father whose eleven-year-old son died with the weight of his school on him. "I keep thinking of my son. It's too much. I have to be strong." The man's wife, wracked with guilt about bringing their child to school on May 12, wasn't eating or sleeping. The couple lived in a tent, lost to each other.

Another farmer chimed in: "There is no peace in my heart. We are sad all the time, especially when we gather for meals because my grandson is no longer around. We're sad. We're angry."

Behind them, the teachers' common rooms and offices remained solidly, insultingly in place. Scornful messages written with red paint on one of the walls referred to stories circulated among parents that the educators had fled or stayed in safe buildings, leaving the students to their fate. "Children, your relatives are here, but your most respected teachers are in hiding and have disappeared," read one.

"Only the classrooms collapsed, but the teachers' building stayed up. How unfair is that?" asked a man, whose twelve-year-old daughter died an hour after being pulled from the wreckage, her chest pulverized. "Even one-hundred-year-old public toilets didn't collapse."

Wufu authorities hadn't acknowledged any problem but said they were looking into the matter and had promised results soon. None of the relatives believed anything would come out of it.

"We want the government to give us justice. If we don't get it here, we will just keep going up and up to higher levels. We're going to continue until we get justice," said one woman, who saw blood trickling from her twelve-year-old granddaughter's ears and realized only after she had died that her neck had been crushed. "We need outside help. No one is listening to what we have to say. They have never listened to us."

A few feet away stood a shelter made of wooden planks and plastic sheeting, filled with rows of framed photos of the students who had died. Black cloth draped over some of the images to signify mourning, while others had stuffed animals, candy, flower bouquets, and sticks of incense clustered in front. Parents stared at photos or replenished offerings. I stood inside with one of the fathers who showed me the photo of his child. The girl had a white hairclip and stood with her hands on her hips, her body turned at a jaunty angle.

After a few minutes, I had to step outside—and away from the pictures of the smiling children.

The last time an earthquake so catastrophic had shaken China was July 28, 1976, when a magnitude-7.5 temblor laid waste to Tangshan, a densely populated industrial city of a million people about ninety miles east of Beijing at 3:42 a.m. Half a day later, a 7.1 aftershock rolled through the devastation, and others between 5.0 and 5.5 continued hitting the area. The country was in the middle of political upheaval, and the disaster went largely unacknowledged and unconfirmed for hours except by the Xinhua News Agency, which made a brief mention of a quake occurring near Beijing.

Officially, 242,769 people died, making it the third deadliest in recorded history, according to the US Geological Survey. At the top of the agency's list is a quake in Shaanxi, a northern Chinese province, in which 830,000 people are believed to have perished in 1556. Second is one that struck in 2010 in Haiti, where the government says 316,000 died.

Tangshan survivors crawled out of the rubble into a drizzly night and clawed through the wreckage to save others. Silence reigned for a few seconds before the screaming and crying began. When rescuers arrived several days later, they found stacks of the dead clogging the streets and scores of the living huddled under makeshift tents. Survivors scrounged for food and drank from ditches, sewers, and swimming pools, many becoming sick with diarrhea.

Rebuilding, with an approved budget of $1.34 billion, didn't begin for two years. Some survivors lived in temporary houses built from wood, brick, straw, and mud salvaged from rubble for as long as a decade.

The disaster struck when China was suffering the final throes of the Cultural Revolution, a ruthless, chaotic period when Beijing closed itself to the rest of the world. The possession of four things made a man rich: a watch, a bicycle, a radio, and a sewing machine. The secretive and suspicious government under Chairman Mao routinely suppressed unfavorable news, including the full extent of losses in the Tangshan quake. Some say the actual death toll was as high as seven hundred thousand.

253

The government refused international aid, insisting on self-reliance, basing its relief operations on the mantra "Resist the Earthquake and Rescue Ourselves." Mao, who in his waning years suffered heart attacks and other ailments, was jolted in his bed in Zhongnanhai, the Beijing compound where Chinese leaders live and work, when the quake destroyed Tangshan. He agreed to be wheeled on his hospital bed to a safer building. Mao died on September 9, only weeks after the disaster, reaffirming a traditional belief that earthquakes and other calamities foretell the end of dynasties or the deaths of great leaders, signaling impending change as a result. These calamities test rulers' "mandate of heaven," the Chinese philosophical concept that defines the legitimacy of those in power predicated on their actions.

The Cultural Revolution ended shortly after, as did the ugly power struggle that had convulsed the Party. Deng Xiaoping soon consolidated his position as the country's paramount leader and ushered in a new era of increased openness and economic growth.

Thirty years later, Chinese bulletin boards, blogs, and even news websites buzzed with chatter on the mystical aspects of the Sichuan disaster. There were natural portents that defied the laws of nature, they said.

The first sign came on April 26, when eighty thousand tons of water suddenly and noisily drained away from a pond in Enshi, around 350 miles east of the epicenter. A couple of days before the quake, thousands of toads swarmed the streets of Mianzhu, also east of the epicenter, where at least two thousand people were reported killed in the disaster.

Numerology, deeply rooted in daily Chinese life, also came into play. In the first six months of 2008, China suffered crises involving the heavens, the earth, and its people. On January 25, the worst winter storm in five decades unleashed snow, ice, and sub-zero temperatures that lasted days. On March 14, antigovernment riots exploded in Tibet and surrounding areas. Then, on May 12, exactly eighty-eight days before the August 8 start of the Beijing Olympics, the earthquake struck.

Because eight is considered a lucky number—sounding similar to the character for prosperity—many Chinese worried that the heavens were displeased. To further boost their case, they said that the dates marking all the events added up to eight. January 25 was 1/25 or 1 + 2 + 5.

Despite the familiar turn to superstition, more interesting was the vivid contrast with which the government dealt with the disaster in 2008 as a wealthier, more technologically advanced, comparatively more politically open nation. Rescue efforts were much speedier and, for a while, more transparent. Within twenty minutes of the quake, Xinhua sent a news flash, citing the China Earthquake Administration. About ten minutes later, China Central Television began its unprecedented twenty-four-hour live coverage of the aftermath. We caught only snippets because we were working all the time, but I remember thinking how strange it was to glean actual news from those reports instead of sitting glassy-eyed through monotonous readings of canned script.

Details of the quake went viral on Chinese blogs, chat rooms, bulletin boards, and other networking sites. Within minutes, the military arm in Sichuan set up an emergency command and control center as the Central Military Commission in Beijing began coordinating rescue efforts. Some 130,000 soldiers and 40,000 militiamen deployed to aid the rescue and recovery efforts.

Premier Wen Jiabao, a geologist and engineer, rushed to the scene two hours later, the first of three visits he made to ravaged towns and villages that first month after the quake. He shed tears on more than one occasion as he walked through rubble, soothed crying orphans, and bellowed words of comfort into a bullhorn to encourage survivors trapped in debris. "I am Grandpa Wen," he reportedly told some children. "You have to persevere, and you will be saved."

President Hu Jintao joined him four days later, surrounded by officials, reporters, and other villagers as he sat on the floor talking to a sobbing family at a temporary shelter. "We know you've suffered from disaster, and we also know your homes have been destroyed," he said. "We know you've lost your relatives. We are just as upset as you are. Our hearts hurt like yours do."

Even though Wen and Hu had burnished their images as men of the people, those moments were particularly poignant because they buoyed—and even strengthened—the spirit of the survivors and rescue crews. The leaders appeared genuinely shaken. They appeared all over state media speaking to the people through handshakes and hugs, carrying and kissing children, and sometimes even directing rescue operations. Hua Guofeng, the premier during the Tangshan quake, also cemented his popularity with the masses when he visited the site.

One month later, some survivors had already moved into prefabricated homes erected by the government. The rest remained in tent communities that sprang up on Sichuan's fields, mountains, and city sidewalks as refugees tried to regain a semblance of normal life. Many communities were small and haphazardly planned. Others resembled miniature villages, with row after row of bright blue, government-issued emergency tents converted into homes, schools, and shops.

Unlike Tangshan, the Chinese leadership very quickly accepted overseas donations and relief materials from countries ranging from Algeria to Vietnam—and even North Korea—which totaled hundreds of millions of dollars. Rescue teams, including groups from Russia and China's archrival, Japan, began their work within forty-eight hours.

Besides the outpouring of foreign help in the wake of the disaster, an unprecedented swell of domestic goodwill and volunteerism by ordinary Chinese overtook the country. Not only did long lines form to donate money and blood, but tens of thousands from all over the nation converged in Sichuan to lend a hand.

Some roads leading to badly damaged areas were blocked not by debris or rescue workers but by ordinary citizens who had driven for hours or days, their cars full of clothes, blankets, bottled water, and bread. The ones I spoke to didn't reveal their names because they had skipped work. One news report show-cased members of an auto club who transported the injured from Beichuan to Mianyang for two days, a forty-mile journey that they made at least ten times a day. Blood banks in Beijing were turning people away two days after the quake because their stocks were full. People gave billions of dollars in donations.

The rush of support and caring, especially from citizens in their teens and twenties, took the nation by surprise. Generally considered irresponsible and selfish, the generation born after the 1980s was raised in one-child families during a period of growing inequality. Also, a society grown complacent with steadily increasing prosperity, used to leaving social problems to the government to solve, was taking the opportunity to give back.

圝

Although Beichuan lay almost ninety miles from the epicenter, it was obliterated because it sat on the Beichuan fault, from which the quake originated. The whole county seat and a handful of townships were wiped out as the shale hills around them crumbled and rained down destruction. More than half the population of Qushan town—about 8,600 residents—perished. At Beichuan, at least one thousand of the dead were middle-school students. One day before, a teacher had posted on his blog photos of the teenagers and their instructors laughing as they played games in the field to relieve exam tensions.

To get to Beichuan County, our car sped past rice plantations and small towns struggling to cope. In Yong'an, the last town before heading into the hilly terrain, we came to a stop. A huge convoy of tour buses packed with villagers, presumably rescued from destroyed areas farther up, was moving slowly down the road. Cars were parked on the side, and local authorities were monitoring a roadblock. I swore under my breath, unable to tell what they were doing. We watched them turn away a few cars then told our driver to let us out. Until we had a better assessment of the situation, it was safer to mingle with the crowds.

Off to the side, a couple of men were sitting under yet another plastic-sheeted shelter. Inside sat Li Zizhong and Zhang Mingfu, drinking grain liquor, smoking, and eating beef boiled on their charcoal stove. "All we need is a little something to eat," said Li. "I'm happy to have my life."

Only later did he indicate that he had lost his wife and daughter, who had been in school when the quake hit. "I heard her voice yelling for a long time. Today, nothing."

Andy and Ken, a smart, soft-spoken, and good-humored AP television colleague, were with me that day. We needed to go past the roadblock, up the mountains, and make the last twenty miles to the town of Beichuan. Desperate to get there, I was willing to hike up in the muggy heat. Whatever it took.

Then I noticed a field running parallel to the road and a line of villagers walking through on a dirt path before climbing back onto the main road. I persuaded Ken and Andy, cameras in tow, to do the same. We fell in line with a group of people and passed the blockade without incident. We started the long hike up, surrounded by stone-faced villagers on a mission to find their loved ones. When suddenly we heard shouts, I instinctively cringed, thinking we were being stopped. Then I realized they were coming from residents living along the road. They were holding out bottles to people as they passed. "Water! Water!" they were saying. "Have some water!" A few accepted the precious bottles with muttered thanks.

As we slowly walked to Beichuan, people were flagging down and catching rides from motorcyclists heading uphill. I did the same, and within minutes I was holding on to my seat, strangely exhilarated as we raced toward our destination. Ken had found another motorcycle, and Andy had climbed into the back of a truck. I tried talking to the driver, but the wind was too strong and he was concentrating on avoiding cracks in the road and runaway boulders that had fallen in random spots.

Finally, we came to the mouth of Beichuan. It looked like Hell. Police and emergency vehicles jammed the one road in and out of town. Paramilitary police and soldiers in camouflage were everywhere, some with red-and-white first aid armbands, red helmets, or face masks. Groups of them were carrying packages of bottled water, shuffling in the heat. Bright blue first aid tents had been set up at intervals.

Dust covered the road—it coated everything the whole time I was there—and haze filled the sky. The area hummed with muted bustle and complete exhaustion. Rescue workers slouched in the shade, taking a break from their grim task. Survivors sat in a row off to the side, their belongings stuffed into sacks and bags, the skeletons of buildings behind them. Many had rolled up their pants and shirts, a common way for Chinese men to beat the heat.

I kept walking, trying unobtrusively to take it all in, still leery about being exposed as a reporter and stopped from doing my job. No one seemed to care, even when Andy and Ken both began working their cameras. One young mother carrying a toddler with a tiny, grimy face managed to make the girl smile and wave at me.

I lost my colleagues as I followed a trail of people—villagers hunched by the weight of their belongings, rescue workers in jumpsuits and helmets, policemen in blue uniforms—who seemed to know where they were going. Slowly we headed into a valley, passing impossibly huge rocks that had crashed down scarred hillsides. A pink tour bus, its entire windshield smashed in by a boulder almost the same height, lay abandoned on the side of the road. Crowds passed us going in the opposite direction, carrying framed photos of their loved ones or the bodies of the dead.

Then we rounded a bend, and everyone inadvertently gasped.

Below us lay the entire ravaged expanse of Beichuan. It was a surreal mess, like a game of pick-up sticks gone terribly awry. Whatever remained standing listed and buckled at crazy angles. Everything else had been annihilated.

As we walked the last few hundred feet, I felt the same strange mix of energy as when I first walked into Beichuan. It was tense, subdued, bustling, somber, stoic. Above us, helicopters circled, adding to the feeling of foreboding.

Shen Xinyong's family of seven sat on a pile of rocks, expressionless and weary from lack of sleep and food. After three days of aftershocks and scouring the earth for potatoes and gourds, they had decided to abandon their irreparably damaged house and make the six-hour walk downhill. Shen's four-year-old daughter stared unblinkingly at me as her three-month-old sister sat limply in her grandmother's arms. I rummaged through my bag and gave them the last of my Chengdu provisions: an unopened packet of Morning Tea Biscuits, a couple of buns, and a bottle of water. Shen took them silently.

I headed in, past groups of marching soldiers carrying shovels and past an old couple holding on to each other as they shuffled along with the help of a soldier, who had slung a sack of their belongings on his shoulder.

There was a flurry of activity ahead of me. People were running and shouting to clear the way for a crowd of rescue workers and medics carrying a cloth stretcher. The person on it was motionless and bundled in sheets, face covered with a towel, indicating that he or she had been buried in darkness, eyes needing protection from harsh daylight. An intravenous drip snaked out of the left arm, promising the hope of life. Only at the last second did I notice the stockinged foot wearing a pink pump, revealing that it was a woman. But they were already gone.

Deeper in, almost everyone was wearing a protective mask and carrying a bag of belongings or searching for a relative or friend. Corpses covered in green plastic sheets lay scattered around. A group of exhausted young soldiers sat on the ground, heads bent low as their arms rested on their knees. None spoke. Another group of rescuers rushed by, this time with a man strapped to a stretcher. His gray shirt and brown trousers were dusty. It was unclear if he was dead or alive.

260

In a quiet corner, sat a woman whose younger sister worked at the Bureau of Industry and Commerce. "I called her countless times after the quake. I just kept pacing, figuring there was hope," said Zhang Mingfeng, who had gone straight to the bureau from her job in another town. "All I saw was a pile of debris—and I realized there was no hope. We've been crying and hugging each other for two days. It's too cruel." Her voice quavered as she recalled the last time she saw her sister. It had been the day before the quake, when the family gathered for a Sunday lunch. They had ordered shrimp, her sister's favorite.

My condolences sounded hollow to my own ears. Nothing I said to the survivors during those weeks could ever begin to address their suffering. Words stuck to my throat, and language often failed me. I wouldn't have been able to express how sorry I was for their losses even in English. Sometimes, all I could do was sit quietly as the person wept. Occasionally, I put my hand on someone's arm or back. The Chinese are not big on touch, but under the circumstances it seemed like the human thing to do.

Beichuan became my de facto base. We moved out of the motel and slept on the twelfth floor of a twenty-story hotel in Mianyang—not the wisest choice, in retrospect, because of ongoing aftershocks. In the mornings, Andy, Ken and I headed north, not returning until late into the night. We jokingly called ourselves Team Beichuan and vowed to get T-shirts made. It was our way of helping each other stay motivated and upbeat. Over two weeks, we watched the town transform from a crowded hub for recovery and rescue efforts to a silent mass tomb, populated only by phalanxes of workers in hazmat suits and masks spraying disinfectant, like something out of a sci-fi movie.

Soldiers pulled mottled corpses from the wreckage or carried body bags in trucks or hand-pulled carts. We often smelled them coming before we saw them, the odor sickly sweet and overripe. Everywhere we went, people knelt silently in the ruins of their homes, weeping for the ones they lost or gathering whatever belongings they could find.

One week after the quake, when wreaths of chrysanthe-mums—traditional Chinese flowers of mourning—were brought into town, we spent the day monitoring two dramatic rescue efforts that had everyone on edge. Any survivor found at this point would be a miracle.

Rescue workers had gone to numerous sites after possible signs of life were detected only to come up empty-handed. "We'd work for more than half a day and in the end, nothing," croaked Zhang Qingshan, a member of the National Rescue Team, who lost his voice in the first few days of the tragedy because he had been shouting out to possible trapped survivors.

The exception was the retrieval early in the day of Li Mingcui from the ruins of a market 164 hours after being trapped, tem-porarily buoying the country's spirits. Doctors said the sixty-one-year-old woman suffered from serious dehydration and had renal and liver failure, as well as multiple fractures in her ribs and shoulders. Her son, Zhao Jun, who learned of the rescue on television and rushed to the hospital, described his mother as "an ordinary old lady and not in good shape. She sees doctors several times a year and wears socks and sweaters to bed, even some-times in summer."

The stories of other rescue operations also began in the thin light of morning, when villagers made the daily pilgrimage to search the wreckage for lost family members. They shouted out to emergency workers, saying they thought they might have found someone buried under debris. Shining flashlights thirteen feet down into the wreckage, rescue workers spotted an ear—whole, unmarred, and not decaying—attached to a person whose hair appeared to move almost imperceptibly, as if the person were breathing. The victim was deep inside the rubble; rescue workers couldn't tell if it was a man or a woman, nor was it ever clear what building it was before it collapsed.

They surveyed the site, shaded by a tree, strategizing ways in and chipping away at the concrete. A heavy yellow crane sat ready to roar to life when needed. As the cool morning turned into a blazing hot afternoon, soldiers joined the workers in their bright orange jumpsuits, white helmets, and face masks. They maneuvered heavy machinery to pry apart stubborn pieces of debris and carried the rubble away by hand.

"Slowly! Slowly!" rescuers shouted, worried that the hole they were making in the pile would suddenly collapse. Equipment to measure vital signs was lowered and registered a very faint response. An ambulance equipped with a resuscitator and oxygen stood by.

The growing crowd watching the process—mostly journalists and soldiers taking pictures on their cellphones—craned their necks. So many fellow reporters from Beijing were there that it was like we had never left the capital. We sat along the sidelines through the afternoon, hunched over notebooks and cameras, chatting idly and occasionally running up to the area to check on progress. It was a feel-good story we all desperately craved.

The work stopped only twice. First at 2:28 p.m., when the whole country marked the one-week anniversary of the start of the quake. Soldiers and workers stood at attention as ambulances, police cars, and cranes honked their horns and sirens wailed in unison. Then around 4:00 p.m., during a brief but strong aftershock, there was another pause.

Throughout the day, excitement grew when it seemed like the rescue was almost complete—then dimmed when it became obvious the person was still trapped. At one point the ambulance pulled closer and the back doors were opened. A line of soldiers held back surging onlookers. Still, no body materialized.

A Beichuan official said later that a forty-one-year-old man was pulled out after dark to the excitement of rescue workers, but he didn't know if the man survived. If he had, we would have heard about it because state media would have run endless stories on him.

In another corner of town, at the end of a long road covered in glass, shoes, and other belongings, geologists and volunteers were inspecting a collapsed apartment building when they heard the tinny sound of music, like that from an electronic game, coming from the lower reaches. Like many structures in the disaster zone, it had sunk into its foundations and the first and second floors were now at subterranean levels.

When they got on their knees and shouted into the gap, they said a woman's voice—weak and faint—responded. "All of us heard the music and some of us heard her. There's definitely someone in there," said Meng Ye, a forty-year-old volunteer from the central city of Xi'an. "That sound will haunt me all night."

Seeing a nearby sign for a restaurant in the debris, rescuers wondered if the woman found food and increased her chances of surviving. They tapped the storefront's mangled metal gate, a rhythmic 1-2-3, and shouted "Hello? Is there anyone there? Hello?" over and over again.

"If you can play your music, play it again. We're all here to save you. Tap if you can hear me. Do you hear me?"

But there was silence.

A group surveyed the site and an argument ensued over how to proceed: should they tear through the ground-level rubble or drill from above? Eventually, they drilled in from the floor above—and found no one. The mood deflated and the number of rescue experts dwindled.

Wang Jianwei, a member of the rescue team who found the sixty-one-year-old woman earlier in the day, had a theory about the silence: "Sometimes people use their last ounce of strength to call out to us and when they hear that we are coming to save them, they are so emotional, they die."

❊

In the meantime, I had found another driver who was knowledgeable and willing to travel to the worst wreckage and the farthest village for the story. He had the slight build and high cheekbones typical of the Sichuanese and possessed a rakish air.

He chain-smoked like a chimney and often talked to his wife on his cell phone when we were on the road.

Driver Zhang's dark green SUV was always clean and always had a supply of bottled water. We drove for hours on end for days on end, winding our way through the destruction. He doggedly helped me pursue leads for stories and even occasionally gave me a hand with my bag or over a pile of rubble.

He found it strange that a woman would work such long hours on such a distressing story and couldn't quite figure out my place as a Chinese person among all the foreign journalists. I told him it was the only way to get my job done, and besides, in a disaster, everyone is equal.

A native of Chengdu, Zhang often espoused the delights of his native province. According to him, food in Sichuan tasted so good because of the oil from the rapeseed plant, harvested and pressed locally. He pointed at the fields of plants with sunny yellow flowers—rapeseed. He told me about hot pot dinners with friends and *xiaochi*, the snacks like *dandan* noodles and *longchao-shou*, Sichuan's version of wontons, often in a bath of chili oil, that made Chengdu famous.

"You should move here," he said. "Life in Sichuan is the best. It's about relaxation. Our women are beautiful, we eat great food, we play cards. People come here, and they are mesmerized by the life here. They come for a visit and end up staying."

I spent about five weeks in the zone, and have almost 2,500 photos, five notebooks—still dusty and smudged—and an assortment of random sheets of paper on which I scribbled things down when I didn't have anything handy. As time went on, it became easier to observe objectively rather than process what was happening. It didn't feel right to show more emotion than the people whom I interviewed when they were the ones who had to live with unbearable losses. It seemed like a weakness or, worse, an insult when faced with their stoic demeanors.

In the evenings, after a long day's worth of traveling, reporting, and writing, I switched off, exhausted. On the drive back,

I lay down in the back seat, popped in my earbuds, and played Jacques Lu Cont's Thin White Duke remix of The Killers' "Mr. Brightside." I can't explain why that version of the song appealed to me, but there was hope in the ethereal tune for me, and I kept it on a loop to lull me after dark and to motivate me on mornings that I had to return to the ruins.

榉

I met Zhang Jiazhi two days after the earthquake. I was in Deyang, an industrial city between Chengdu and Mianyang, chasing a story about how hospitals and clinics not obliterated or rendered unsafe were struggling mightily to cope with the aftermath of the disaster. While the government had promised to pay survivors' medical expenses, just getting care proved the bigger problem.

Functioning facilities, medicine, blood, needles, doctors—everything was in short supply after the quake, except for the injured. Numerous makeshift care centers had sprung up on the front lines of badly damaged towns but were overwhelmed. The situation highlighted how sorely neglected the health care system was despite China's meteoric economic rise. Underfunded by the government and unaffordable to most, health care was especially poor in inland areas like Sichuan province, highlighting yet again the yawning gap between prosperous urban dwellers and struggling rural Chinese.

"What do we need most? We just need some rest," Dr. Wu Tianfu told me irritably as he worked at a furious pace in a tent set up by the Red Cross Society of China in Hanwang, where hundreds of schoolchildren had died. "Then we need gloves, masks, iodine, sutures, cold medicine. It's a long list."

At the eight-hundred-bed Deyang City People's Hospital, the largest in an area with several quake-devastated counties, more than one thousand people had been brought in from the hard-hit cities of Mianzhu and Hanwang alone. Supplies of blood, disinfectants, and needles were depleted in the first two days, and replacements were only trickling in. In contrast, ambulances rushed up every few minutes, transporting yet more people bundled in quilts, their faces swollen and crusted with dried blood, needing treatment for broken bones, head and abdominal wounds, and amputations. In the emergency room driveway, a massive handwritten list gave the names of people admitted that day, also indicating in which ward others already being treated could be found. "This is a partial list," it announced. People crowded around anxiously, trying to find their loved ones.

Nearby, makeshift shelters fashioned from plastic sheets were crammed. Patients, their limbs wrapped in thick gauze bandages, were hooked up to intravenous tubes. Relatives surrounded them, and volunteers offered porridge, cakes, and sweets.

"They just keep coming, hordes of people who were hurt," said Dr. Deng Xiaoling, examining a crying eleven-year-old girl, her back, head, and legs gashed after escaping from the ruins of her school in Hanwang. "Under normal circumstances, the children shouldn't have complications, but, now the weather is very hot, they aren't eating, their immune system is weak, and this could lead to complications or problems that we don't want to face."

The doctor moved on, too busy to say more. I lost Andy and Ken as I slowly absorbed my surroundings: triage centers and outpatient clinics set up in tents and the hospital lobby, operating rooms moved from the twelfth to the second floor in case of large aftershocks.

Andy came back with a teenage girl who told us that we needed to hear her cousin's story. The girl, who had a worried expression on her broad face, led us up a flight of stairs, past dozens of people huddled on chairs and lying listlessly in beds jammed in a corridor. We turned into one of the rooms and there was Zhang Jiazhi, lying in a bed, his head and the stumps of what was left of his arms swathed in bandages. A tube ran out of his nose, but his cheeks, though scratched and bruised, were still rosy. His eyes, round and long-lashed, were wide with an expression I still can't describe. He was a beautiful child.

267

Eleven-year-old Jiazhi was on the second floor of his primary school when the quake rolled through his farming village. The last to leave, he was running out when the building collapsed. Knocked over and trapped by debris, he was dragged out by a classmate and stumbled to freedom, scalp gouged by chunks of concrete, arms broken and crushed, flesh ripped, bones exposed.

"Not once did he cry," his father, Zhang Qingyou, said with a mixture of pride and terrible sadness. He had rushed to the school when the ground began to shake and saw his son emerge, bloody, from the ruins. His face tensed at the memory of that first sight of his son. The man's wife, Lin Yiping, a tiny woman with a strikingly pretty, doll-like face, stood next to Jiazhi, her hand lightly on his shoulder.

Their son's escape began a twenty-hour ordeal. Aftershocks rattled the nearest hospital to their village, which turned him away. His parents then rushed him to the city's main square, which had become an enormous triage center. It teemed with the walking wounded who overwhelmed doctors as they jostled to get on ambulances. "It was wave after wave of people. The doctors were too busy and did not have time to come over to check on Jiazhi," Zhang said, shaking his head. "We didn't know what to do. It was a mess. There was nothing we could do."

Jiazhi and his parents managed to squeeze into an ambulance with nine other people making their way to Deyang City People's Hospital. The trip took an hour because an accident slowed traffic to a crawl. Once there, four more hours passed as they waited in the packed emergency room with Jiazhi lying on a stretcher. Tremors were still shaking the area. Finally, the boy was sent to an operating room, where, along with seven other patients lying side-by-side, doctors performed simultaneous surgeries.

But time had run out.

The doctors, who worked for two hours, couldn't salvage his arms. "They said the nerves and blood vessels had died, and there's no way to get them back to normal," his father said. "I tried to ask the doctor to at least save his right hand, which he writes with. But they said it was too late."

Jiazhi survived. But with care delayed for nearly a day, the boy, who loved to play ping-pong and carve wooden toys for his friends, had to have both arms amputated. He lost his right one just below the elbow, the left under the shoulder. While I learned his story, nurses came by on their twice-daily rounds to check his vital signs, clean his wounds, and replenish his IV drip, hooked up to his left foot. Jiazhi followed their movements with his eyes as they worked in silence.

His father, a farmer who makes 2,000 yuan a year (about $300), worried how he was going to rebuild a life for his family. "We have nothing left. Everything is gone. We just have to figure out what to do."

While his parents continued to talk to me, Jiazhi stared silently ahead, his cut and swollen face expressionless. I don't remember him blinking. I tried to talk to him, but he didn't respond except to turn his eyes to his mother.

"He hasn't talked since the operation," Lin said, beginning to sob. "He hasn't eaten. He's only cried once since the earthquake, when they told him he no longer had his arms."

After the story ran, a German television station that had picked it up wrote me with queries from viewers on how to help Jiazhi. Then an American man contacted me for the same reason, followed by a woman. It's rare that we get feedback from readers moved by our stories, and I was happy to know that people had been touched by the Zhang family's story. It was also a reminder that there were countless other stories to tell about people whose lives had been destroyed.

❀

Trauma experts said that 80 percent of the survivors in Sichuan could be expected to suffer short-term effects of post-traumatic stress disorder. Half would have longer-term problems, including obsession with the trauma, nightmares, flashbacks, emotional numbing, irritability, memory problems, and hyper-vigilance. Fear, experts said, was the most serious problem. It would interfere with everyday activities like sleeping, bathing, even walking into a building.

For Luo Tiangui, the nights after his rescue were the hardest. "I am a bad person," he said over and over again as he flailed violently in his hospital bed in the Deyang Hospital of Chinese and Western Medicine.

The farmer had been buried in his house, just sixty miles from the epicenter, as he woke from a nap. Luo spent hours trapped under the remains of his home until his wife and younger brother rushed back from the wheat fields, dug through the rubble with their bare hands, found him, and freed him. He escaped with a broken thigh and fractured ribs, but his mental state had shattered. Doctors were giving him drugs to help him sleep. They told his family to share happy memories with him in the hope that it would help.

The day I saw him, he was lying in his hospital bed, shirtless and sweating under a blue-and-white striped sheet. Clean-shaven and slightly bug-eyed, he was staring at the ceiling as he muttered "It's on fire, it's on fire." It was one of the many hallucinations that he had been suffering. Luo's wife and daughter stood by his bedside and stroked his hands, which didn't stop trembling. The TV above his bed was kept off so as not to bombard him with news and images from the quake.

"It's too hard to bear," said his wife, who started crying when she looked at her husband, a former soldier, construction worker, and furniture-maker. Her face—brown and freckled from years of working in the fields—was forlorn but broke into a slow, sweet smile when her husband turned to look at her.

It was hard to believe, but Luo was one of the luckier ones. Because of the strain on resources, hospitals and clinics could only take care of immediate, physical needs instead of helping those suffering from mental trauma, the hidden toll for many survivors. With so many shattered homes and lives in turmoil, it was impossible even to begin to estimate how many would need psychological assistance. Relatives, weeping inconsolably, fell to the ground in front of plastic-wrapped bodies. Villagers stared blankly in shock at what used to be their homes. Some talked with gratitude about having escaped with their lives—only to dissolve into tears when an aftershock rolled through. People couldn't sleep, couldn't eat.

Only once did I have a nightmare in Sichuan. I awoke, jaw clenched in the dark, still thinking I was trapped under a building and unable to scream. Still feeling the presence of villagers I dreamt were next to me. Still feeling the pressure of the blackness that weighed us down. Too tense to fall back asleep, I called Alexa, a dear friend and fellow AP Beijing reporter, herself worn down by cancer treatments in New York. A day before, she had sent me an e-mail that I read over and over again: "No matter where you are, that's where you should be, and you will find good stuff. Don't let it get to you."

We talked for an hour, time zones and continents blurring. My tears soaked the pillow as I told her how overwhelmed I was but how I couldn't step away from it all because I had to do my job. Alexa, in turn, confided about how draining it had been to go through five rounds of chemotherapy and still to face seven more in addition to two major surgeries.

"We were in the same boat, facing down death, and terrified. And even though we were half a world apart, I never felt closer to you because you were leaning on me and I was leaning on you," she told me years later, back to her quirky, spunky self.

❋

Because of who I am, I took comfort in eating. Many of the meals that I ate in the quake zone did more than just satisfy my hunger. They sustained my spirit and helped forge connections with the people I met.

For the first few days in Mianyang, almost everything was closed or destroyed. Because we only had time to eat at night, we rationed meals to one container of instant noodles bought at a tiny store next to the entrance of our motel. I felt guilty for being alive and for feeling hungry when so many had died. At the same time, the hot, salty soup comforted me. Andy, normally cheerful but now subdued, and I ate on a worn couch that the motel owners had moved to the sidewalk, watching the silent streets.

Forget the Zone Diet, I joked to friends after I returned to Beijing. *The Quake Zone Diet is the way to go,* I said, pulling at my waistband to show how loose it had become. Gallows humor was another refuge.

One day, Andy and I found a small eatery on a side street about a five-minute walk from the motel. It was the only thing open in the vicinity; its tables and stools set up on the sidewalk offered a welcome sight. Although it was a hole-in-the-wall, the food was freshly cooked and tasty, and business was brisk. The sense of normalcy was heartening—for us, for our fellow diners, and for the restaurant staff, who rushed about shouting out orders and serving meat and vegetables shot through with the addictive combination of chili oil, Sichuan peppercorns, spring onions, and garlic. The provincial spirit lived on in the food.

McDonald's chocolate sundaes became a staple. I bought them late at night after I finished writing, eating them quickly before the heat reduced them to a melted brown mess. In the mornings, reporters congregated at the breakfast buffet of the hotel where we all stayed. Over eggs, cereal, noodles, porridge, or fruit, we read local papers, caught up with each other, and compared notes before heading out.

But one of the best meals from that time was with Marsha, the CBS Asia bureau chief, and her colleague Celia Hatton, fellow food lovers and among the most energetic and energizing people I know. It took place on May 20, eight days after the quake. I was given the green light to move our base to Chengdu, the provincial capital where Greg and I had first landed in Sichuan.

I was amazed at how normal it was when I arrived. In Mianyang, where Andy and I had been, most shops were still closed, and many people were still sleeping on the streets. In Chengdu, business was brisk, traffic was heavy, and neon lights blazed—as though the quake had never happened.

When I walked into my room at the Crowne Plaza hotel, it felt like the presidential suite. It was my birthday, and I had spent it at a packed hospital interviewing survivors, including the man who had used his phone's alarm to mark time. For the first time that day, I relaxed. I took off my dust-covered boots and walked barefoot on the carpet. I sank into the armchair and slowly savored the celebratory yet worry-tinged messages from friends and family.

Later that night, I met Marsha and Celia. We walked to a small restaurant near our hotel that was open late and served Hong Kong–style roast meats and noodles. We ordered a large plate of barbecued pork in honor of the enthusiasm that Marsha and I shared for pig products and talked nonstop about nothing at all throughout the meal. I felt lighthearted for the first time in days.

Food was also a good source—and a good gauge—of healing for the people I met. It's by no means a scientifically proven cure, but the sentiment echoed throughout camps and shelters for evacuees in the disaster zone: a period of mourning, loss, and fear followed by eating as a means of comfort and a reaffirmation of life.

In Shifang County, where hundreds were buried and two chemical plants collapsed, we spotted an orderly line of people in the middle of the street of one village, bowls, pots, and chopsticks in hand as they waited for a free lunch from a Taiwanese volunteer organization. China still claims Taiwan as its territory and has threatened military retaliation if it seeks independence. It was another example of how the quake had blurred long-standing lines of political tension.

Members of the Buddhist Tzu Chi Foundation in navy blue T-shirts, white trousers, and white baseball caps were leading the crowd in songs and cheers. "We should thank everyone! Let us raise our thumbs and say 'Thank you!'" A handful of people obliged. More shouts and clapping followed and some villagers smiled.

"Food is also special," Dr. Chien Sou-Hsin, a volunteer with the foundation, said as he examined people in a makeshift clinic. "Eating is crucial to the culture. It lets them be together, it makes them feel better."

Under another canopy, volunteers with headscarves and cleavers were furiously chopping, slicing, and dicing carrots, onions, and shiitake mushrooms. One man, wielding waist-high spatulas in each hand, was stir-frying a mound of cabbage in a giant wok, one of about half a dozen available.

Peeled garlic, chopped leeks, spring onions, green beans, lettuce, and cucumbers piled high in baskets and metal bowls. A ceramic bowl as big as my encircled arms, filled with a wicked-looking chili paste, sat by a table topped with condiments and sauces. The line began moving quickly as volunteers dished out steamed rice topped with shredded bitter melon in a spicy sauce, cabbage and carrots cooked up with Sichuan peppercorn and dried chilies, and tofu with pickled vegetables.

"We're so grateful for the rice and the hot food," said Liang Yuezi, who sat huddled on a bench with her friends, wolfing down her lunch out of a small metal bowl. "I feel so much better after eating this."

Wu Jiangju, a farmer wearing a cloth cap to protect herself from the sun, talked about how her father had been crushed when his home collapsed. "I can't really sleep. I'm still so scared." What helps, she said, is that "we have people caring for us. We have food. We are happy."

In one of the thousands of temporary tent colonies that sprang up, I met thirteen-year-old Liu Yisi, a lanky, tanned boy with short-cropped hair who escaped from his school. He was sitting cross-legged on his bed, desultorily leafing through a couple of magazines. His left hand was heavily bandaged. A mass of scabs covered his face, and spots of dried blood had stained his gray T-shirt. He barely looked up when I walked in with Li Fuhong, a psychology professor who drove two hundred miles to help survivors deal with post-traumatic stress.

"How's your mood?" Li asked softly.

"Fine," Yisi said without looking up, his voice hoarse. He only gave one-word answers as he paged through the magazines. When offered chocolate, he shook his head.

After a few more minutes of awkward exchanges, Li said firmly, "The bad events are over. The future will be better. I need to be strong," making the boy repeat after him, two, three, four times.

The boy's mother, Zhao Xiaoxia, said that since the earthquake Yisi couldn't fall asleep unless she was holding his hand. For the first few days, he refused all food except water and milk. Then his appetite slowly returned, but because his mouth was swollen he could manage only porridge. The morning we visited, he had polished off an egg and when he finished had asked for his favorite food—KFC.

"I went and bought him the fried chicken, a drumstick and wings," Zhao said, beaming. "This is how I know he's getting better."

In Yingxiu, an epicenter town that was the worst-hit in the disaster, survivors cooked communal meals partly out of necessity, partly to find solace in each other. It was still a terrible, desolate scene when we arrived a month after the quake.

The main highway leading there had buckled and broken dramatically in the tectonic upheaval. Surrounded by mountains and a river rushing through town, it should have been beautiful—but it was bleak. Paramilitary police were helping with relief and reconstruction. Many of the evacuees had moved into blue-and-white prefabricated homes and were beginning to settle back into life.

I walked by a dozen people seated around two tables set up on rocky ground surrounded by trucks, the remnants of buildings, and clothes and sheets drying on lines. Food bubbled in a couple of giant woks and pots set on fires protected by bricks.

People weren't talking much but sat close to each other, plucking morsels from dishes set in the center, comfortably eating in unison. There was even a jar of hot sauce in the middle, a nod to local tastes. It was a typical Chinese dining scene, incongruous in the ruins of Yingxiu.

Lunch that day was a soy sauce–based stew of cured pork, yellow broad beans, and dried bamboo shoots, which people were slopping onto steamed white rice. Pink slices of canned luncheon meat studded a huge pan of soupy egg noodles.

"Eat! Eat!" He Kairong urged me. As hungry as I was, I declined, touched by her generosity. It didn't feel right to partake of their limited provisions. Insistent, she pulled out a large piece of pork from the stew, put it in a bowl, and pressed it into my hands. "This is the food of our people. Is it good?"

It was delicious, at once warm and earthy, soft and salty.

He was working at her car wash business with her three sisters when the quake struck. She crawled out from under a pile of rocks, unscathed except for an injured ankle. In the days following, He and other people in town helped carry the elderly up and down the surrounding hills, saving them from flooding and mudslides. "You can't imagine what it was like in the beginning. Everyone was terrified. No one wanted to eat. It was disaster after disaster."

On another day, the sun hung low in the mountains as two women in Zundao town fried up their dinners in woks set on roaring fires built from cinder blocks and wood scraps of other people's ruined homes. Off to the side sat an old wooden desk that looked like it had been lifted from a classroom, bearing a basket of cut-up potatoes and green beans, a bowl of cubed fresh pork, a bottle of sesame oil, and a pot of the ubiquitous chili paste. It was strange to see such mundane, life-affirming signs in the middle of all the devastation.

The women shook and stirred their pans at their own stations, moving occasionally to the side table to pick out some seasoning. Oil, garlic, dried chilies, and leafy vegetables were mixed and wilted in one pan. In the other, fresh pork, beans, potatoes, salt, and chili flakes were cooked up with fatty chunks of braised duck, resulting in a rich dish full of protein. An omelet was cooked last, sputtering in the heated oil.

"We still have to eat," Wang Wenying said as she waited for the duck and potato dish to cook. "We still have to survive."

A rotund thirty-eight-year-old pharmacist with a ready laugh despite the hardships, Wang was wearing a white T-shirt, denim shorts, and pink rubber flip-flops, her hair pulled back in a bun. The house she had lived in, a solid two-story concrete building, remained standing, but the walls had cracked. "I don't dare stay inside," she said.

Instead, she squeezed with her parents, her mother-in-law, her daughter, and nephew into a camouflage-patterned tent with three beds, a sofa, a TV, and a computer, all taken from her home.

"Our lives have been set back by twenty years," Wang said as she added a pinch of salt to the pan. "The living conditions are poor. It's hot in the tents, the lines are long for water. . . . I don't know when things will improve. The sooner, the better."

Minutes later, she was done. She took her plates of food to another wooden table off to the side in the rubble and set them down with the dishes the other woman had cooked. Without preamble, they picked up their chopsticks and began eating.

翻

I returned a few weeks before the first anniversary of the quake. I wasn't sure what to expect or if I felt one emotion in particular. I was looking forward to seeing familiar faces and meeting new ones, but I was also tense about potential friction with authorities, who had come down harder than ever on survivors in subsequent months. Most of all, I was filled with nostalgia knowing it would be the last time I would see Sichuan for a while because I was leaving China in a few months.

The toll of daily reporting had slowly been wearing me out, and the relentlessness of 2008, with the Tibet riots, the Olympics, the melamine-sickened babies, and most of all the earthquake, made me realize it was time for a break. It was increasingly difficult to talk to people in sensitive situations, to invade their lives for my work. I worried too much about the consequences for them, whether it was worth risking for a story. Worst of all, there were too many days when I no longer cared one way or the other. I was losing motivation and objectivity—I needed some distance to regroup.

Once I landed in Chengdu, though, all those feelings temporarily slipped away. Sichuan and its people have a special place in my heart, and I realized that, no matter what, I was glad to be back. The area felt familiar, yet the mood had changed. There were still so many traces of the disaster but also the driving energy and unbeatable convergence of manpower that makes China the kind of country that finishes Olympic venues ahead of schedule rather than on it.

Once-shuttered towns and villages—and everything in between—buzzed with hammering, drilling, and pounding. Buildings and homes slowly were taking shape with new layers of bricks and concrete, as leaks and holes were patched. Steamrollers were resurfacing roads, rumbling slowly in the dusty heat. Another ubiquitous sight, trucks and cranes moved their piles of gravel, bags of cement, and other building materials.

Little roadside stands had sprung up in places I thought were wrecked for good, including Beichuan, preserved, rubble and all, as a memorial, which had become a tourist site. Banners encouraging people to rebuild, to be strong, and to be fast appeared everywhere, while critically damaged schools had been torn down, leaving behind only bitterness and anger.

It was what China does best: to move on and to put on a good face, regardless of the cost. Like the darkest periods of its history, the ugliness of the quake had been pushed back into the shadows. But time had sharpened the grief of parents who lost their children. The government finally released the death toll for students just days before the anniversary: 5,335 fatalities—but no names. Many believed the actual figure was twice as high.

For Farmer Wang, the death of his teenage son was even more unbearable because of a purchase he made more than a decade earlier. In 1995, he bought a cartful of bricks and two tons of cement from a contractor who said they were extra materials from a school construction project. The price was low, and Wang's neighbors had already taken advantage of the deal. It was only after the quake that the man understood what had happened all those years ago. That material was meant for the construction of Beichuan Middle School, where his son studied. The contractor sold it for profit instead.

We sat in Wang's temporary home near the ruins of the school after slinking in quickly. He agreed to meet with us but was nervous, saying that some neighbors in the cluster of prefab houses would report visits by strangers to local authorities. The room had a bunk bed, a handful of chairs and stools, and a television set, which Wang kept on to mask the sound of our conversation. He spoke with a strong Sichuan accent, and I strained to understand him. As he answered my questions, his eyes were dead, and his voice was matter-of-fact, despite the unthinkable implications of his words.

He and other parents said the contractor had sold them the material for personal profit, and, judging from the steel reinforcement rods, bricks, and pillars they found in the rubble, he had skimped or used shoddy replacements. "He used his position to sell those things on the side. At the time, no one suspected there was a problem."

The provincial government didn't allow them to examine material found in the rubble. "We are not satisfied about the question of quality and think the building collapsed because it had quality problems. So we went to the provincial government . . . but they drove us back that night."

Wang and other parents then met with lawyers from Beijing and showed them construction plans that detailed the amounts of building material intended for the middle school. The lawyers promised to call back. They never did. "I've talked to so many people. I've talked so much that I don't want to talk anymore. Nothing I say will have an effect on anything."

The tension and muted sense of despair was just as strong a year later in Wufu, where grieving relatives had sat under the trees between crumbled grade school classrooms and the still-standing teachers' building. One father said a group of parents had filed a lawsuit in Sichuan but hadn't heard back from the courts. Another group traveled to Beijing to petition the central government and have since been under tight surveillance.

"I'm filled with a sense of hopelessness," said the man, who lost his eleven-year-old son. "Nothing has been resolved."

I had planned for days on meeting him, but on my way to Wufu he called to say that he had been warned against talking to me and "they" knew that I was coming. We had been communicating over what I thought was a clean line—a temporary SIM card I had bought from a small shop in Beijing—but apparently to no avail.

It was an uneasy meeting in an unoccupied classroom of a kindergarten. His answers were clipped, and he was visibly uncomfortable talking to me. Within minutes he suggested that we leave. I was in the back seat of our SUV when a car pulled up and a man got out to talk to the father. We drove a few hundred feet then parked on the side of the road as I tried to call another parent. The mystery car drove past us but also pulled over, waiting. When we started driving again, it followed us. It wasn't worth the cat-and-mouse game or putting another parent in an awkward position. The car stopped following us as soon as we left the city limits.

❁

One of my last stops was to see Zhang Jiazhi, the boy whose arms had been amputated. He and his parents were living in a rented room just big enough to hold two beds, a cupboard, an armchair, a desk, two small collapsible tables, and a minifridge. In a corner was a hot plate for cooking and bottles of oil and soy sauce. They paid $30 a month for the space, including the cost of electricity and water.

The family said hello, and Jiazhi, now a tall, thin twelve-year-old, immediately turned to his computer and began playing games and chatting with friends online once the pleasantries were over. He adroitly moved the mouse with the remains of his right arm. One of his flesh-colored prosthetic arms casually rested upright on the armchair next to him, its fingers curled around a pen. I did a double-take when I realized what it was.

The boy's face was narrower, and he had the aloof air and monosyllabic vocabulary of teenagers around the world. He was at a new school and had made new friends, his father said, but the bonds weren't as strong. "He's not as lively as before, and he doesn't like mixing with adults and strangers," his father said. "He's more withdrawn and introverted."

The family was struggling to rebuild a life. "There is pressure to make him feel happy again, to recover. He's better today than he was a few days ago. When he's not happy, he fights with his mother."

Jiazhi continued playing a blaringly loud game on the computer, seemingly oblivious to the conversation. The second time I visited Jiazhi in a temporary shelter, I brought peaches and a mini watermelon, from which his mother slowly spooned chunks into his mouth. This time, I brought a melon again along with pears and oranges but the fruit sat untouched.

"Our life is in chaos now," his father continued. "There are no rules. We have no jobs. I still do construction work in the disaster zone. I help villagers in our old home with reconstruction. I still make a bit of salary. . . . I don't know where we are going to settle down, where our new house is going to be, where my child is going to go to school. I don't know what I'm going to do for work. You can't always build a home where there's a school. You can't always find work where there is a school. Now, we can only take it one day at a time."

The good news was that the government had taken care of the medical fees, and Jiazhi's body had recovered "especially fast." He started using the prosthetic arm for basic actions, like eating and writing, within two months of leaving the hospital. In the beginning, he could only bear to have it on for an hour because it was itchy and hot. Although he could wear it for up to three hours now, Jiazhi was still grappling with how to deal with people's reactions.

"When we go out, people will stare at him, especially when he's not wearing the prosthetics. People will say things. They don't mean it in a bad way, but he takes it that way," his father said.

I asked Jiazhi if he could show me how he used the prosthetic. His father helped him with it, and, because the pen was already in place, the boy began writing on a blank page of my notebook. First his name, four times in different sizes. Then his parents' names. Then mine.

Peng Peng, my colleague from our television division, asked Jiazhi a series of questions, which he answered briefly, hesitantly, either because he was shy or reluctant to talk.

"Have you adapted to this life?"

"Yes."

"How is your current life different from before?"

"There is a bit of inconvenience."

"Do you have confidence in how you will adapt and adjust to your life in the future?"

"I have confidence."

"Why?"

"I just do."

He felt the same as before and got along with the other students, except now he needed more help from his classmates to get his meals at the cafeteria and carry his books.

Peng Peng asked him what he wanted to be when he grew up.

"A translator," Jiazhi said, indicating a preference for English, although he hadn't learned the language. When pressed, he added: "I don't have hands and can't really do anything else. I only have my mouth, so I think being a translator is the best thing for me. I can't have people help me do things all the time."

"How do you feel when you think back to the quake?" Peng Peng asked.

"I feel like someone who is very lucky. I'm lucky in all respects. So many people died, yet I lived."

He paused, struggling to put everything that he had endured into words. What he said captured in some way what the government had been trying to push all along. It was a call to move forward and not look back. It was a call, in many ways, to forget.

"The earthquake is over," Jiazhi said. "I don't think about it anymore."

ACKNOWLEDGMENTS

I owe so much to the Chinese *laobaixing* who shared their time, stories, and food with me, often under the bleakest of circumstances. Too many of those connections were sparked quickly and lived only for minutes or hours, but they made deep impressions on my mind and my heart. *Xiexie.*

I cannot begin to describe the gratitude and affection I have for my colleagues at the Associated Press. In New York, I'm indebted to Kathleen Carroll and John Daniszewski for their gracious support and kind words when green-lighting time off for this project. Also thanks to Mike Silverman for putting me on my path to China and Anne Levin for her dim sum talks.

In Beijing, Charles Hutzler's mercurial mix of humor, crotchetiness, kindness, and cynicism pushed me hard to be a better writer and reporter. He provided champagne when I got my fellowship and wise counsel in my post-AP endeavors. Scott McDonald has my affection for being a tireless cheerleader. He always took the time to give an encouraging word and boost our morale—and sugar levels—by buying chocolate or cake for the bureau. Ted Anthony challenged me with tough assignments and always had my back. There's no better friend with whom to put away a pound of pork. Eternal food soul mates Anita Chang, Alexa Olesen, Tini Tran, Gillian Wong, and Chi-Chi Zhang inspired me daily with their generosity, fierce intellect, and unwavering belief in what we did as reporters. It was also an honor to work with Chris Bodeen, Joe McDonald, Henry Sanderson, and Steve Wade. If it were not for Greg Baker and Ng Han Guan, many of my assignments outside of Beijing would've been dreary and ill-fated. They taught me how to see the world through a different lens and understood that trying the local cuisine wherever we were was a priority. Elizabeth Dalziel, Eugene Hoshiko, Andy

Wong, and Alex Yuan always made gorgeous images and patiently helped me with my pictures. Television rocked with Yusof Abdul-Rahman, Norman Bottorff, Chen Songzhu, Jimmy Jian, Lucy Kearney, Isolda Morillo, Peng Peng, David Wivell, Raf Wober, Wayne Zhang, Zhao Bin, and Nicky Zhu.

Many thanks also to Elaine Kurtenbach in Shanghai and to all my colleagues in Hong Kong and Taiwan.

A special shout-out to Yu Bing, Xi Yue, Zhao Liang, Walker Li, Henry Hou, Yang Jie, Ji Chen, and Bonnie Cao for being tenacious and patient researchers. Thanks to drivers Shi Jie, Yuan Zhenjiang, and Chang Hexin for their recipes and food recommendations.

I could not have survived China without my four pillars: Jonathan Ansfield, Lindsay Beck, Emma Graham-Harrison, and Steven Jiang. Many others in the talented Beijing press corps also became dear friends: Sam Beattie, Ben Blanchard, Chua Chin Hon, Marsha Cooke, Jonathan Landreth, Jason Leow, Phil Pan, Peter Parks, Tracy Quek, John Ruwitch, Sarah Schafer, Cindy Sui, and Marga Zambrana. I also treasure the meals I had with Alex Chen, Sawada Hanako, Duncan Innes-Ker, Ramy Inocencio, Leon Lee, Amy Li, Amy Lui, Eitan Plasse, Anh Truong, and Wei Jiangang.

To Connie Young and Nathan Mauger, thank you for jumping enthusiastically into the trailer project.

This book was conceived during the Nieman Fellowship, a gift of time and freedom for which I will always have former curator Bob Giles and his wife, Nancy, to thank. Thanks also to everyone at the foundation and to my esteemed fellow Niemans. Other Cambridge friends who inspired me with their optimism and delicious sustenance: Ed Cunningham, Anne Gergen, Ann Gund, Susan Hecht, Micah McCauley, Len White, and especially Cheryl Lim, whose innate calm and love for pastries carried me through the roughest patches. Jim and Mary Alice Van Sickle's kindness and their cottage were the best refuge a girl could wish for.

Thank you to David Patterson for being a staunch advocate in all situations and an unfailingly responsive agent, a rarity in the publishing world. James Jayo is a consummately gracious and sharp editor, and I was lucky to have him on my side.

My deepest gratitude to busy friends who nonetheless took the time to read chapters or provide their insight and expertise: Robbie Barnett, Lindsay Beck, Peter Beck, Nicholas Bequelin, Chan Kam Wing, Jenny Chio, Lilian Chou, Amy Finkelstein, Lois Fiore, Mack Fraga, Dru Gladney, Hsing You-tien, Ian Johnson, Jana Juginovic, Kim Kwang-Tae, Ed Lanfranco, Andrei Lankov, Cecilia Lee, So Kam Ng Lee, Kate Pak, Vincent Pan, Park Choong-Hwan, Janice Podsada, Roy Prosterman, Sammy Ruwitch, Sarah Schafer, Sarah Swider, Tay Yue-Jin, Inara Verzemnieks, John Wallace, Jon Watts, and Yang Dali.

I want to especially thank Ken Hom for being extraordinarily gracious and generous with his time and words.

The friendships that kept me sane: Dyuti Sengupta, Rajneel Ganjoo, and Ayana; Crystal Tecca and Jeff Mangahas; Denise, Kevin, Paddy, Liam, and Colin Fournier; Julie Chao; Annie Lau; Kyle Hinman; David Fry; Jim and Lucita Valiere; Karen Davis; Jessica Guynn; and my girls Priscilla Cheung, Patricia Mays, and Nekesa Moody, who played hooky to see me off to China.

In Singapore, Leila Ashraf, Noraini Aziz, Chris Chaplin, Patrina Chew, Patricia Chow, Darius Chua, Betty Lee Lo, Keith Ng, Augustine Tan, Heather Tan, Linda Tan, Wong Maye-e, and Yeoh En-Lai fueled my writing with the tastiest local treats. Vijay Joshi and the AP bureau staffers welcomed me with a space to write. Wong Chun Han helped with research.

To Seth, for opening the door.

Without my family, I am nothing. My grandparents helped raise and feed me from the day I was born. I will never forget. My cousins and my aunt love food in a way that makes my stomach smile. My parents gave me unconditional freedom, and their wholehearted love and support in everything I do have allowed me the luxury of exploring the world and figuring out my place in it.